Anxiety

Cognitive behavioural therapy has proved to be an effective treatment for anxiety disorders in children and young people. This book provides an overview of CBT and explores how it can be used to help children with anxiety disorders.

In *Anxiety: Cognitive Behaviour Therapy for Children and Young People* Paul Stallard describes the nature and extent of anxiety problems that are suffered in childhood and discusses evidence for the effectiveness of the cognitive behavioural model as a method of treatment.

This concise and accessible book, written specifically for the clinician, provides a clear outline of how CBT can be used with children suffering from anxiety disorders in an easy to follow format. The book provides many ideas that can be incorporated into everyday practice, as well as clinical vignettes, case examples, and worksheets for use with children and young people.

This straightforward text will prove essential reading for professionals involved with children who have significant anxiety problems including mental health workers, social services staff and those working in educational settings.

Online resources:
The final chapters of this book contain worksheets that can be downloaded free of charge to purchasers of the print version. Please visit the website www.routledgementalhealth.com/cbt-with-children to find out more about this facility.

Paul Stallard is Professor of Child and Family Mental Health at the University of Bath and Consultant Clinical Psychologist for Avon and Wiltshire Mental Health Partnership NHS Trust. He publishes widely in many professional journals and is involved in evaluating school-based CBT programmes for anxiety and depression in the UK and abroad.

CBT with Children, Adolescents and Families
Series editor: Paul Stallard

"The *CBT with Children, Adolescents and Families* series, edited by Professor Paul Stallard and written by a team of international experts, meets the growing need for evidence-based treatment manuals to address prevalent psychological problems in young people. These authoritative, yet practical books will be of interest to all professionals who work in the field of child and adolescent mental health." – *Alan Carr, Professor of Clinical Psychology, University College Dublin, Ireland.*

Cognitive behaviour therapy (CBT) is now the predominant treatment approach in both the NHS and private practice and is increasingly used by a range of mental health professionals.

The *CBT with Children, Adolescents and Families* series provides comprehensive, practical guidance for using CBT when dealing with a variety of common child and adolescent problems, as well as related family issues. The demand for therapy and counselling for children and adolescents is rapidly expanding, and early intervention in family and school settings is increasingly seen as effective and essential. In this series leading authorities in their respective fields provide detailed advice on methods of achieving this.

Each book in this series focuses on one particular problem and guides the professional from initial assessment through to techniques, common problems and future issues. Written especially for the clinician, each title includes summaries of key points, clinical examples, and worksheets to use with children and young people.

Titles in this series:

Anxiety by Paul Stallard
Obsessive Compulsive Disorder edited by Polly Waite and Tim Williams
Depression by Chrissie Verduyn, Julia Rogers, and Alison Wood
Eating Disorders by Simon Gowers and Lynne Green
Post Traumatic Stress Disorder by Patrick Smith, Sean Perrin & William Yule

Anxiety

Cognitive Behaviour Therapy with Children and Young People

Paul Stallard

DATE DUE

14/8/15			

Demco, Inc. 38-293

Routledge
Taylor & Francis Group

LONDON AND NEW YORK

First published 2009
by Routledge
27 Church Road, Hove, East Sussex BN3 2FA

Simultaneously published in the USA and Canada
by Routledge
711 Third Avenue, New York, NY 10017 (8th Floor)

Routledge is an imprint of the Taylor & Francis Group, an Informa business

Typeset in Times by RefineCatch Ltd, Bungay, Suffolk
Printed and bound in Great Britain by TJ International Ltd, Padstow, Cornwall
Paperback cover design by Andy Ward

British Library Cataloguing in Publication Data
A catalogue record for this book is available from the British Library

Library of Congress Cataloging in Publication Data
Stallard, Paul, 1955–
    Anxiety : cognitive behavioural therapy with children and young people /
Paul Stallard.
        p. ; cm.
    Includes bibliographical references and index.
    1. Anxiety in children.   2. Cognitive therapy for children.   I. Title.
    [DNLM: 1. Anxiety Disorders – therapy.   2. Adolescent.   3. Child.
 4. Cognitive Therapy – methods. WM 172 S782a 2009]
    RJ506.A58S73 2009
    618.92′8522 – dc22
                                                                2008021874

ISBN: 978-0-415-37256-5 (hbk)
ISBN: 978-0-415-37255-8 (pbk)

Contents

Acknowledgements

I would like to thank my family, Rosie, Luke and Amy for their continuing support and encouragement during the writing of this book. I would also like to thank the many colleagues I have had the good fortune to meet and work with and who have helped to develop the ideas contained in this book. Finally, this book would not have been possible without the children, young people and their parents whom I have had the privilege to work with.

1

Anxiety problems in childhood

Anxiety disorders in children and young people are common and constitute the largest group of mental health problems during childhood. They can have a significant effect on everyday functioning, impact on developmental trajectories and interfere with educational attainment, the development of friendship and family relationships. Many anxiety disorders persist and, if left untreated, increase the likelihood of problems in adulthood.

The anxiety response is complex and involves cognitive, physiological and behavioural components (Weems and Stickle, 2005). The cognitive component involves appraising situations and events for anticipated risk; the physiological component prepares the body for any necessary action (e.g. flight or fight) while the behavioural component helps the child to anticipate and avoid future danger. Anxiety is a normative response designed to facilitate self-protection with the particular focus of the fear and worry varying according to the child's development and previous experiences.

One of the important cognitive components of anxiety is that of worry, with community surveys indicating that worries among children are common. Muris et al. (1998) found that 70% of children aged 8–13 reported that they worried every now and then. The content of these worries focused on school performance, dying, health and social contacts, with the most intense worries occurring two to three times per week. Similar findings were reported by Silverman et al. (1995) who found that the three most common areas of worry related to school, health and personal harm.

Children with identified anxiety disorders referred to specialist clinics share similar concerns. Their main areas of worry relate to health issues, school, disasters and personal harm, with the most frequent worries being about friendships, classmates, school, health and performance (Weems et al., 2000). The difference between community and referred groups is not necessarily the specific content of the worries but it is their intensity (Perrin and Last, 1997; Weems et al., 2000). Comparisons between community and referred children found that clinically anxious children had more intense worries (Weems *et al.*, 2000)

The specific focus of worries in children and young people changes across childhood. Weems and Stickle (2005) suggest that the symptoms of specific anxiety disorders are shaped by sequential developmental challenges in cognitive, behavioural and social processes. With young infants the key tasks are concerned with survival, so that fear and anxiety are related to sudden loud noises, unexpected events and a wariness of strangers. As the child develops an attachment to their primary caregivers a fear of separation emerges as common by the end of the first year. By the age of six children become more independent and begin to recognise their potential vulnerability, resulting in worries about the loss of or separation from parents continuing. In addition, specific fears such as those of animals and the dark emerge. Between the ages of 10 and 13 children become increasingly aware of their own vulnerability with fears about personal injury, death, danger and natural disasters emerging. By adolescence the nature of the fears is based more on social comparisons, and anxiety about failure, criticism, and physical appearance is common (Warren and Sroufe, 2004). Fears and worries during childhood are therefore normal but become problematic when they become persistent, severe and incapacitating, and interfere with or limit the child's everyday life and functioning.

> Worries in children are common and appear to be a normal part of child development.
>
> Children with anxiety disorders tend to have more intense worries.
>
> As children develop and their cognitive capacity increases, the focus of worries and fear shifts from concrete to more abstract concerns.

Prevalence

Point prevalence community surveys in the UK and the USA indicate that 2–4% of children aged 5–16 fulfil Diagnostic and Statistical Manual of Mental Disorders (DSM-IV-TR) diagnostic criteria for a severe anxiety disorder with accompanying significant impairment (American Psychiatric Association (APA), 2000; Costello *et al.*, 2003; Meltzer *et al.*, 2003). In general, anxiety disorders tend to be more prevalent in girls than in boys, and in older children. In particular, girls are more likely than boys to report phobias, panic disorders, agoraphobia and separation anxiety disorder.

In terms of the nature and course of anxiety disorders, a great deal can be learned from longitudinal studies. In the USA, the Great Smoky Mountains Study recruited a random sample of 1,420 children aged 9, 11 and 13 and followed them up until the age of 16 (Costello *et al.*, 2003). The three-month point prevalence of children fulfilling DSM-IV criteria for anxiety disorder varied from 0.5% at age 9/10 to 1.9% at age 11, 2.6% at 13 and 3.7% at 15, with the lowest rate being in 12-year-old children. In terms of specific disorders, separation anxiety decreased in prevalence with age whereas social anxiety and panic increased. Cumulative estimates suggest that by the age of 16, approximately 10% of children will have met DSM-IV criteria for an anxiety disorder.

Rates are significantly higher if the impairment criteria are omitted. For example, Costello *et al.* (1996) in the Great Smoky Mountains Study found that 20% of children suffered with an emotional disorder. A similar rate was found in a community survey of 1,035 children aged 12–17 in Germany, where estimated lifetime rates of anxiety disorders in adolescents were 18.6% (Essau *et al.*, 2000).

In terms of specific disorders, Costello and Angold (1995) concluded that overanxious disorder, generalised anxiety disorder, separation anxiety and simple phobia "are nearly always the most commonly diagnosed anxiety disorder, occurring in around 5% of children while social phobia, agoraphobia, panic disorder, avoidant disorder and obsessive-compulsive disorder are rare, with prevalence rates generally well below 2%".

> Approximately 1 in 10 children and young people will fulfil diagnostic criteria for an anxiety disorder over the course of their childhood.

Co-morbidity

There is considerable co-morbidity between anxiety disorders and also with other emotional disorders, particularly depression (Costello *et al.*, 2003; Essau *et al.*, 2000; Greco and Morris, 2004; Newman *et al.*, 1996). In view of this overlap, specific anxiety disorders may be confused. For example, with separation anxiety disorder the child may express a number of worries or fears that could be mistaken for generalised anxiety disorder. Similarly, the social avoidance that characterises social phobia could be confused with the apathy that is a common feature of depression.

The other co-morbid condition is that of alcohol misuse, whereby children with anxiety disorders are at an increased risk of alcohol misuse as adolescents. It has been hypothesised that alcohol may be used as a way of reducing or alleviating unpleasant anxiety symptoms (Schuckit and Hesselbrock, 1994).

> Co-morbidity with other anxiety disorders and depression is common.

Course

Although results are not always consistent (Last *et al.*, 1998), most longi-tudinal studies have demonstrated that many anxiety disorders in children persist into adulthood.

In New York, a sample of 776 children aged 9–18 who received psychi-atric assessments were followed up two and nine years later (Pine *et al.*, 1998). There was a strong association between adolescent anxiety and the presence of anxiety at each subsequent assessment. Anxiety and depressive disorders in adolescence led to a two- to three-fold increase in the risk of these disorders in young adulthood. There was some evidence of specificity, with simple and social phobias in adolescence predicting simple and social phobias in young adulthood. The relationship over time with other anxiety disorders such as generalised anxiety disorder, overanxious disorder and fear-fulness was less strong. Nonetheless the data suggests that most anxiety dis-orders in young adulthood are preceded by anxiety disorders in adolescence.

In a longitudinal study in New Zealand, a birth cohort of 1,265 were assessed for anxiety disorders between the ages of 14 and 16 and then on a range of measures of mental health, educational and social functioning between the ages of 16 and 21 (Woodward and Fergusson, 2001). After controlling for possible confounding variables, significant associations were found between anxiety in adolescence and anxiety, depression, illicit drug dependence and educational underachievement in young adulthood.

Similar results were found in the Dunedin Multidisciplinary Health and Development Study in New Zealand (Kim-Cohen *et al.*, 2003; Newman *et al.*, 1996). A birth cohort of approximately 1,000 children was assessed at various times during childhood and into young adulthood at ages 18, 21 and 26. Of those with a diagnosed anxiety disorder at the age of 21, 80.5% had received a prior diagnosis before the age of 18. This figure was similar at age 26, where 76.6% of those with an anxiety disorder had received a prior diagnosis before the age of 18. This was relatively consistent across the specific disorders: generalised anxiety disorder (81.1%), panic disorder (78.9%), simple phobia (84.1%) and social phobia (72.8%).

> Childhood anxiety can have an unremitting course and persists into adulthood.

Aetiology

There are multiple pathways to the development of anxiety disorders in children and adolescents that involve a complex interplay of biological, environmental and individual factors. This is based on the principles of multifinality (any single factor leads to multiple outcomes) and equifinality (many pathways may lead to the same outcome). A biological vulnerability (e.g. behavioural inhibition) is assumed to predispose the child to an anxiety disorder which is then activated and maintained by environmental factors (e.g. parental behaviour), cognitive processes (e.g. biased cognitions and processes) and learning experiences (e.g. conditioning and avoidance).

A biological vulnerability through genetics and temperament in the form of hypersensitivity to stress and challenge predisposes children to the development of anxiety disorders. This genetic influence has been investigated by examining the concordance of anxiety disorders within families. This has involved "top-down" (i.e. investigating the children of adults with anxiety disorders) and "bottom-up" (i.e. investigating adult relatives of children with anxiety disorders) approaches. Studies have consistently demonstrated high familiarity of anxiety disorders, with up to one-third of the variance being attributed to genetic influences.

Temperament is one of the constitutional constructs that has received considerable attention, and refers to a relatively stable way of responding to events across settings and time. The temperamental factor that has perhaps attracted most interest is that of behavioural inhibition: the tendency to exhibit fearfulness and withdrawal when confronted with novel or unfamiliar events or situations. The research suggests that behavioural inhibition, particularly when it remains stable over time, is associated with increased risk of subsequent anxiety disorders. However, while there is an important association between behavioural inhibition and anxiety, not all children with a predisposing temperamental vulnerability develop anxiety disorders. Environmental and individual specific factors also play a significant role in the aetiology and maintenance of anxiety disorders.

One of the most important environmental influences for children is the family. This provides the context within which anxious behaviour could be modelled and/or reinforced. Parental psychopathology may result in children being repeatedly exposed to anxious behaviour in which fearful behaviour and avoidance are modelled. These behaviours can also be reinforced through parenting practice where parents of anxious children encourage avoidant behaviours in their children. Similarly, a restrictive style of parenting characterised by parental over-control and over-protection limits the development of autonomy. In turn this increases dependency, restricts the opportunities available to children to develop problem-solving skills and increases the expectation that fearful events are unpredictable and uncontrollable.

Individual conditioning and observational learning experiences are also important and are particularly relevant to the aetiology of phobic disorders. These disorders can develop through different pathways in which identified events become conditioned with a terror or extreme fright response. This can occur through direct experience, by indirectly observing a phobic reaction in another or through the provision of information. However, while direct and vicarious conditioning experiences are important, it is not always possible to identify their occurrence, suggesting that once again other pathways are equally important in the development of fears and anxiety disorders.

Finally, cognitive processing is important in determining how children perceive and interpret their environment. Information-processing approaches have explored the way children select, attend to and interpret cues as dangerous or threatening. Anxious children are more likely to attend selectively to threat cues and perceive more threat in ambiguous situations.

> There are many different pathways to the development of childhood anxiety disorders.
>
> Genetic influences and temperamental factors are predisposing factors that can increase vulnerability.
>
> Important environmental influences include familial factors, learning experiences and cognitive factors.

Types of anxiety disorder

Apart from separation anxiety disorder, the DSM-IV-TR (APA, 2000) does not have specific categories for childhood anxiety disorders. These are generally listed under "anxiety disorders" with some specific comments about the different way these might be manifest in children.

ICD-10 (World Health Organization, 1993) includes a specific section for emotional disorders with onset specific to childhood and includes separation anxiety disorder, phobic anxiety disorder and social anxiety disorder. The other common anxiety reactions displayed by children – social phobia, panic disorder and generalised anxiety disorder – are included within the general section describing neurotic, stress-related and somatoform disorders. While the onset, triggering events and symptoms within each anxiety disorder may differ, they share an overarching theme in that it is the child's perception of threat, either real or imaginary, that generates anxiety.

The remaining anxiety disorders are obsessive-compulsive disorder (OCD) and posttraumatic stress disorder (PTSD). In OCD the young person experiences recurrent and persistent thoughts (obsessions) and/or repetitive behaviours (compulsions) that cause marked distress and anxiety. With PTSD the anxiety and distress are caused by exposure to a trauma or event that involved actual or threatened death or serious injury, or a threat to the child's physical integrity, with the child's response involving intense fear, helplessness or horror. Both OCD and PTSD are the subjects of separate books and will not be addressed in this book.

> Anxiety disorders are similar in that it is the perception of threat that generates anxiety.

Separation anxiety disorder (SAD)

It is normal for toddlers and preschool children to show a degree of anxiety over real or threatened separation from people to whom they are attached. With separation anxiety disorder the fear over separation develops during the early years and constitutes the primary focus of the anxiety. It is differentiated from normal separation anxiety when it is of such severity that it is statistically unusual (including an abnormal persistence beyond the usual age period) and when it is associated with significant problems in social functioning.

Jessica was described by her mother as having always been an anxious child. She would often cry and become agitated if separated from her mother. At the age of three she started at playgroup but became very distressed at being left, resulting in her mother having to stay. Her mother stayed with Jessica every day for the first two weeks. When she was finally able to leave her daughter at playgroup, Jessica constantly cried, called for her mother and continued to cry until she made herself sick. She was subsequently withdrawn from playgroup and stayed at home with her mother. During this time Jessica could not be left with friends or relatives and her mother always had to be present.

Upon starting school Jessica once again became distressed but her mother and teacher persevered and Jessica started to stay on her own. However, her attendance quickly became erratic as she regularly missed one or two days per week due to tummy aches and feelings of sickness. Jessica was taken to her doctor on a number of occasions but no specific physical reasons for her complaints could be found. She was invited for her first sleepover at a friend's house at the age of eight but felt unable to go. Jessica was worried that her mother would leave their home and would not be there when she returned. The fear of her mother leaving or having an accident grew. Jessica's school attendance became worse, she would not play with other children and spent her time constantly with her mother or checking that she was at home.

The key diagnostic feature is persistent and excessive anxiety concerning separation from the home or from those to whom the child is attached, typically the mother. This anxiety results from excessive worries about losing, or harm befalling, a major attachment figure (usually parents or other family members). It may be displayed before or during separation and may be exhibited through a variety of symptoms. However, the focus of the anxiety is defined and specific and is not part of a wider anxiety reaction that pervades multiple situations and is triggered by differing events.

Common symptoms of separation anxiety disorder include an unrealistic, preoccupying worry about possible harm befalling the child or their major attachment figures that would result in them becoming separated in some way. The child may display a persistent reluctance or refusal to go to school or sleep on their own, or may complain of repeated nightmares about separation. Children may complain of frequent somatic symptoms such as nausea, stomach ache, headache or vomiting, or present with excessive distress as shown by anxiety, crying, tantrums, misery, apathy or social withdrawal before, during or immediately following separation from a major attachment figure.

DSM-IV-TR (APA, 2000) notes that the onset of separation anxiety disorder is before the age of 18, it lasts at least four weeks and it causes significant distress or impairment in social, academic, family or other important areas of functioning.

Developmental differences in the symptoms of separation anxiety disorder have been noted. Francis *et al.* (1987) found that children aged five to eight were more likely to report fears of unrealistic harm, nightmares about separation, or school refusal, whereas older children (aged 13–16) more often endorsed somatic complaints. Gender differences in the expression of symptoms have not generally been noted, although Silverman and Dick-Niederhauser (2004) conclude that more girls than boys present with separation anxiety disorder.

> Separation anxiety disorder is characterised by persistent and excessive anxiety concerning separation from or harm befalling a major attachment figure.

In terms of prevalence, studies demonstrate rates of 3–5%, which decrease with age with a peak age onset of seven to nine years of age (Silverman and Dick-Niederhauser, 2004). Recovery rates are good, with Foley *et al.* (2004) finding that 80% of their community sample diagnosed with SAD had remitted over the 18 month follow-up. Co-morbidity is common, particularly with overanxious disorder, specific phobia and depression.

Phobic anxiety disorder

Fears in children are common and have been defined by Marks (1969: 1) as a "normal response to active or imagined threat". Most children experience some degree of fear during childhood, with the majority being mild, developmentally normal and transitory. Indeed, Ollendick *et al.* (2002) note that children often demonstrate fear reactions to a range of events including loud noises, strangers, darkness and animals. Phobias differ from normal childhood fears in that they persist over an extended period, are maladaptive and are not age- or stage-specific (Miller *et al.*, 1974). Thus children with phobic anxiety disorder present with a marked and persistent fear of specific objects or places (e.g. dogs, dentist). Exposure results in an immediate anxiety response and may also include crying, tantrums, freezing and clinginess.

> *Sophie (14) recalled an event that happened when she was six years of age. While playing hide and seek with some friends she became trapped in a small dark cupboard. Her friends became bored with the game and wandered off, leaving Sophie to be discovered some 15 minutes later by her aunt. Sophie was distraught, crying inconsolably and shaking, and required considerable physical comfort before she calmed down. From that date onwards Sophie became fearful of small dark places.*

Phobias are specific to certain objects or situations. The subsequent anxiety reaction is extreme and clinically abnormal and does not form part of a more generalised disorder. While adolescents may recognise that their fear is excessive, younger children may not.

The DSM-IV-TR (APA, 2000) criteria, although not specific for children, note that exposure to the phobic stimulus almost invariably provokes an anxiety response resulting in the phobic situation being either avoided or endured with intense anxiety. It is also noted that the child's anxiety response may involve crying, tantrums, freezing or clinging. In addition, because fears are common during childhood, DSM-IV-TR notes that the specific fear has to be present for at least six months.

In terms of the nature of the phobia, DSM-IV (APA, 1994) identifies sub-types involving animals (e.g. cats, snakes), natural environment (e.g. thunder, water), blood–injection–injury, situations (e.g. flying, lifts) and others (e.g. being sick, balloons).

> Specific phobias are extreme maladaptive fear reactions to specific objects or situations that persist and cause severe distress for the child.

Although researchers have used different criteria, community studies suggest prevalence rates of 2–5% and that phobias result in significant impairment of everyday functioning (Essau *et al.*, 2000; Ollendick *et al.*, 2002). Girls and younger boys tend to report a higher number of fear symptoms (Essau *et al.*, 2000).

Social phobia/social anxiety disorder

A wariness of strangers and social apprehension are common during childhood. However, for some children this fear becomes severe and is associated with clinically significant problems in social functioning. According to ICD-10 (WHO, 1993), social anxiety disorder has its onset before the age of six and is characterized by a recurrent or persistent fear and/or avoidance of strangers (adults and peers).

Social phobia typically starts in adolescence. It is characterised by significant and excessive fear of negative evaluation by others in social situations with one's peer group or in performance situations such as music or sports events. Children typically fear that they will act in humiliating or embarrassing ways, which in turn generates significant anxiety symptoms. This discomfort results in a marked and extreme avoidance of social situations.

> *Michele (14) was an only child and was comparatively isolated from her peers. Upon starting school she did not mix particularly well with the other children and preferred to play on her own. Although she was always polite and talkative with adults, she became a loner among her peers and was often on the periphery of social groupings. Michele became a regular target for teasing and this continued until she started secondary school. Although Michele was interested in developing friendships she became increasingly concerned about how others would react to her. She worried that she might say the wrong thing and began to notice a number of anxiety signals when she was around children of her own age. These included a racing heart, a dry throat, and feeling hot and flushed. She began to spend increased time on her own, avoiding social situations, and became very panicky if she had to do anything with her peers.*

In order to fulfil diagnostic criteria, children must be able to demonstrate that they have the capacity to develop age-appropriate relationships and that the anxiety-related symptoms occur with other children and not just with adults. Children may not recognise their fear to be excessive or unreasonable and anxiety may be expressed through crying, tantrums, freezing and shrinking from social situations. Fear of embarrassment is common during adolescence and, as such, symptoms must persist for at least six months before a diagnosis can be made.

> Social phobia is a marked and persistent fear of social or performance situations in which the child fears humiliation or embarrassment.

Children with social phobia will often report moderate distress across a range of social settings. Beidel *et al.* (1999), for example, found that children with social phobia most often endorsed situations in which they performed in front of others (reading in class, 71%; musical or athletic performances, 61%) or more general conversational interactions (speaking with adults, 59%; starting a conversation, 58%) as generating at least moderate distress. In terms of frequency, children with social phobia reported distressing events as occurring every second day (Beidel, 1991), with school being a common setting. This distress was perceived by those with social phobia as highly incapacitating, with two-thirds reporting themselves as having been significantly impaired at school over the past four weeks (Essau *et al.*, 2000).

In terms of prevalence, Essau *et al.* (2000), in a community survey of 1,035 German adolescents aged 12–17, found that 1.6% fulfilled diagnostic criteria for social phobia. There was tendency for more girls than boys to fulfil diagnostic criteria, with the frequency of social phobia increasing with age. Within this sample co-morbidity was common, with 41% also fulfilling diagnostic criteria for somatoform disorders and 29% for depressive disorders.

Panic attacks

Panic attacks are characterised by acute symptoms of severe anxiety that occur unexpectedly. These are not specific to particular events or situations and therefore seem unpredictable. The dominant signs are very intense, short-lived physiological symptoms of anxiety accompanied by a secondary fear of dying, losing control or going mad. This may result in avoidance of situations that have triggered panic attacks and a continuing fear of further attacks.

> *Becka (12) was a sociable, high-achieving, popular girl who had a busy and active social life. She had no history of problems or worries but recalled experiencing her first panic attack six months ago while out shopping with her friends. She recalled suddenly becoming very hot, feeling dizzy, light-headed, short of breath and unable to stop shaking. Becka didn't know what was happening and recalled fearing that she would pass out. This intense feeling passed after a couple of minutes although Becka called her mother to collect her. Approximately four weeks later Becka had another panic attack while travelling home on the school bus. She recalled feeling intensely hot, light-headed and shaky, and noted that her heart was racing. Becka became very tearful, raced off the bus and remembered worrying that she was having a heart attack. This intense period passed after three or four minutes but she was still tearful when her mother arrived to collect her. The same happened approximately two weeks later during school assembly, with Becka*

suddenly feeling panicky and thinking that she would pass out. Once again the symptoms lasted a few minutes, but Becka has felt unable to join school assembly since this time.

DSM-IV-TR (APA, 2000) identifies three types of panic attack: unexpected (uncued), situationally bound (cued) and situationally predisposed. Unexpected attacks are those where the child does not associate their occurrence with any particular triggers. Situationally bound attacks invariably occur in anticipation of or on exposure to specific cues, whereas situationally predisposed attacks occur in specific situations but not after every exposure to specific cues.

Panic attacks are therefore unpredictable and occur in circumstances where there is no objective danger. Outside these episodes of intense fear children will often be comparatively free from anxiety symptoms, although anticipatory anxiety is common. These panic attacks need to include at least four of 13 physiological symptoms including palpitations, sweating, shaking, shortness of breath, choking, chest pain, hot flushes, nausea and dizziness. Other symptoms include feelings of de-realisation or depersonalisation, loss of control or a fear of dying.

Kearney *et al.* (1997) found that the most frequent and severe symptoms in children aged 8–17 were accelerated heart rate, nausea, hot/cold flushes, shaking and shortness of breath. Typically the panic attack becomes very intense within five minutes before it starts to subside.

> Panic attacks are characterised by recurrent and intense physiological symptoms that often occur in the absence of any identifiable or specific triggering cues.

Community studies of young adolescents indicate a prevalence of between 0.5% and 5% (Essau *et al.*, 2000; Goodwin and Gotlib, 2004; Hayward *et al.*, 1997). Co-morbidity with other anxiety disorders and depression is high (Goodwin and Gotlib, 2004).

Generalised anxiety disorder (GAD)

Generalised anxiety disorder has replaced the previous diagnostic category of overanxious disorder (OAD). OAD was generally considered to be unsatisfactory, with criteria being vague and having a high degree of overlap with other anxiety disorders. GAD reflects excessive and uncontrollable worries across a range of future and past events accompanied by physiological symptoms of arousal. The resulting anxiety becomes dysfunctional in that it persists and interferes with important areas of everyday function-ing (e.g. family life, school, peer relationships).

> *Adam (8) was described by his mother as a worrier. He would worry about everything and anything and would constantly discuss these worries with his mother and seek her reassurance. This had recently become a particular problem at school. Adam required considerable reassurance from his teacher before he would start his work and would constantly check with her that it was correct. If this was not provided he would become tearful, shake and appear unable to concentrate on his work. Each night he would worry about the following day and would identify a number of worries about friendships, school work and activities that he would constantly talk over with his mother. This typically resulted in him becoming more anxious and often ended up with Adam becoming tearful, shaking, and unable to get to sleep.*

Typically symptoms of anxiety will occur most days and will have been present for several weeks. Symptoms include a sense of apprehension and worries about possible future misfortunes and personal competence, for example at school or in sporting events. Children may express worries about practical issues such as time-keeping or completion of assignments as well as catastrophic events such as wars or terrorist attacks. There may be signs of motor tension such as appearing restless, fidgeting, trembling and feeling unable to relax. These may be accompanied by physiological symptoms such as light-headedness, sweating, tachycardia (fast heartbeat), dizziness and a dry mouth.

In children, recurrent somatic complaints such as headaches and stomach aches and a need for reassurance may be prominent features. DSM-IV-TR (APA, 2000) notes that the excessive worry is present more days than not, is difficult to control and has been present for longer than six months. For children, DSM requires the presence of one of the following six symptoms: restlessness, fatigue, difficulty concentrating, irritability, muscle tension and sleep disturbance. DSM also notes that GAD may be over-diagnosed in children and suggests that a thorough assessment is required to determine the presence of other anxiety disorders.

> Generalised anxiety disorder is a persistent, excessive and intense worry about a wide range of future and past events.

Community surveys suggest that although OAD/GAD symptoms are common, less than 1% of children fulfil more stringent diagnostic criteria for a current disorder (Essau *et al.*, 2000; Wittchen *et al.*, 1998). In terms of presentation, Kendall and Pimentel (2003) found that children with GAD demonstrate a constellation of symptoms including an inability to sit still or relax, difficulty concentrating, becoming easily upset, snapping at people and experiencing muscle aches and disturbed sleep. Similarly, Masi *et al.* (1999) note that 70% of children with GAD in their study reported feelings of tension, apprehensive expectation, negative self-image, and the need for reassurance, irritability and physical complaints. Kendall and Pimentel (2003) noted that the number of symptoms children endorsed increased with age, although others have not noted this trend (Masi *et al.*, 2004).

Co-morbidity with other anxiety and depressive disorders is high, with Masi *et al.* (2004) noting that only 7% of their sample presented with pure GAD. This is partially explained by the similarity across symptoms of GAD and other affective disorders (i.e. worry, poor concentration, sleeping difficulties).

- Extreme and incapacitating anxiety disorders are common and will affect up to one in ten children during childhood and adolescence.
- Anxiety disorders during adolescence confer a strong risk for recurrent anxiety disorders during early adulthood.
- There is considerable co-morbidity between specific anxiety disorders and with depression.
- There are multiple pathways to the development of anxiety disorders, with important factors including:
  - genetic influences
  - temperament, particularly behavioural inhibition
  - child-rearing practices
  - parental psychopathology
  - cognitive factors
  - conditioning experiences.

2

Cognitive behaviour therapy

Cognitive behaviour therapy (CBT) is a structured form of psychotherapy that emphasises the important role of cognitions in determining how we feel and what we do. It is a *practical* approach which focuses on current events and difficulties. This *here-and-now* focus appeals to children, who are often more interested in understanding and coping with the problems they are currently experiencing rather than attempting to discover why they occurred. The style of therapy is *collaborative*, in which the child and therapist work together in partnership. Children have an *active role* in treatment sessions and are involved in testing the reality and limitations of their cognitions, beliefs and assumptions. Behavioural *experiments* provide children with objective ways of assessing the validity of their cognitions and provide a powerful way of promoting self-discovery and facilitating cognitive restructuring. CBT is *skills-based*, helping children learn and develop a variety of skills and strategies. Existing functional skills are developed, thereby promoting *self-efficacy*, while new skills are learned, tried and evaluated. Finally, CBT is *time-limited*, thereby promoting independence and encouraging self-help and reflection. The time-limited nature also appeals to the short-term time perspective of many children and can help to facilitate the initial process of engagement.

- CBT is a practical, skills-based intervention.
- The here-and-now focus offers good face validity.
- Behavioural experiments provide powerful and objective ways of helping children test their cognitions.
- CBT is time-limited.

The process of CBT

A core principle of CBT that guides the process of therapy is that of collaboration. The clinician and child work together in partnership. The clinician is not "the expert" who "knows" the answers and therefore "advises" the child. It is through this collaborative partnership that the child develops an understanding of his or her difficulties and discovers helpful strategies and skills. The child and the clinician each bring important and different skills to the partnership. The child brings their unique understanding of their situation and problems, the meaning they attribute to the events that occur and knowledge about what they have previously found helpful or unhelpful. The clinician brings a theoretical framework in which the child's experiences, cognitions, emotions and behaviours are organised to provide an explicit understanding of the current problems. This understanding can be very enabling and empowering; it facilitates the development of self-efficacy and helps the child begin to explore possible solutions. The partnership is developed and maintained through the open sharing of information and psycho-education about anxiety and the CBT model. Collaboration is also encouraged through core therapeutic skills involving empathy, reflective listening and Socratic questioning. Through these the importance of the child's contributions to the therapeutic sessions is emphasised. Self-efficacy is further enhanced through the development of a partnership based on self-discovery involving openness and experimentation.

- CBT is a collaborative partnership.
- Information is openly shared.
- The child's contributions are encouraged and valued.
- Openness and experimentation are encouraged.

Involving parents

The role of parents in child-focused CBT will be discussed in detail in a later chapter. However, the empirical evidence indicating that parental involvement results in additional therapeutic gains is equivocal. This is in contrast to the widely held clinical view that parents, and other important adults such as teachers, are important in facilitating change and maintaining progress.

The extent of parental involvement in the treatment programme will be influenced by the child's age. With younger children parents will have a more central role, whereas with young people more work may be undertaken directly with the young person on their own. When parents are involved the clinician needs to assess the ability of parents to support the programme. Possible practical issues such as attending sessions or undertaking behavioural experiments need to be addressed, and parental views and support for the intervention need to be determined. Potentially negative or unhelpful cognitions need to be identified, challenged and resolved. Similarly, the role of parental cognitions and behaviours in the development and maintenance of the child's anxiety needs to be assessed and addressed.

The degree to which parents are involved in individual treatment sessions will vary. Parents may be involved in all the sessions, attend separate sessions or join their child at the end of each session. However, at a minimum, regular parent review sessions should be scheduled into the intervention in order to monitor progress and identify any important factors that may affect the likely success of the intervention.

> - The extent and nature of parental involvement in CBT will vary.
> - At a minimum, parents should be involved in regular review meetings.

Clarify confidentiality and boundaries

At the outset of therapy, issues of confidentiality need to be agreed and boundaries established. This is particularly important when working with young people on their own so that they and their parents are clear as to what information is shared and what remains private. It therefore needs to be made explicit that any information that highlights significant risk issues may need to be shared with other agencies. Risks could relate to the behaviour of others, i.e. neglect or abuse; the child's own behaviour, e.g. drug misuse or deliberate self-harm; or the child's behaviour may threaten the safety of others, e.g. threats of serious assaults or illegal behaviour.

In addition to clarifying confidentiality, the requirements of therapy in terms of number of meetings, timing of appointments, frequency of reviews, etc. need to be agreed. In some instances this can be formalised into a behavioural contract where the expectations of all those involved, including the clinician, can be made explicit.

> Clarify issues of confidentiality, boundaries and the timing and sequencing of therapy.

Outline session structure

CBT tends to follow a standard format with each session involving most, or all, of the following seven elements.

1   *General update:* Review progress and identify any significant events that have occurred since the last meeting which might have an impact on the intervention. These may be wide ranging and could relate to changes at home, in family relationships, friendships, health, school, or in social activities.

2   *Symptom update:* Assess the current anxiety symptoms and whether there have been any significant changes in the extent or nature of these. This provides a quick check that can alert the clinician to areas that might need to be explored in more detail during the session.

3   *Assignment review:* Check the outcome of any out-of-session assignments, with an emphasis on encouraging self-reflection: "so what have you found out from that?"; "has it told us anything new?".

4   *Agenda-setting:* Agree the main focus of the session and explain how this fits with previous meetings. It is often useful to do this with reference to the problem formulation, since this provides the framework that informs the content of the intervention.

5   *Session focus:* This will form the bulk of the session and will focus on a major element of the CBT intervention, i.e. psycho-education, development of an anxiety formulation, skills acquisition, experimentation and practice.

6   *Agree assignment:* Agree whether this would be helpful and, if so, clearly define the task and discuss potential barriers that might interfere with its successful attainment.

7   *Session feedback:* An opportunity for the young person to reflect on the session content ("is there anything we have talked about today that you found particularly helpful?"), process ("have you had a chance to say everything you wanted to say?") and progress ("do you think anything has changed since we started this programme?").

CBT sessions typically involve:

- a general review
- symptom update
- review of previous assignments
- agenda-setting
- main session focus
- agreeing any out-of-session assignments
- feedback about the session.

Core elements of CBT for anxiety

CBT is a generic term that refers to a collection of techniques and strategies that can be employed in various combinations to address the cognitive, behavioural and physiological factors associated with anxiety. The transition from some of the earlier, more behavioural interventions to CBT has seen a shift in the balance between, and emphasis on, the cognitive and behavioural components. The cognitive content of many CBT programmes with children can, at times, appear quite limited (Stallard, 2002). This does not imply that cognitions are not addressed during these interventions. Undoubtedly behavioural experiments and exposure – core treatment components of programmes for children with anxiety disorders – will result in some accompanying cognitive change even though this may not have been the direct focus. An issue that has received less attention is whether directly addressing some of the dysfunctional cognitive processes and biases that have been found to be associated with anxiety disorders enhances treatment effectiveness. This is part of the wider debate about what aspects of CBT are effective since, as noted by Kazdin and Weisz (1998), CBT is "provided as a uniform bundle of techniques". There is therefore a need for deconstruction studies that allow the relative value of the individual components of CBT to be determined. This would determine what specific strategies are effective in alleviating which symptoms.

While there are differences in the specific content and emphasis of CBT interventions, most tend to involve a number of common elements (Albano and Kendall, 2002; Kazdin and Weisz, 1998; Stallard, 2005). First, most involve some form of psycho-education. Children and their parents are educated into the CBT model and learn about the relationship between thoughts, feelings and behaviour. Second, most include emotional recognition and management training. This helps children to become aware of their own unique anxiety response and to identify helpful ways in which their anxiety response can be managed. The third element helps children to recognise their cognitions (i.e. self-talk) in anxiety-evoking situations and some of the biased and distorted processes that have been found to be associated with anxiety disorders. Once these are identified, the fourth element involves children learning to challenge and replace their anxiety-increasing self-talk with positive coping and anxiety-reducing self-talk. Fifth, there is an emphasis on practice and exposure, both imaginal and *in vivo*, during which children apply and practise their new cognitive and emotional skills. The sixth core element involves the development of self-monitoring and self-reinforcement techniques in order to acknowledge and celebrate positive attempts at facing and overcoming worries. Finally, interventions include a focus on relapse prevention and preparing for future challenges and setbacks.

Core components of CBT programmes for anxiety disorders include:

- psycho-education
- emotional recognition and management
- identification of anxiety-increasing and distorted cognitions
- thought challenging and the development of anxiety-reducing cognitions
- exposure and practice
- self-monitoring and reinforcement
- preparing for setbacks.

Structure of an anxiety programme

Standardised CBT programmes for anxiety disorders usually consist of 12–16 sessions. A similar number will be required for individually developed formulation-based programmes, although significant change can sometimes be achieved with fewer sessions.

The specific content and emphasis of the CBT programme will be informed by the assessment and formulation. For example, some children are emotionally literate and aware and may need to focus more on the cognitive and behavioural domains. They may need to develop a better understanding of the role of their cognitions in generating anxious feelings and to practise facing and coping with anxiety-provoking situations. With younger children, or where cognitive development and ability are more limited, the cognitive element may receive less direct attention. Similarly, some children may already have a good understanding of their thoughts and feelings but require more exposure and practice to develop and transfer the use of coping skills to everyday life. The actual content of individually constructed CBT will therefore vary, although a standard intervention might consist of the schema shown in Figure 2.1, accompanied by out-of-session assignments. The main focus of each session is highlighted although it is important to emphasise that each builds on the previous sessions as the cognitive, behavioural and emotional components are integrated.

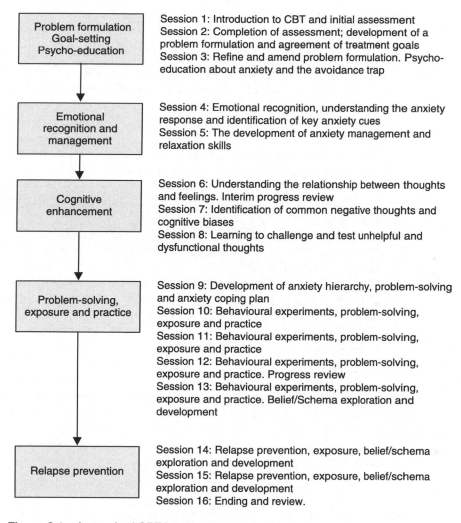

Problem formulation Goal-setting Psycho-education	Session 1: Introduction to CBT and initial assessment Session 2: Completion of assessment; development of a problem formulation and agreement of treatment goals Session 3: Refine and amend problem formulation. Psycho-education about anxiety and the avoidance trap
Emotional recognition and management	Session 4: Emotional recognition, understanding the anxiety response and identification of key anxiety cues Session 5: The development of anxiety management and relaxation skills
Cognitive enhancement	Session 6: Understanding the relationship between thoughts and feelings. Interim progress review Session 7: Identification of common negative thoughts and cognitive biases Session 8: Learning to challenge and test unhelpful and dysfunctional thoughts
Problem-solving, exposure and practice	Session 9: Development of anxiety hierarchy, problem-solving and anxiety coping plan Session 10: Behavioural experiments, problem-solving, exposure and practice Session 11: Behavioural experiments, problem-solving, exposure and practice Session 12: Behavioural experiments, problem-solving, exposure and practice. Progress review Session 13: Behavioural experiments, problem-solving, exposure and practice. Belief/Schema exploration and development
Relapse prevention	Session 14: Relapse prevention, exposure, belief/schema exploration and development Session 15: Relapse prevention, exposure, belief/schema exploration and development Session 16: Ending and review.

Figure 2.1   A standard CBT intervention

The effectiveness of CBT

A growing number of research studies have demonstrated the effectiveness of CBT with children and young people. Those studies that have involved random allocation and compared CBT to a waiting list or a comparison treatment will be briefly summarised.

Generalised anxiety disorders

Individually administered CBT

The earliest randomised controlled trial using CBT to treat anxiety disorders was undertaken by Phillip Kendall (1994). A total of 47 children aged 9–13 with a primary diagnosis of overanxious disorder, separation anxiety disorder or avoidant disorder were randomly assigned to a waiting list control or an individually administered 16-session CBT intervention, i.e. the Coping Cat programme. The programme involves an educational component summarised by the acronym FEAR:

- F – Feeling Frightened: Identify anxious feelings and somatic anxiety reactions.
- E – Expect bad things to happen: Clarify cognitions in anxiety-provoking situations and, in particular, unrealistic or negative attributions and expectations.
- A – Attitudes and actions that will help: The development of a coping plan in which anxiety-increasing self-talk (cognitions) is changed to anxiety-reducing self-talk.
- R – Results and rewards: Evaluate performance and reinforce successful coping.

The first eight sessions of the programme focus on skills training with the remaining eight being concerned with practice using both imaginal and *in vivo* exposure. During the exposure stage each step in the child's fear hierarchy is translated into a STIC task ("show that I can") with the child systematically progressing from low- to high-anxiety situations as each step is successfully mastered. The main focus of the 16 sessions is summarised in Table 2.1.

Table 2.1 Coping Cat Programme (Kendall, 1994)

Session 1	Introduction and assessment
Session 2	Identifying different feelings
Session 3	Construction of a fear hierarchy and identification of personal somatic response
Session 4	Relaxation training
Session 5	Recognise and reduce anxiety-increasing self-talk
Session 6	Develop coping strategies such as coping self-talk and verbal self-direction
Session 7	Develop self-evaluation and reinforcement skills
Session 8	Review concepts and skills
Session 9–15	Practise coping with anxiety situations using both imaginal and *in vivo* experiences
Session 16	Review and incorporate skills into everyday life

Children in the CBT group made significant improvements, including reductions in anxiety and depression as determined by self- and parent-completed assessments. These gains were evident at the end of treatment and were maintained when assessed at one year follow-up. In addition to statistic-ally significant change, the clinical significance of this improvement was assessed by examining the number of children who were diagnosis-free by the end of treatment: 64% of children no longer met criteria for their primary pre-treatment anxiety diagnosis, compared to 5% in the waiting list control group.

A second evaluation of Coping Cat involved 94 children aged 9–13 who were randomly assigned to CBT or a waiting list control (Kendall *et al.*, 1997). As before, self- and parent-completed measures of anxiety and depression showed significant post-treatment improvements which were maintained at one year. At post-treatment, 53% of children no longer met diagnostic criteria for their primary pre-treatment anxiety disorder. In addition, there was a significant reduction in symptom severity of those children who still retained their primary diagnosis.

The effects of age (children aged 9–10 versus those aged 11–13), diag-nosis (overanxious disorder, separation anxiety disorder and simple phobia) and the treatment segments (education and skills training versus exposure) on treatment outcome were also examined. Comparable outcomes were obtained across age groups and diagnostic categories. Psycho-education and skills training (first eight sessions of the programme) were not, however, sufficient to produce meaningful changes without exposure and practice.

Children from this second trial were followed up to assess the longer term benefits of Coping Cat (Kendall *et al.*, 2004). Of the original 94 children, 86 (91%) were reassessed an average of 7.4 years after completing the programme. On the basis of diagnostic interviews undertaken with the referred child or their parent, 90% (child-based interview) and 80% (parent-based interview) no longer met diagnostic criteria for their primary pre-treatment anxiety disorder. These results are encouraging and highlight that Coping Cat results in significant and lasting benefits.

The degree to which improvements found in specifically designed research trials can be achieved in everyday clinical settings was explored in a pilot study by Nauta *et al.* (2001). A 12-session Dutch version of the Coping Cat programme was administered in a child and adolescent outpatient clinic to 18 children aged 8–15 presenting with a variety of anxiety disorders. Children were randomly assigned to individual CBT or to CBT plus an additional seven session cognitive training for parents. Cognitive parent training involved psycho-education, training in problem-solving, rewarding of courageous behaviour and identifying and challenging parental core beliefs about their child's anxious behaviour. Children in both groups demonstrated significant reductions in anxiety symptoms although, at post-treatment, only 28% of the children were diagnosis-free. Rates of diagnosis remission did however increase over time, to 80% at three months' and 71% at 15 months' follow-up.

In a subsequent study, the authors adopted a more robust design to test their earlier findings (Nauta *et al.*, 2003). A total of 79 children aged 7–18 with various anxiety disorders were randomly assigned to individual CBT, CBT plus cognitive training for the parents or a waiting list control. Compared to a waiting list control group, children receiving CBT, with and without parental involvement, made significant improvements. Post-treatment, 54% of the children in the CBT groups were diagnosis-free compared to 10% in the waiting list group. This improvement was maintained at three months, with 68% no longer meeting criteria for any anxiety disorder.

> Individually administered CBT interventions result in significant and lasting reductions in anxiety symptoms.

Group CBT

The previous studies demonstrated the effectiveness of individually administered CBT for mixed anxiety disorders. The limited availability of specialist child-focused CBT clinicians is an important consideration that has led some to explore whether group CBT is effective with anxious children.

Silverman *et al.* (1999a) randomly assigned 56 children aged 6–16 to group CBT or a waiting list condition. Group CBT involved parents and children meeting in separate groups for 40 minutes and then coming together for a 15 minute co-joint meeting. The intervention emphasised the use of natural group processes including peer modelling, feedback, support, reinforcement and social comparison. The content of the parent and child groups was similar.

The results demonstrate that group CBT can be effective, with 64% of the children receiving CBT recovering from their initial diagnosis by the end of treatment compared to only 13% of children in the waiting list condition. Although follow-up data was not available for all children, 77% of those assessed no longer met their initial primary diagnosis at three months, 79% at six months and 76% at 12 months. Improvements were also noted on a variety of clinician-, child- and parent-completed assessments.

Group CBT was also found to be effective in a study by Manassis *et al.* (2002), who assigned 78 children aged 8–12 to either individual or group CBT. Each intervention was matched for time and content, with the child CBT intervention, the Coping Bear, being an adaptation of Kendall's Coping Cat programme. On the basis of child-, parent- and clinician-completed assessments, children in both groups demonstrated significant post-treatment improvements. Outcomes were not affected by diagnosis, although the sub-group of children with high social anxiety responded better (as assessed by greater decreases in self-reported depression) to individual CBT.

> Group CBT appears effective although children with social anxiety might find groups difficult and benefit more from individual interventions.

Family-based CBT

Increased interest in the role of the family in the development and maintenance of anxiety has resulted in family treatment components being added to child-focused CBT interventions. The earliest work was that of Paula Barrett and her colleagues in Australia, who assigned 79 children aged 7–14 to individual CBT, individual CBT plus family anxiety management, or a waiting list condition (Barrett *et al.*, 1996a).

The child CBT intervention, Coping Koala, was an Australian adaptation of the Coping Cat programme. Coping Koala consists of 12 sessions lasting 60–80 minutes each. During the first four sessions the child is taught:

- to identify positive/negative thoughts and the associated feelings
- relaxation training
- to use coping self-talk in anxiety-provoking situations
- realistic self-evaluation
- development of self-reward strategies.

The remaining eight sessions focus on practice of these skills and through systematic in vivo exposure to feared situations.

The Family Anxiety Management (FAM) programme runs in parallel to Coping Koala. After each individual session the child joins their parents for the FAM session. FAM has three main aims, with four sessions being devoted to each of the following themes.

1   Parents are taught contingency management strategies to reduce conflict and increase family co-operation. In particular, they are taught to use:

- reinforcement strategies to reward courageous behaviour – these include the use of verbal praise, privileges and tangible rewards that are contingent on facing feared situations
- planned ignoring to extinguish excessive anxiety and complaining – parents are instructed to listen and respond empathically to their child's complaints the first time but are encouraged to direct their child to an alternative coping strategy and withdraw their attention if the complaining continues.

2   Parents are helped to become aware of their own anxiety response in stressful situations and taught to model problem-solving and to demonstrate approach to feared situations.

3   Parents are taught problem-solving and communication skills that can be used to deal with future problems. These involve:

- being consistent and supportive in their management of their child's fearful behaviour
- the introduction of daily discussions between parents to facilitate a more consistent and supportive approach
- the introduction of weekly problem-solving discussions to address any issues that arise.

Child CBT, with and without FAM, produced significant change compared to the waiting list condition, with gains being maintained at six and 12 months' follow-ups. In terms of diagnostic status, 57% of children who received CBT no longer met diagnostic criteria at post-treatment, increasing to 71% at six months and being maintained at 12 months (70%). For those who received CBT plus FAM, 84% were diagnosis-free at post-treatment and six months, rising to 95% at 12 months. Younger children (7–10 year olds) responded better to the CBT + FAM condition although the older children responded equally well to both interventions. Finally, there was a gender effect, with girls responding better to CBT + FAM whereas boys did equally well in both treatment conditions.

The long-term effects were assessed in a follow-up study (Barrett *et al.*, 2001). A total of 52 children were successfully reassessed an average of six years after receiving the intervention. As determined by parent, child and clinician ratings, post-treatment gains were maintained, with almost 86% of children no longer fulfilling diagnostic criteria for any anxiety disorder. However, the marginal benefits of the additional FAM programme were not maintained, with child-only CBT and CBT with FAM proving equally effective.

In a separate investigation, Wood *et al.* (2006) assigned 40 children aged 6–13 to 12–16 sessions of child-focused CBT or family-focused CBT. Child-focused CBT was based on a condensed version of Coping Cat in which skills training was reduced to four sessions, with eight sessions being directed to application and practice. The family-focused intervention, "Building Confidence" was based on the work of Barrett *et al.*, (1996a) with each session involving time with the child, time with the parents and ending with a family meeting. Parents were taught the following communication skills designed to facilitate their child's acquisition of new skills:

- giving the child choices when they are indecisive rather than making choices for them
- allowing the child to learn by trial and error rather than taking over
- accepting the child's emotional responses rather than criticising them
- encouraging the child to acquire and develop novel self-help skills.

In addition, as included by Barrett *et al.* (1996a), parents were taught to reinforce and reward courageous behaviour and to use planned ignoring to reduce anxious behaviour. At the end of treatment, 53% of children in the child-focused CBT group and 79% in the family-focused CBT were diagnosis-free.

Finally, although not a randomised controlled trial, Bogels and Siqueland (2006) report a study in which 17 children aged 8–17 received a three-phase family CBT intervention. In the first phase the child and their parents were taught the core CBT skills of identifying and challenging negative beliefs, *in vivo* exposure and rewards. In phase 2, dysfunctional beliefs that might impede or block the process of change were modified. The final phase was designed to improve family communication and problem-solving and to plan relapse prevention. By the end of treatment, 41% of children were diagnosis-free, rising to 59% at three months' and 71% at 12 months' follow-up. The authors noted that despite only one session being spent with children to challenge negative thoughts, the resulting cognitive improvements were impressive.

> Child-focused CBT with parental involvement results in significant reductions in child anxiety.

The potential advantages of group interventions led Barrett (1998) to explore whether the intervention described earlier would be effective if delivered in a group format. A total of 60 children aged 7–14 were assigned to group cognitive therapy, group CBT plus FAM or a waiting list control group. Both CBT interventions produced significant changes compared to the waiting list group. Post-treatment assessments revealed that 65% of children who received CBT no longer fulfilled diagnostic criteria for any anxiety disorder, compared to 25% in the waiting list group. These results were maintained at 12 months, where 64% of the CBT group and 84% of the CBT plus FAM were diagnosis-free.

Cobham *et al.* (1998) also investigated this issue by randomly assigning 67 children aged 7–14 and their parents to either 10 sessions of group child-focused CBT or child-focused CBT plus parental anxiety management (PAM). Group CBT was based on the Coping Koala programme with the PAM involving the addition of a further four sessions that were open to both mothers and fathers. The intervention was designed to help parents become aware of their role in the onset and maintenance of their child's difficulties and then to teach parents how to manage their own anxiety. In particular, the four sessions focused on:

- psycho-education about the aetiology of childhood anxiety, and in particular the role of the family
- cognitive restructuring
- relaxation training
- contingency management.

Once again a significant percentage of children no longer met diagnostic criteria when assessed post-intervention (CBT = 60%; CBT + PAM = 78%). These gains were maintained at six-months' follow-up (CBT = 65%; CBT + PAM = 75%) and at 12 months (CBT = 67%; CBT + PAM = 75%). In addition, there was some evidence to suggest that the PAM component enhanced the efficacy of child-focused CBT, at least in the short term, if one or more parents had elevated rates of anxiety.

Finally, Bernstein *et al.* (2005) screened a school population and identified 61 children aged 7–11 with significant anxiety disorders. These children were assigned to group CBT, group CBT plus parent training or a waiting list control group. The CBT intervention was an adapted nine session version of the FRIENDS programme (Barrett *et al.*, 2000), and was once again based on Kendall's Coping Cat programme. For the parent training group the child participated in FRIENDS and the parents separately attended similar sessions. The parental component addressed parental anxiety, stress management, the effects of the family on childhood anxiety and the use of behavioural contracting. Of those children fulfilling diagnostic criteria at baseline, 67% in the CBT plus parenting group and 79% in the child CBT group were diagnosis-free at post-treatment compared with 38% in the waiting list group.

> Results consistently demonstrate that CBT, with or without parental involvement, delivered in a group or individual format is effective in the treatment of children with mixed anxiety disorders.
>
> These results appear to last, although the comparative efficacy of CBT over other active interventions has yet to be consistently determined.

Phobic disorders

There is a lack of robust research trials that have specifically examined the efficacy of interventions for the treatment of phobic disorders. Most research has consisted of single-case reports; the use of structured diagnostic interviews, manualised interventions, assessment of treatment fidelity and adequate follow-ups have been noticeably lacking (King and Ollendick, 1997).

Silverman *et al.* (1999b) assessed the comparative efficacy of exposure-based contingency management, exposure-based cognitive self-control and educational support in the treatment of children with phobic disorders. The study addresses the methodological issues identified above and is exemplary in the use of an active comparison condition, as opposed to a waiting list control group. Eighty-one children completed a 10-week treatment programme. During each session children and parents were seen separately and then came together for approximately 15 minutes at the end.

The cognitive self-control intervention was based on the Coping Cat programme. Sessions 1–3 focused on teaching cognitive skills including self-observation, identifying and modifying self-talk, self-evaluation and self-reward, and the development of a fear hierarchy. Sessions 4–9 focused on practice and exposure.

The contingency management intervention focused exclusively on behavioural strategies, with the first three sessions focusing on devising and refining the fear hierarchy and the use of rewards and sessions 4–9 focusing on exposure. The content of the parent sessions mirrored those of the child and emphasised how parents could support their child.

Children in all three groups, as determined by child, parent and clinician ratings, showed substantial gains on all outcome measures. These gains were maintained when assessed at three, six and 12 months and, contrary to predictions, neither the active nor the comparison (control) intervention proved more effective than the others.

> Although CBT is effective in the treatment of phobic disorders, it does not appear to be more effective than other active interventions.

In terms of social phobia, Hayward *et al.* (2000) assigned 35 socially phobic adolescent girls to a 16-week cognitive behaviour group intervention ($n = 12$) or to a no-treatment group ($n = 23$). The first two sessions involved psycho-education and the rationale for treatment. Sessions 3–8 were skills training including the development of social skills, social problem-solving skills, assertiveness and cognitive restructuring. Sessions 9–15 involved practice and exposure, with the final session being a review. At post-treatment, 55% who received the CBT intervention still fulfilled diagnostic criteria for social phobia, compared with 96% in the untreated group. However, by one year this difference was no longer significant, with 40% in the treated group fulfilling diagnostic criteria compared with 56% in the untreated group. The authors concluded that CBT resulted in a moderate short-term effect in treating social phobia in female adolescents.

More encouraging results were found by Spence *et al.* (2000). Fifty children aged 7–14 with social phobia were randomly assigned to group-based child-focused CBT, CBT plus parental involvement or a waiting list control group. The child-focused intervention involved 12 weekly 90-minute sessions and two booster sessions at three and six months. The social skill training component taught children:

- micro-social skills including eye contact, posture and facial expression
- general conversational and listening skills
- more complex social skills such as question-asking and demonstrating active listening
- friendships skills such as sharing, offering help and giving compliments.

The problem-solving component encouraged children to become a "Social Detective" to solve social challenges such as saying no, being assertive and handling conflict. Children were taught a problem-solving technique involving the following steps:

- *detect* – what is the problem?
- *investigate* – relax, assess alternative solutions and consequences and choose an option; identify and challenge unhelpful thoughts and encourage positive self-talk

- *solve* – carry out the plan, use the social skills, evaluate performance and praise.

The additional parent intervention taught parents to model, prompt and reinforce their child's use of new skills; to ignore socially anxious behaviour and avoidance; to encourage participation in social activities; to prompt and encourage homework assignments; and to model socially proactive behaviour. At post-treatment, approximately 72% of the children who received a variant of CBT were diagnosis-free compared with 7% in the waiting list group. These gains were maintained at 12 months, where approximately 67% of children who received CBT continued to be diagnosis-free.

Finally, in a small pilot study, Baer and Garland (2005) assigned 12 adolescents aged 13–18 with social phobia to a CBT intervention or a waiting list control. The CBT intervention was a group-based programme consisting of 12 sessions. The first session involved psycho-education with the remaining sessions focusing on social skills training and exposure. One session focused on cognitive strategies to manage anxiety. Post-treatment assessments indicated that 36% of children who received the intervention no longer fulfilled criteria for social phobia. Although there was no spontaneous remission in the control group during this time, the positive response rate in the treated group is disappointingly low.

> Research is limited, although the results suggest that CBT is of benefit for children with social phobia. However, a significant proportion who receive CBT continue to fulfil diagnostic criteria for social phobia.

School refusal

CBT for the treatment of school refusal and school phobia has been the subject of three studies. King *et al.* (1998) assigned 34 children aged 5–15 with school refusal to CBT or a waiting list intervention. The children presented with a range of primary diagnoses including separation anxiety disorder, adjustment disorder, overanxious disorder, simple phobia and social phobia.

The child-focused CBT consisted of six sessions.

- In session 1 the child identified anxiety-provoking situations and their own anxiety response.
- Sessions 2–3 focused on coping skills training including relaxation training, the link between thoughts, feelings and behaviour, changing self-talk from anxiety-increasing to anxiety-reducing, assertiveness training and self-evaluation and reward.
- Sessions 4–6 involved practice and imaginal and *in vivo* exposure.

In addition parents received five sessions focusing on child behaviour management skills.

- Session 1: rationale and the role of the carer in securing their child's school attendance.
- Sessions 2–3: establish routines, ignore somatic responses and use reinforcement for positive coping and school attendance.
- Sessions 4–5: troubleshoot problems and address parental guilt or fear of rejection by their child as a result of applying firm discipline.

At post-treatment, 88% of the CBT group had achieved 90% school attendance compared to 29% in the waiting list group. This improvement was maintained at three months.

Positive findings were also reported by Last *et al.* (1998) in a study involving 56 children aged 6–17 with school phobia. As in the study by King *et al.* (1998), the children presented with a range of anxiety disorders including simple phobia, social phobia, separation anxiety disorder, avoidant disorder, overanxious disorder and panic disorder. The children were randomly assigned to 12 sessions of individual CBT or an attention placebo condition involving educational support. The CBT intervention involved exposure and training in coping self-statements. During the first session the child constructed their fear and avoidance hierarchy. In session 2 they were taught to identify anxiety-increasing thoughts and to replace them with coping self-statements. The child systematically works through their hierarchy using their adaptive skills during the remaining sessions. The attention placebo condition involved a combination of educational presentations and supportive psychotherapy. By the end of treatment 65% of children who received CBT had reached 95% school attendance compared with 48% in the control group, a finding that was not statistically significant. Similarly, there were no significant differences between the groups at four and 12 weeks' follow-up.

Finally, Heyne *et al.* (2002) assigned 61 school-refusing children with anxiety disorders to individual child therapy, parent/teacher training or child therapy plus parent/teacher training. The child therapy consisted of eight sessions and involved:

- relaxation training as a coping skill to use at times of stress
- social skills training to improve social competence and learn how to deal with questions about absence
- cognitive therapy to reduce anxiety-increasing thoughts and to promote the use of coping statements
- desensitisation, both imaginal and *in vivo*, to secure school attendance.

Children in all three treatment groups improved, with 69% of children no longer meeting criteria for any anxiety disorder at 4.5 months' follow-up. However, parent/teacher training was equally effective as child focused CBT either with or without parent/teacher training.

> Research is currently limited but suggests that CBT may be beneficial for some children with school refusal, although it is unclear whether CBT is more effective than other interventions.

Conclusion

Research examining the treatment of childhood anxiety is, in many ways, exemplary and addresses many of the criteria suggested by Chambless and Hollon (1998). These include randomised trials, manualised interventions, ensuring treatment integrity, clinical samples, multimodal outcome measures, the assessment of clinical significance, and long-term follow-up. Overall the results are positive and indicate that at post-treatment and follow-up the majority of children who receive some variant of CBT do not fulfil diagnostic criteria for an anxiety disorder. Similarly, compared to waiting list control groups, CBT appears to be an effective intervention for the treatment of anxiety disorders (Cartwright-Hatton *et al.*, 2004; Compton *et al.*, 2004). This has led some to suggest that CBT is the treatment of choice for childhood anxiety disorders (Compton *et al.*, 2004). Others, however, have been more cautious and, while noting the encouraging results, have also highlighted the limitations of the available research (Cartwright-Hatton *et al.*, 2004). In particular, comparatively few studies have compared CBT with other active interventions, and when they did so the results were less clear. For example, Last *et al.* (1998) noted similar improvements in school attendance in children who received supportive psychotherapy and CBT. Similarly, Silverman *et al.* (1999b) found that phobic children who received educational support showed similar improvements to those receiving CBT. There is therefore a need to undertake more trials comparing CBT with other active treatments.

Cartwright-Hatton *et al.* (2004) note that none of the studies in their systematic review included children under the age of 6. Thus comparatively little is known about the efficacy of CBT interventions with very young children. Similarly, the evidence base is currently limited and many studies have included children with mixed anxiety disorders. This does not allow a comprehensive comparison of the use of CBT for the treatment of specific anxiety disorders. Thus at present it is unclear which specific anxiety disorders respond better to CBT or how the treatment components may need to be more clearly tailored to the particular disorder.

The applicability of interventions developed for research studies to everyday clinical practice has also been highlighted as a concern (Kazdin and Weisz, 1998). Studies such as those by Nauta and colleagues (2001, 2003) are therefore important in demonstrating that significant treatment gains can be obtained in real-life clinical settings. Similarly, the inclusion criteria of some research studies result in children with more complex and co-morbid presentations being excluded, and yet these are the children who are often referred to, and treated in, child mental health services. In addition, a number of children drop out of CBT or fail to respond. Soler and Weatherall (2007) in their Cochrane review using an intention-to-treat analysis found that remission rates for anxiety disorders following CBT were 56%, compared with 28% in the control groups which typically involved staying on a waiting list. Thus just over half of children with anxiety disorders will respond to CBT compared to a natural recovery rate of just over a quarter. This indicates an urgent need to enhance the effectiveness of CBT interventions, and to identify more clearly what delivery formats are optimum for which specific anxiety disorders. Similarly, alternative interventions need to be developed for the 40% of children who continue to present with more persistent anxiety disorders.

Finally, comparatively little is known about the effective treatment components of CBT interventions. Treatment-dismantling studies are required to determine what components bring about change in which domain with which children. This is important at a pragmatic level in terms of ensuring that limited clinical services remain focused and cost-effective but also at a theoretical level in terms of understanding the process and mediators of change. This latter issue was highlighted in a review by Prins and Ollendick (2003), who identified that comparatively few studies had explored the assumed relationship between cognitive change and outcome. The studies that were available did find cognitive change following CBT, but these changes were not significantly greater than those found in the control conditions. This led the authors to conclude that there is "only indirect support, at best, for the hypothesis that change in cognitive processes results in or 'causes' outcomes in CBT for childhood anxiety" (p. 101). Reflecting on the meta-review by Durlak *et al.* (1991), in which behaviour change appeared unrelated to cognitive change, Kazdin and Weisz (1998, p. 30) conclude that, "there may be a good deal yet to be learned about mediators of change".

There is accumulating evidence to suggest that CBT results in clinically significant and lasting improvements in children with anxiety disorders.

The relative efficacy of CBT compared to other active interventions or with younger children has yet to be consistently determined.

Dismantling studies are required to determine what treatment components are effective in what domains for which children.

Further research is required to develop interventions for children who fail to respond to CBT.

3

Dysfunctional cognitions and processes

The influential work of Beck and colleagues has highlighted the central role of cognitions and cognitive processes in the development and maintenance of psychological disorders (Beck, 1967, 1971, 1976). The explanatory cognitive model that emerged suggests that biases in information processing and cognitions result in the development and maintenance of significant negative emotional states. Particular emotional states are assumed to be associated with specific maladaptive cognitions, and it is these cognitions that are hypothesised to differentiate between emotions. It is therefore assumed that beliefs associated with personal failure, loss and hopelessness are associated with depression. The content of anxiety beliefs is assumed to be more future-oriented and relates to fear of physical or psychological harm and danger. Finally, aggression is assumed to be associated with cognitions relating to unfairness, being wronged and the perception of hostile intent.

In addition to the specific content of cognitions such as automatic thoughts, attributions, assumptions and schemas, psychological disorders are also assumed to develop and be maintained by dysfunctional cognitive processes. Attentional biases are assumed to result in greater sensitivity to threat-related stimuli, while dysfunctional cognitive content is assumed to be maintained though cognitive processes involving dysfunctional and/or distorted processing.

Despite the assumed central importance of cognitive content and processes in the development of psychological disorders, research examining their relationship with anxiety disorders in children is comparatively limited. Studies that have been undertaken were often limited by small sample sizes, assessed hypothetical situations or laboratory tasks and involved community, non-referred study groups. The direct applicability of these findings to clinical situations is therefore in doubt. Furthermore, the findings are not always consistent. Where predicted differences are found, their size is sometimes small and their clinical significance is questionable. Finally a number of studies have failed to adopt a developmental perspective and have applied adult-derived cognitive models to children. These static models fail to recognise the growing cognitive capacity of children and, for example, the development of meta-cognitive processes.

Notwithstanding these limitations, there is evidence to suggest that children with anxiety disorders exhibit dysfunctional cognitions and processes. In particular, they have more expectations that negative events will occur, make more negative evaluations of their performance, are biased towards possible threat-related cues, and perceive themselves as being unable to cope with frightening events that arise.

Attention bias

Attentional biases in information-processing have been hypothesised to underpin emotional disorders (Beck *et al.*, 1985). With anxiety disorders individuals are assumed to demonstrate an established bias towards the processing of threat-related stimuli. This increased hypervigilance towards possible threat cues results in a greater level of threat detection. This in turn heightens feelings of anxiety, thereby reinforcing and increasing hypervigilance. This leads to the establishment of an anxiety cycle in which expectation and bias result in the seeking and finding of confirmatory information.

This model was developed to explain anxiety in adults, although recent models integrating cognitions and temperament have been proposed to explain anxiety in children (Lonigan *et al.*, 2004). This model proposes that high negative effect is associated with a pre-attentive bias towards threat-related information. If the child is not able to exert sufficient effortful control to override this attention bias, he or she will selectively attend to threat-related information.

Information-processing biases in children have been investigated by laboratory experiments using the Stroop and dot-probe paradigms. Martin *et al.* (1992) compared the performance of children with a specific fear of spiders against those who did not on a Stroop task. Children with spider phobia across all ages (6–13) demonstrated greater interference with spider-related words than non-spider-related words. A similar bias was found by Taghavi *et al.* (2003) when comparing children with generalised anxiety disorder with a control group. The anxiety group demonstrated an attentional bias for threat- and trauma-related words, a tendency that was not significant in the control group.

Vasey *et al.* (1995) compared the performance of children aged 9–14 with anxiety disorders with a non-clinical control group on an attention deployment task. Threat words were detected significantly faster by the anxious group when they were preceded by threatening rather than neutral words suggesting the presence of an attention bias. This finding was replicated in a later study comparing children with generalised anxiety disorders and a normal control group (Taghavi *et al.*, 1999). Anxious children exhibited a greater attention bias towards negative stimuli. This was specific to threat-related information with no between-group differences being detected for depression-related information.

Other research has been equivocal and has not fully supported the premise that a bias towards fear-related stimuli is specific to anxious children. Waters *et al.* (2004) used a dot-probe task that employed fear-related, neutral, and pleasant pictures to explore attention in clinically anxious and non-clinical children. Both groups of children showed an attentional bias towards fearful stimuli, although there was no difference between the groups. However, compared with the non-clinical group, anxious children showed a stronger attentional bias overall towards affective picture stimuli.

Although data is limited, these findings suggest that selective attention to threat cues may increase anxiety, resulting in further attention to threat (Taghavi *et al.*, 1999). Threat-related bias may therefore serve to maintain anxiety (Puliafico and Kendall, 2006).

> Evidence is limited but suggests that anxious children selectively attend to threat-related stimuli.

Threat perception

A potential source of cognitive bias arises from the way children interpret situations and their perception of the degree of threat or danger that these pose. Daleiden and Vasey (1997) raise the question of whether anxious children are hypervigilant to signs of potential threat. The identification of potential threat signals confirms the child's assumptions and beliefs that the situation is dangerous even though subsequent information may demonstrate that this is not the case.

Community studies using the research paradigm of ambiguous social stories have found support for the threat perception bias. Muris *et al.* (2000) noted that children with higher levels of social anxiety were more likely to interpret a short social story as scary, and would make this judgement more quickly, than those with low-level social anxiety. In a subsequent study, non-referred children were assessed using questionnaires and a structured diagnostic interview (Muris *et al.*, 2000). Once again children fulfilling diagnostic criteria for an anxiety disorder or with significant sub-clinical symptoms displayed a higher frequency of threat perception and threatening interpretations and an early detection of threat.

Barrett *et al.* (1996b) examined how clinically anxious children interpreted hypothetical ambiguous situations and compared them with children with oppositional disorder and a non-clinical control group. As an example, children were told that a group of children playing a game started to laugh as they approached. They were asked to indicate what they thought was happening and what they would do. Both the clinically anxious and the oppositional children were more likely to interpret ambiguous situations as threatening (i.e. they are laughing at me). However, while this suggests that anxiety in children is related to threat interpretations of ambiguous situations, this was not specific to anxiety. Children in the oppositional group also demonstrated this tendency.

Interpretative bias was also examined by Bogels and Zigterman (2000), who compared children with social phobia, separation anxiety disorder and generalised anxiety disorder with a clinical (externalising disorders) group and a non-clinical control group. Children were read a series of nine hypothetical stories concerning social situations (e.g. meeting members of a sports team), separation (e.g. becoming separated from a parent while shopping) or generalised anxiety (e.g. remembering to turn off the oven). Children were asked to imagine the situation and to describe what they would think if this happened to them. The children rated how they would feel on a range of emotions and how dangerous, unpleasant or frightening they perceived each situation to be. Finally, children were asked to rate the degree to which they felt able to deal with the situation. The anxious children reported significantly more negative cognitions than those with externalising conditions, a tendency that approached significance when compared with the non-clinical group. Anxious children tended to judge situations as more dangerous and felt less able to cope.

> Anxious children tend to interpret ambiguous situations as more threatening and will reach this decision more quickly.

Frequency of negative cognitions

Self-talk, and in particular negative cognitions, has been hypothesised to be important in the onset and maintenance of childhood anxiety disorders (Kendall and MacDonald, 1993). It has been suggested that higher rates of negative cognitions are associated with anxiety disorders, and that reducing these will improve psychological functioning (Kendall, 1984). This has been described as the power of "nonnegative thinking" and builds on the findings of earlier studies where children's self-talk in natural fear-provoking settings (e.g. visiting the dentist) was found to be significantly related to their reported level of fear (Prins, 1985). Research has shown some support for this suggestion, although the findings are not conclusive and have been questioned (Alfano *et al.*, 2002).

In a community study, Prins and Hanewald (1997) assessed the cognitions of a non-clinical group of children using a thought-listing and a self-statement approach during and after a maths test. Children assessed as high anxiety reported significantly more negative self-evaluatory cognitions during the test than a low-anxiety group on both the thought-listing and self-statement measures. Similarly, Muris *et al.* (2000) found higher rates of negative self-statements in children with higher levels of social anxiety than those with lower levels.

Studies with children with clinical disorders have also noted an association between frequency of negative cognitions and anxiety. Kendall and Chansky (1991) used a thought-listing procedure where children were asked to verbalise their thoughts before, during and after taking part in an anxiety-provoking task (giving a speech). There were no differences in the overall number of thoughts generated by children with an anxiety disorder and a clinical comparison group. However, children who were clinically anxious reported more negative anticipatory thoughts. This tendency was specific to the anticipatory period since, contrary to predictions, there was no difference between the groups during the task, where approximately 30% of both groups reported negative thoughts.

The comparatively low rate of negative cognitions during stressful tasks was also reported by Beidel (1991). After undertaking a vocabulary test, or a read-aloud task, children with and without anxiety disorders were asked to report their cognitions. Only 11–19% of children reported any negative cognitions and there were no differences in frequency between the anxious and non-clinical groups. Similarly, Alfano *et al.* (2006) compared the frequency of negative cognitions in socially phobic children and adolescents and a non-clinical group. The authors noted that only 20% of socially phobic adolescents reported the presence of any negative self-talk. Thus the vast majority (80%) of socially anxious children and adolescents did not report any negative performance thoughts during the role-play task.

Finally, in a study with socially phobic children, Spence *et al.* (1999) noted that, compared to a non-clinical group, socially phobic children reported more negative cognitions on a reading task. Although these findings are consistent with those of Muris *et al.* (2000), the actual difference in rates of negative self-talk reported by anxious and control children is small. Alfano *et al.* (2002) note that in both studies the difference was one thought. Thus, although this is statistically significant, the clinical importance and relevance is less clear.

> Although anxious children report more negative cognitions, the difference is small and the clinical significance is unclear.
>
> The majority of anxious children do not report negative cognitions during stressful tasks, although there is evidence of higher rates before a task is undertaken.

Frequency of positive cognitions

An alternative hypothesis that has been examined is the association between positive cognitions and psychological health, i.e. the "power of positive thinking". It has been hypothesised that children with high levels of anxiety would have lower rates of positive self-talk.

This has been examined in a number of studies, which have consistently failed to find support for this assumed relationship. In non-clinical groups rates of positive thoughts are similar across high- and low-level anxiety children (Prins and Hanewald, 1997). With clinical groups, Spence *et al.* (1999) failed to find differences in rates of positive cognitions between socially phobic and a non-clinical control group. Similarly no differences in positive self-statements between children with anxiety disorders and non-clinical (Treadwell and Kendall, 1996) or clinical comparison groups have been found (Bogels and Zigterman, 2000; Kendall and Chansky, 1991).

> There is no evidence to suggest that anxious children report fewer positive thoughts.

Ratio of positive to negative cognitions

Another factor that has been explored is the ratio of positive to negative thoughts. This is known as the states of mind (SOM) ratio and suggests that a balance between negative and positive thoughts is required for optimal health and adjustment (Schwartz and Garamoni, 1986).

Comparatively little research has been undertaken exploring this hypothesised balance and the presence of anxiety disorders in children. Treadwell and Kendall (1996) found mixed results when they compared SOM ratios of children with anxiety disorders with a non-clinical group. The SOM ratios for the two groups were comparable. The SOM ratio of children with anxiety disorders did not fall within the expected categories that would suggest dysfunction. Indeed, the anxious children fell within the positive dialogue category, which is assumed to be the optimal balance between negative and positive thoughts for psychological adaptation.

> There is no evidence to suggest that the ratio between positive and negative cognitions is associated with anxiety disorders in children.

Cognitive specificity

An issue that has received some attention is the extent to which specific and distinct cognitions are associated with anxiety. The cognitive model proposed by Beck (1967, 1976) is founded on the assumptions that cognitive distortions underpin emotional disorders and the nature of these distorted cognitions differentiates between specific emotional disorders. The content of anxiety beliefs is assumed to be future-oriented and relates to fear of physical or psychological harm and danger. Clinically, the question of cognitive specificity is important since it may inform the focus and content of therapy. Therapy may be more effective if the intervention is targeted and focuses on the specific thoughts and distortions associated with a disorder rather than providing a more general cognitive package.

In a study with a non-referred community sample, Epkins (1996) classified children on the basis of self-report scores as either high- or low-level anxiety with and without dysphoria. Both the dysphoria and social anxiety groups reported more negative self-cognitions and cognitive distortions than the control group. In addition, the cognitive distortions of overgeneralisation and personalisation were specific to social anxiety, not dysphoria. However, although both groups displayed more depressive cognitions than the control group, there was no evidence to indicate that these were specific to dysphoria. Further support for the specificity hypothesis for anxiety was found in a community study of non-clinical children in Hong Kong (Leung and Poon, 2001). The predicted relationship between anxiety and beliefs emphasising fear of physical or psychological harm was supported. Support was also obtained for the predicted relationship between aggression and beliefs of injustice, hostility and immediate gratification. However, the assumed cognitions of loss and failure were not, as would be predicted, uniquely associated with depression.

A few studies have compared the cognitions of clinical groups with non-referred community samples. In the first, Epkins (2000) examined the cognitions of clinic-referred children with externalising, internalising and co-morbid conditions with a community group. The internalising and co-morbid groups showed significantly more cognitive distortions and depressive and anxious thought content than the externalising and community groups. Schniering and Rapee (2002) undertook a comparison of the specific cognitions of a community and mixed clinical group with anxiety, depressive and disruptive disorders. In the first study the authors found significant differences between the frequency with which the community and anxiety and depressive clinical groups endorsed thoughts relating to physical threat, social threat and personal failure. Within the clinical group, cognitions relating to physical and social threat differentiated children with oppositional conduct disorders from anxious or depressed youths but did not differentiate between the anxious and depressed groups. In a subsequent study the authors reported that thoughts of personal failure/loss were the strongest predictor of depressive symptoms; thoughts about social threat or negative evaluation were the strongest predictors of anxiety while thoughts about hostility/revenge were the strongest predictors of aggression (Schniering and Rapee, 2004).

> Support for the content specificity of cognitions is not consistent and, in particular, there is overlap between the cognitions of anxious and depressed children.
>
> Cognitions relating to psychological or physical threat are more likely to be associated with anxiety.

Specificity of cognitive errors

Researchers have investigated the relationship between cognitive errors and specific emotional disorders. In particular, the thinking errors of over-generalisation (i.e. attributing a single negative outcome to other current or future situations); personalisation (i.e. assuming personal responsibility for negative outcomes); catastrophising (i.e. expecting the worst possible outcome); and selective abstraction (i.e. selectively focusing on the negative aspects of events) have been explored. Epkins (1996), for example, hypothesised that selective abstraction in which negative events or features of situation are focused upon may be associated more with depression than with anxiety. Similarly, personalisation, and the associated threat and vulnerability this generates, could be hypothesised to be more highly associated with anxiety. However, given the considerable overlap between anxiety and depression and the differences between anxiety disorders and their manifestation, it is questionable whether cognitive errors would be highly specific or shared.

Leitenberg *et al.* (1986) found that anxious children endorsed over-generalisation, personalisation, catastrophisation and select abstraction more frequently than non-anxious children. However, this anxious group did not differ in the frequency of endorsement from those with raised levels of self-reported symptoms of depression and low self-esteem. It was therefore unclear whether these cognitive errors were specific to emotional problems *per se* or to anxiety disorders in particular. Similarly, in a community sample, Epkins (1996) found that children with social anxiety and depressive symptoms reported more cognitive errors than a non-clinical control group. In addition, the socially anxious children tended to display more distortions involving overgeneralisation and personalising. However, while children with elevated rates of depressive symptoms displayed more selective abstraction than the control group, they did not differ significantly from the anxious group. Finally, in a community study Leung and Poon (2001) noted that catastrophising was associated with both anxiety and depression although the specific focus of the catastrophising was unique to the condition. Catastrophisation involving threat was related to anxiety whereas that involving personal failure was related to depression.

While these studies support the association between raised rates of anxiety and cognitive distortions, none assessed children with clinical disorders who fulfilled diagnostic criteria for anxiety disorders and phobias. This issue was addressed by Weems *et al.* (2001), who assessed 251 children referred to a specialist clinic with anxiety disorders. After controlling for co-morbid depression, the cognitive distortions of overgeneralisation, personalisation and catastrophisation were common across a range of anxiety disorders. These findings suggest that irrespective of the specific anxiety disorder, these distortions may be important.

Finally, as previously mentioned, Epkins (2000) found that children with internalising disorders reported significantly more distortions of catastrophising, personalisation, overgeneralisation and selective abstraction than those with externalising disorders. These findings add support to cognitive models and the assumed differences between internalising and externalising disorders in terms of cognitive content and processing. In terms of specificity, the internalising group included children with both anxiety and depression. A separate comparison of the distortions within each group was not undertaken, and so it is unclear whether these cognitive errors were specific to anxiety or depression.

Findings such as these have led some to conclude that while emotional disorders are associated with particular cognitive distortions, there is a lack of specificity in the content of these cognitions between discrete anxiety disorders (Alfano *et al.*, 2002). Epkins (2000) suggests that further work is required to identify which cognitions are "broad-band" specific (i.e. shared across internalising disorders) and which are "narrow-band" specific (i.e. within specific anxiety disorders).

> Children with anxiety disorders are more likely to display cognitive distortions involving overgeneralisation, personalisation and catastrophising. It is unclear whether these are specific to anxiety disorders or are general to internalising disorders.

Coping bias

A further set of cognitions that have received attention are those relating to coping. Anxious children have been hypothesised to overestimate danger but also to underestimate their ability to cope. This perceived inability to perform successfully has been hypothesised to reinforce and heighten subsequent perceptions of threat.

Bogels and Zigterman (2000) asked children referred with anxiety disorders to rate how they would deal and cope with a number of hypothetical situations. Anxious children tended to underestimate their competence and ability to cope effectively with threat compared to a clinical and non-clinical control group. Perceived self-competence was also assessed by Spence *et al.* (1999). Children diagnosed with social phobia were asked to undertake a series of role-plays and a reading task and to complete a range of measures assessing self-talk, outcome expectancies and self-evaluation. Comparisons with a matched non-clinical group revealed that socially anxious children had lower expectations of their performance than non-anxious children. The authors also noted that the social skills performance of socially phobic children was less competent than their non-anxious peers suggesting that social skills training might be an appropriate intervention. These findings are consistent with those of Alfano *et al.* (2006), who found that socially anxious children had lower expectations of their performance and also rated their actual performance lower on a social interaction task than a control group. In this study the performance of the children was independently rated by blind observers who confirmed that the socially phobic children were less skilled.

The research is not, however, consistent, since different findings were reported by Cartwright-Hatton *et al.* (2005). Although socially anxious children rated their social skills lower than less socially anxious children, independent observers were unable to distinguish between the two groups. This led the authors to suggest that highly anxious children may believe themselves to be nervous rather than actually lacking the requisite skills.

Finally, the solutions chosen by children in response to ambiguous situations have been studied. Barrett *et al.* (1996b) found that anxious children were more likely to choose avoidant ways of coping with potential problems whereas oppositional children choose aggressive solutions. This tendency increased significantly after a family discussion, suggesting that parents may reinforce and encourage avoidance in anxious children.

> Anxious children tend to perceive themselves as less able to cope with potentially threatening situations and believe themselves to be less competent.

Perceived control

Barlow (2002) suggests that a perceived lack of control over external fear-inducing events or internal bodily reactions underpins the development of anxiety disorders. It is the belief that anxiety-related events and sensations are uncontrollable that creates distress. Weems *et al.* (2003) examined the role of control beliefs in anxiety disorders by comparing children with a separation anxiety disorder, specific phobia, social phobia or generalised anxiety disorder with a non-referred comparison group. Children answered a series of questions to assess their perceived control over internal emotional and bodily reactions associated with anxiety (e.g. "I can take charge and control my feelings") and with external threats (e.g. "I can usually deal with hard problems"). Children with anxiety disorders reported a lower perceived control over anxiety-related external events and their internal reactions to anxiety than the comparison group. These findings are preliminary and need to be replicated but could have important implications for therapy.

> The role of perceived control in the development and maintenance of anxiety in children requires further exploration.

Conclusion

Research detailing the association between cognitions, cognitive errors and specific anxiety disorders in children is limited and the findings are not consistent. Weems and Stickle (2005, p. 118) conclude that "a number of studies have shown that these cognitive processes are associated with anxiety and differentiate youth with anxiety disorders from non-anxious youth". Others are more cautious and highlight the methodological and conceptual difficulties that have contributed to the inconsistent and divergent findings, resulting in the literature being difficult to interpret (Alfano *et al.*, 2002).

While it is not clear whether particular cognitive biases are specific to anxiety disorders, it is evident that these cognitive biases are frequently observed in anxious children. However, it is interesting to note that the specific cognitions, attentional biases and cognitive errors that have been found to be associated with anxiety disorders are not always specifically targeted during interventions. As observed by Schniering and Rapee (2002), "treatment with adults can be more effective in a shorter period of time when intervention targets automatic thoughts and cognitive biases specifically associated with a given disorder, compared with 'standard' cognitive therapy targeting more general cognition" (p. 1107). Whether this would also apply to children is unclear. Alfano *et al.* (2002) note that change in cognitive symptoms can be achieved without directly targeting cognitions, and suggest that "directly targeting cognitions is not the critical factor in changing children's cognitive symptoms" (p. 1224). Indeed, the authors note that commonly used cognitive methods such as increasing coping self-statements may not be task-facilitating in the sense that they result in meaningful changes in anxiety. Alfano *et al.* (2002) therefore conclude that further work is required to compare the effects of behavioural and cognitive treatment components on the cognitions and processes associated with anxiety.

A further issue that has received comparatively little attention is developmental variations in cognitions associated with anxiety disorders. The evolving cognitive development of the child may result in younger children having less well developed metacognitive skills. This suggestion is consistent with the findings from Weems *et al.* (2001), who noted that the cognitive errors of catastrophising and personalisation were more strongly associated with anxiety in adolescents than with younger children. Similarly, Alfano *et al.* (2006) found that negative self-thoughts relating to performance were only evident in adolescents with social phobia, not younger children (i.e. aged 7–11 years).

Further research is required to document developmental variations in cognitive content and processing and to investigate specific associations with anxiety disorders in both younger children and adolescents. This will help to determine the nature and extent of dysfunctional cognitions and processes specifically related to anxiety disorders which, in turn, would inform the cognitive focus of the intervention.

> Further research is required to determine whether interventions for both children and adolescents may be enhanced by targeting cognitions specifically associated with anxiety.

4

Parental behaviour and childhood anxiety

The role of the family in the onset and maintenance of childhood anxiety disorders has been the subject of much attention (see reviews by Bogels and Brechman-Toussaint, 2006; Creswell and Cartwright-Hatton, 2007: Wood *et al.*, 2003). The accumulating research has highlighted a number of complex issues and suggests that the family can be both a risk and a protective factor. In terms of risk, there is a genetic transmission for temperamental characteristics such as behavioural inhibition that increase the likelihood that a child will develop an anxiety disorder. Similarly, the association between child and parent anxiety disorders has been well documented in studies examining both the children of anxious parents and the parents of anxious children (Last *et al.*, 1987, 1991; Turner *et al.*, 1987). While this research highlights the importance of genetic factors it is also apparent that not all children with a hereditary predisposition develop an anxiety disorder. Indeed, Eley and Gregory (2004) suggest that genetics accounts for approximately one-third of the variance and, as such, environmental factors appear to be of equal or greater importance. Shared environmental influences therefore make a significant contribution to the development of anxiety disorders in children, and one area that has received considerable interest is that of parental influence.

Rapee (2001) describes a theoretical model which proposes that children with a genetic vulnerability to anxiety are likely to exhibit high levels of arousal and emotionality. Parents respond to this behaviour with increased involvement and protection in order to minimise or prevent their child's distress. In turn, over-involvement and protection serve to increase the child's perception of threat, reduce their sense of personal control over threatening situations and increase their use of avoidant strategies. Therefore parents who protect their children from stressful experiences or who take over in stressful situations are implicitly teaching their children that the world is a dangerous place and they are unable to cope on their own. In view of these potentially important influences the role of parental over-control, negativity, modelling, management and cognitions in the development and maintenance of child anxiety disorders will be briefly outlined.

Parental over-control

Over-control is the degree to which parents intrude in their child's life and regulate their behaviour and activities. Parental intrusiveness serves to limit the child's opportunities to master challenging problems and impairs their self-efficacy (Wood *et al.*, 2006). Thus, when confronted with novel situations, anxious children may have lower expectations that they can independently cope and remain safe, and as such experience anxiety. Learning to cope with novel situations is a common and important developmental task during childhood. As such, a limited or unsuccessful learning history may increase anticipatory anxiety.

There is now considerable evidence detailing the relationship between excessive parental involvement, over-control and childhood anxiety (Rapee, 1997: Wood *et al.*, 2003). For example, Krohne and Hock (1991) note that mothers of highly anxious girls were more controlling than those of girls with low-level anxiety on a cognitive task. In terms of clinically anxious children, Hudson and Rapee (2001, 2002) observed parents and children working together on a problem-solving task. The authors noted that mothers of children with significant anxiety disorders were more intrusive and more involved than mothers of a non-clinical comparison group. The finding that mothers of clinically anxious children are less granting of autonomy than mothers of non-clinical children has been replicated in other observational studies (Mills and Rubin, 1998; Whaley *et al.*, 1999).

These studies suggest that an over-involved parenting style is associated with anxiety, although this may not be specific to anxiety disorders. Controlling parenting has also been found in parents of children with oppositional disorders (Hudson and Rapee, 2001). Parental over-involvement may not necessarily be a causal factor in the development of anxiety disorders, but may nonetheless be an important maintaining factor. While there is evidence to support this possibility, Bogels and Brechman-Toussaint (2006) note that the relationship between over-control and anxiety may not be linear. Parental under-control, in which the child is provided with too much autonomy before they are ready, may also contribute to the development of anxiety.

> There is evidence to highlight the relationship between parental over-control and childhood anxiety. However, it is unclear whether this is specific to anxiety disorders.

Parental negativity

Parental negativity is conceptualised as excessive criticism or rejection and the absence of emotional warmth. A negative and critical environment may result in children developing cognitions that their world is hostile and, through these, increase their sensitivity to potentially threatening aspects of their life.

Observational studies have noted a relationship between parental negativity and childhood anxiety. Hudson and Rapee (2001) found that mothers of anxious children were more negative during a discussion with their child. The results are not, however, always consistent. Whaley *et al.* (1999), for example, observed anxious mothers talking to their children about an anxiety-provoking situation. Anxious mothers of anxious children were rated as significantly less warm and positive, and more critical than non-anxious mothers of non-anxious children. However, anxious mothers of children with no disorders also displayed this tendency. Similarly, Siqueland *et al.* (1996) found no differences in the maternal warmth of mothers of anxious and non-anxious children.

In conclusion, there is less consistent evidence to suggest that parental negativity is specifically associated with childhood anxiety (Wood *et al.*, 2003). The results are variable and could suggest that maternal anxiety, *per se*, is an important factor that could account for reduced maternal warmth and positivity.

> The nature of the relationship between parental negativity and childhood anxiety is less clear. Parental anxiety may have an important role in moderating or explaining the relationship between parental negativity and child anxiety.

Parental modelling

Another way by which parents may contribute to the development of their child's anxiety is by modelling anxious behaviour. This may be particularly relevant where the parent has an anxiety disorder, and may verbalise their fears and model anxious reactions and avoidance. Research is limited, although recent observational studies found that anxious mothers tend to catastrophise, focus on negative outcomes and convey a sense of having no control (Moore *et al.*, 2004). Similarly, Whaley *et al.* (1999) found that anxious mothers of clinically anxious children were more likely to discuss problems in ways that emphasised a lack of control and ability to cope effectively. Anxious mothers may therefore signal expectations that the child will not cope and, by repeatedly voicing their negative expectations, both model and reinforce anxious behaviour and failure.

> Limited evidence suggests that parental modelling of anxious behaviour may contribute to the development and/or maintenance of anxiety in children.

Parental reinforcement of avoidant behaviour

In addition to modelling anxious behaviour, parents may also reinforce avoidant coping in their children. Barrett *et al.* (1996b) asked children how they would respond to a set of ambiguous situations both before and after a short family discussion. A significant number of anxious children changed their response after talking with their parents, from pro-social to more avoidant responses. Further analysis revealed that parents supported and reinforced their child's avoidant suggestions (Dadds *et al.*, 1996). A subsequent study replicated these findings and noted that higher levels of parental distress were also associated with increased avoidance following a family discussion (Shortt *et al.*, 2001). By parents encouraging avoidance it is hypothesised that children will have fewer opportunities to learn more adaptive ways of coping with fearful situations and to develop a positive learning history. Shortt *et al.*, (2001), suggest that these findings indicate a need to help parents overcome their own problems so that they are able to help their children approach anxiety-provoking situations.

> Parents are inclined to encourage avoidant responses in their anxious children.

Parental beliefs and cognitions

Parental beliefs and cognitions will affect how engaged children and parents are in therapy and may affect the parenting strategies they choose (Bogels and Brechman-Toussaint, 2006; Siqueland and Diamond, 1998). Mills and Rubin (1990, 1992, 1993) highlight how mothers of anxious children are more likely to attribute social withdrawal to a dispositional state and believe that this is a difficult behaviour to change. Kortlander *et al.* (1997) assessed maternal expectations about their child's ability to cope with a stressful task.

Compared to mothers of non-anxious children, mothers of the clinically anxious group expected their children to be more upset, less able to cope, and were less confident in their child's ability to perform the task.

Parental beliefs about the degree of control they can exert in child-rearing situations is an important determinant of their parenting behaviour. Although potentially important, the extent to which parental cognitions mediate change in parenting behaviour, and/or child anxiety, has not yet been clarified. However, Bogels and Brechman-Toussaint (2006, p. 849) conclude that "there is tentative evidence to suggest that the beliefs and attributions parents make for children's anxious behaviour, together with their perceptions of personal control, may indirectly contribute to the development and maintenance of child anxiety by increasing the likelihood of over-controlling parenting behaviours or a failure to respond to children's anxious responses. In turn, these parenting responses may exacerbate or at least maintain child anxiety by impacting on children's personal self-efficacy."

> Although evidence is limited, parental cognitions and beliefs may influence parenting behaviours which contribute to, or maintain, anxiety in their children.

The role of parents in treatment

The accumulating evidence highlighting the association between parental behaviour and childhood anxiety has led some to note that interventions that do not attempt to change parental behaviour would be unlikely to be effective (Spence *et al.*, 2000). Indeed, given the strong association between child and parental anxiety it would seem important to include a treatment component that specifically targeted and addressed parental anxiety. However, while the involvement of parents in child-focused CBT appears to have some theoretical and pragmatic substance, their actual role, and the extent of their involvement, varies considerably. Parents have been involved in child CBT in various roles including those of a facilitator or co-clinician or as a client in their own right (Stallard, 2002). The focus and emphasis of the intervention have ranged from working on the child's problems through to additional parent sessions designed to teach the parents new skills to mange their own mental health problems. Similarly the balance between, and way in which child, parent and family work is conducted and sequenced, have varied.

The facilitator: psycho-education

The most limited role is that of facilitator, in which parents are provided with some degree of education about the underlying rationale and content of the intervention. Typically this involves two or three parallel sessions in which the rationale for using CBT is explained, and information about techniques and strategies that will be taught to the child during the programme is provided. Involving parents in this way increases their awareness and commitment to the treatment programme. It provides parents with the information they need to facilitate and actively encourage the child's use of skills outside of clinical sessions. Courageous and active coping can be prompted and reinforced, and their involvement can increase the likelihood of continued change after the intervention has finished.

Parental involvement is limited, with the child remaining the central focus of the intervention. The programme is therefore designed to address the child's problems, with important parental behaviours and cognitions that may have contributed to the onset and development of the child's anxiety not being directly addressed. This model of parental involvement is exemplified in the Coping Cat programme (Kendall, 1994). The 16-week programme is undertaken with the child, with parental participation consisting of two separate sessions focusing on psycho-education.

The co-clinician: develop and support the child's acquisition of new skills

A more extensive variant of the facilitator is that of the co-clinician. The child's anxiety continues to be the primary focus of the intervention, which is designed to help the child develop the necessary skills to overcome their difficulties successfully. However, parents are more actively involved and attend most or all of the treatment sessions either with their child or in parallel. They are therefore aware of the specific content of each session and are encouraged to monitor, prompt and reinforce their child's use of coping skills outside of treatment sessions. Both Mendlowitz *et al.* (1999) and Toren *et al.* (2000) describe joint parent/child interventions for children with anxiety disorders that encapsulate this role. As with the facilitator, the parent's own behaviour/problems are not directly addressed. The role of parents is to support the intervention in reducing their child's psychological distress. Changing parental behaviours and cognitions that may have contributed to the onset or maintenance of the child's problems are not directly addressed.

Parent's as co-clients: address both child and parental behaviour

Programmes that involve parents as co-clients directly address parental behaviours that are assumed to contribute to the development and maintenance of their child's anxiety. While the child receives CBT to address their own problems the parents/family acquire new skills to address important family or personal difficulties. Cobham *et al.* (1998), for example, describe a programme in which children with anxiety disorders receive 10 sessions, with parents receiving four separate sessions. The parents' sessions explore their role in the development and maintenance of their child's problems and how to manage their own anxiety and model appropriate anxiety management strategies. Similarly, the Family Anxiety Management programme described by Barrett *et al.* (1996a) trained parents in contingency management, problem-solving and communication skills and how to become aware of their own anxiety behaviour. These are in addition to the child-focused sessions that teach children to identify and manage their own anxiety-increasing cognitions and emotional responses.

The role and purpose of parents in programmes for children with anxiety problems have varied.

- Parents have been involved as facilitators or co-clinicians to support and encourage their child's acquisition and use of new skills.
- Parents have been involved as co-clients to address their own anxiety problems or to learn new behaviour-management skills.

Model of change

The lack of clarity about the primary purpose of parents in CBT programmes has resulted in parents being involved in treatment sessions in different ways. Parents have attended parallel treatment sessions, often separate from their child (Heyne *et al.*, 2002). In a variation, parental involvement in the study by Spence *et al.*, (2000), consisted of parents observing child sessions through a one-way screen. In these programmes parents and children work through the same materials but do not attend any treatment sessions together in the same room. In others, sessions are dedicated for both parents and children to work together (Barrett, 1998; Barrett *et al.*, 1996a; Cobham *et al.*, 1998).

The theoretical model detailing the process by which parental involvement facilitates changes in the child's behaviour and their acquisition of skills has rarely been described. Barrett (1998) describes how the clinician joins with parents and children during joint sessions to form an "expert team". This requires the open sharing of information and the empowerment of parents and children by building on their existing strengths in order to solve and address problems. Ginsburg *et al.* (1995) describe a process of transfer in which expert knowledge and skills from the clinician are transferred to the parent, to the child. In turn this informs the sequencing of treatment sessions in order to maximise the successful application of skills. Thus parents and children learn skills together, although the parents are encouraged to implement the skills first. Once mastered, the parent's use of anxiety-reduction strategies is phased out and the child's use of self-control strategies encouraged.

> The process by which parents facilitate change needs to be clarified. This will inform whether parents and children are seen jointly or separately.

Does parental involvement enhance effectiveness?

Given the different ways in which parents can be involved in child-focused CBT, a key question is whether parental involvement enhances effectiveness and, if so, what model of involvement is optimal. This question is of paramount importance to clinicians in planning interventions and yet has received surprisingly little attention. Studies that have investigated this issue are summarised below.

Spence et al. *(2000)*

Fifty children aged 7–14 with social phobia were randomly assigned to 12-session child-focused CBT, CBT involving parents, or a waiting list control. Compared to the waiting list control group, children in both CBT groups showed significant reductions in social and general anxiety and a significant increase in parental ratings of social skills performance. Although fewer children in the parental involvement group retained their initial diagnosis (12.5%) compared with child-only CBT (42%) at post-treatment, this finding was not statistically significant. Similarly, there were no statistically significant differences between CBT with and without parental involvement on any measure, leading the authors to conclude that "parental participation in the program was not found to add significantly to the effectiveness of child only treatment" (p. 724).

Heyne et al. *(2002)*

Child-only CBT was compared with (1) parent/teacher training and (2) child CBT plus child/parent training in the treatment of 61 school-refusing children aged 7–14. Statistically and clinically significant post-treatment changes occurred for each group, although child CBT was the least effective in increasing school attendance. By follow-up (average 4.5 months) there were no significant differences between the treatment groups on any measure. Attendance and adjustment of those in the child-only CBT group were similar to that of the other groups. Heyne *et al.* conclude that "contrary to expectations combined child therapy and parent/teacher training did not produce better outcomes at posttreatment or follow-up" (p. 687).

Cobham et al. (1998)

Sixty-seven children aged 7–14 with anxiety disorders were randomly assigned, according to parental anxiety level, to either child-focused CBT or child-focused CBT plus parental anxiety management. At post-treatment, 6 and 12 months' follow-up, there were no statistically significant differences in the number of children who met diagnostic criteria, clinician ratings of improvement, or child self-report measures in either group. Parental anxiety was, however, an important factor. When both parent and child were anxious, CBT with parental involvement resulted in significantly lower rates of diagnosed child anxiety at post-treatment (39% v. 77%). Although still evident, these differences had reduced at 6 months (44% v. 71%) and 12 months (59% v. 71%) and were no longer statistically significant. This led the authors to conclude that "the provision of the additional component [parent involvement] did not add anything to the efficacy of CBT for the child alone when neither parent reported elevated levels of trait anxiety" (p. 903).

Mendlowitz et al. (1999)

Sixty-two parents and children (aged 7–12) with anxiety disorders were randomly assigned to a 12-week child-only, parent-only, or child and parent CBT intervention. At post-treatment, all groups demonstrated decreases in self-report anxiety and depression symptoms. Parents in the combined child and parent CBT group rated their child as more improved, and children reported a greater use of active coping strategies. The authors concluded that "concurrent parental involvement enhanced the effect on coping strategies" (p. 1223).

Barrett (1998)

Sixty children aged 7–14 with anxiety disorders were randomly assigned to 12-session child-focused group CBT, group CBT plus family management or a waiting list control group. Children in both intervention groups improved compared to the waiting list control. Parental involvement did not have any significant effect on diagnostic status at post-treatment or 12 months' follow-up. However, parental involvement did result in significantly greater changes on clinician-completed evaluation scales, parental reports, and child reports of anxiety. Barrett concluded that "the group condition with the added family training component showed marginal improvement on a number of measures in comparison with the cognitive-behavioural group intervention treatment" (p. 466).

Barrett et al. (1996a, 2001)

These studies report the 12 months' and six years' follow-up of children assigned to child CBT, CBT plus family management, or a waiting list condition. The initial study involved 79 children aged 7–14. Post-treatment, significantly fewer children in the intervention groups fulfilled diagnostic criteria, with parental involvement being superior to child-only CBT (84.0% v. 57.1%), a difference that continued to be significant at 12 months (95.6% v. 70.3%). Similarly, CBT and family management proved superior to child-only CBT at post treatment and follow-up on clinical evaluations of change, self-report and parent-completed measures.

A long-term evaluation of this cohort was undertaken, resulting in 52 children being reassessed six years after completing the programme. Gains were maintained, with 85.7% no longer meeting diagnostic criteria, although parental involvement did not enhance the outcome. There were no significant differences between the groups on any measures. The authors summarise that "contrary to predictions, the CBT + FAM condition [parental involvement] did not appear more effective than CBT only" (p. 139).

Bernstein et al. (2005)

In this study 61 children aged 7–11 were assigned to group CBT, group CBT plus concurrent parent training, or a waiting list control. Of these children, 46 met DSM-IV criteria for separation anxiety disorder, generalised anxiety disorder and/or social phobia. The child-focused CBT intervention was the FRIENDS programme, a nine-session adaptation of the Coping Koala programme. Children receiving a variant of CBT demonstrated significant post-treatment improvements on child-, parent- and clinician-completed measures compared to the waiting list. Between the two forms of CBT the results were mixed. In the CBT plus parent training group the percentage of children meeting diagnostic criteria reduced from 80% to 33% after treatment, similarly to the child CBT-only group (82% to 29%). Parents who received parental training rated more improvement on some parent-completed measures than those who were not involved in the intervention.

Nauta et al. (2001)

In this pilot study, Nauta *et al.* (2001) found no additional benefits of adding a cognitive-oriented parent-training programme to child-focused CBT. Eighteen children aged 8–15 were assigned either to 12-session individual child-focused CBT or to child-focused CBT with cognitive parent training. The child-focused CBT intervention was a 12-session adaptation of the Coping Cat programme. The additional parent cognitive parent training involved seven sessions in which the parent's thoughts and feelings regarding their child were addressed. Difficult situations were described, accompanying feelings and thoughts elicited and the consequences of these detailed. Parents were taught to challenge their dysfunctional thoughts and encouraged to undertake a series of behavioural experiments. At three-month follow-up, 88% of those who received only child-focused CBT no longer fulfilled diagnostic criteria for an anxiety disorder, compared to 71% who also received cognitive parent training. Similarly, no additional effects of parental involvement were noted at post-treatment or follow-up on child- or parent-completed questionnaires.

Nauta et al. (2003)

The role of parents was investigated more fully in this subsequent study involving 79 children aged 7–18 who fulfilled diagnostic criteria for a separation anxiety, social phobia, generalised anxiety disorder or panic. The children were assigned to the groups described above, namely CBT only, CBT plus cognitive parent training or a waiting list group.

As determined by diagnostic status and parent reports, children in both active interventions made significant gains over the waiting list group. After intervention, 54% of children no longer fulfilled any anxiety diagnosis compared with 10% in the waiting list group. However, there were no differences in diagnostic rates between CBT with and without parental involvement at post-treatment (59% v. 54%) and three months' follow-up (69% v. 68%). Similarly, the addition of the parental component did not result in any significant differences on child- or parent-reported measures. The authors conclude that parental involvement did not enhance the effects of CBT, but note that potentially important changes in parental cognitions were not assessed.

Wood et al. (2006)

This study compared a family-focused CBT programme (the Building Confidence programme) with traditional child-focused CBT based on Kendall's Coping Cat intervention. Forty children aged 6–13 years received 12–16 therapy sessions. Both groups made improvements on all measures of anxiety when assessed at follow-up. More children in the family-focused CBT programme were diagnosis-free (79%) at the end of treatment compared to the child-only condition (53%), although this difference was not statistically significant. However, the authors noted that according to parental ratings, anxiety symptoms declined more rapidly in the family group. Similarly, the family CBT group showed more improvements on ratings by independent evaluators although there were no differences on child self-report measures of anxiety. The authors note that both treatment groups showed improvements on all outcome measures but conclude that "parent reports and independent evaluator ratings suggest that, when compared with an individual child-focused treatment, family CBT produced greater symptoms reduction and improved functioning at posttreatment"

Summary

The results of these studies do not provide consistent support for the widely held clinical belief that parental involvement enhances child-focused CBT. At post-treatment, only one study found that parental improvement resulted in significantly lower diagnostic rates (Barrett *et al.*, 1996a). There were no significant differences in any study on child-report measures although some studies note additional improvements on parent-completed measures (Bernstein *et al.*, 2005; Mendlowitz *et al.*, 1999; Wood *et al.*, 2006). The possibility of a positive response bias cannot be excluded and the clinical significance of these differences is not clear. Indeed, although some studies reported statistically significant differences between CBT with and without parental involvement on specific questionnaire sub-scales, the number continuing to score above the clinical cut-off did not show a significant change (Barrett, 1998; Barrett *et al.*, 1996a).

The strongest data suggesting the enhanced role of parents in child-focused CBT comes from the work of Barrett *et al.* (1996a). Although the authors noted a number of significant post-treatment benefits, the extent of these became less marked over time. When assessed, six years after the intervention, parental involvement did not result in any additional significant differences over child-only CBT. However, long-term research is limited. Further studies are required to explore possible longer-term benefits associated with parental involvement in child-focused CBT.

Bogels and Siqueland (2006) highlight a number of reasons for the absence of additional gains with parental involvement. The authors suggest that the parental component may need to be more intense in clinical settings, where problems are often co-morbid and more severe. Similarly, interventions may not be sufficiently tailored to the individual needs of specific families. Important outcomes such as changes in parental cognition or family functioning have seldom been assessed. In addition, the extent of parental difficulties and degree to which they require direct intervention in their own right have been assessed in only one study. The work of Cobham *et al.* (1998) suggests that this is important and that targeted parental interventions may be more important if the parent also has significant anxiety problems. In a separate study evaluating family CBT, Bogels and Siqueland (2006) note that, following the intervention, levels of anxiety in fathers reduced significantly, although this effect was not evident for mothers. This led the authors to suggest that fathers may be crucial in helping adolescents to conquer their fears, and suggest that they should be included in treatment programmes.

Cobham *et al.* (1998) speculate whether the failure to find the expected additional benefits of parental involvement may be due to the length of the intervention. Parent sessions may not be sufficiently potent to secure and maintain significant post-treatment reductions in diagnostic status. The actual content of parent sessions has also varied, and may be more effective if the programme directly addresses parent behaviour and cognitions associated with childhood anxiety instead of general behavioural management techniques. Indeed, despite the failure of the studies by Nauta *et al.* (2001, 2003) to detect additional benefits, the authors note that important changes in parental cognitions, which were not assessed, may have occurred.

Finally, the way in which child and parent sessions are provided has received surprisingly little interest. In many programmes, parental involvement consists of separate sessions that run in parallel to those for the child. This has led some to suggest that parental involvement may be enhanced by co-joint work in which parents and children are involved in treatment sessions together (Ginsburg and Schlossberg, 2000). The need to pay greater attention to the process of change and therefore how parents are involved in the intervention was also suggested by Bogels and Siqueland (2006). It is therefore important to clarify how skills and knowledge are transferred from the clinician to the child (Ginsburg *et al.*, 1995). Clarification will highlight important maintaining or impeding parental behaviours and in turn this will inform the sequencing and attendance at treatment sessions. Indeed, the studies that reported the greatest benefits from parental involvement provided joint child/parent sessions (Barrett, 1998; Barrett *et al.*, 1996a).

Conclusion

Comparatively little attention has been paid to defining the role of parents in the treatment of childhood anxiety and in evaluating the impact of their involvement on outcome. The evidence is limited, although in their meta-review Cartwright-Hatton *et al.* (2004) conclude that there is little evidence to support the widely held belief that parental involvement in child-focused CBT enhances treatment effectiveness. This conclusion runs counter to the widely held clinical view and suggests that further work is required to determine the maximum way of involving parents in child-focused CBT. This is particularly important in view of the considerable resource implications that parental involvement may require. Programmes that run separate parent and child sessions almost double the amount of therapeutic time required, thereby raising questions as to whether the marginal gains produced are a good use of limited resources.

> There are theoretical and clinical reasons why parents should be involved in the treatment of childhood anxiety.
>
> There are variations in the purpose and nature of parental involvement.
>
> The additional benefits of parental involvement have not yet been consistently demonstrated.

5

Assessment and problem formulation

Worries and fears during childhood are common. As such, the clinician needs to assess carefully the extent, nature and clinical significance of the child's anxiety in order to determine whether an intervention is appropriate or required. A variety of standardised interviews and questionnaires are available to aid the systematic assessment, and quantification, of anxiety symptoms and disorders. These can provide a useful adjunct to the clinical interview, although they do have limitations. Silverman and Ollendick (2005), for example, highlight a number of issues ranging from the psychometrics of particular questionnaires and interviews through to their clinical utility and sensitivity. These limitations need to be recognised when using and interpreting the results from these measures.

The diagnosis and assessment of anxiety disorders in children should be based on a full clinical interview and use multiple methods and sources, taking information from different contexts into consideration. Multiple methods might include interviews, observations and rating scales that sample and capture the different ways in which anxiety disorders and symptoms might present. These need to be tailored to the child's development. For example, with younger children there may be less use of self-report questionnaires but a greater reliance on observation and third-party report. Similarly, multiple sources provide opportunities to compare and contrast different perspectives on the child's behaviour. However, agreement between raters, particularly when assessing internal anxiety states and symptoms, is often low. Observations and third-party assessments may show considerable variability, reflecting the way children present across situations and with different people.

The clinical interview

The initial interview is designed to provide a general overview of the child, their presenting problems and context. During the initial interview the clinician will have an opportunity to gain a basic understanding of a number of aspects of the child and their life, including:

- personality and temperament
- academic performance, social relationships and behaviour at school
- family structure, family relationships and a basic understanding of family dynamics
- significant events such as trauma, difficult changes/transitions, health issues or developmental problems
- significant events for the parents such as relationship problems, redundancy, financial or housing worries, mental health problems
- the young person's friendships, interests and social life
- personal strengths and positive attributes.

The first part of the assessment interview therefore provides a general understanding of the young person and their context. The second part moves into a more detailed assessment of their specific psychological problems, and will include:

- a clear description of each current problem and worry – this needs to be specific and detailed; talking through a recent example in depth can be helpful
- an understanding of the child's emotional response and any particularly strong anxiety signals they notice
- a basic understanding of the nature and content of strong or recurrent worrying thoughts and the events or situations that trigger them
- how the child reacts and deals with their worries and their perception of how helpful they find these methods of coping
- any previous attempts at coping that the child has used and whether any have been more or less successful
- onset, severity, intensity and frequency of the worries and anxiety symptoms
- exploration of the presence of other co-morbid conditions such as other anxiety disorders, depression or post-traumatic stress disorder (PTSD)
- motivation to change and belief in likely success.

The initial clinical interview also provides an opportunity to model key aspects of CBT immediately and to highlight the child's central and active role in the process. It should be made explicit that the clinician wants to hear what the child has to say; that their views and contributions are important; that their understanding may be different from that of their parents; and that everything they say will be taken seriously. The process involves ensuring that the child is involved in the interview; that questions are directed towards them; that they have opportunities to disagree with what has been said. This last point can be difficult for anxious children, and so questions have to be phrased in a way that can help them to voice their views. Introducing questions with a brief premise can help to make this process easier. Premises such as "sometimes young people see things differently from their parents" or "there are often lots of different ways of thinking about this" can help. The clinician also needs to remain aware that the interview can prove anxiety-provoking, especially for an anxious child. The clinician therefore needs to attend to any signs that the child is anxious and to acknowledge them. Uncertainty can be reduced by describing at the outset of the interview what will happen, what you intend to talk about and how long the interview will last. If the child becomes anxious during the interview the clinician can validate their feelings and acknowledge how difficult it must be for them. Similarly the young person can be given some degree of control by providing them with choices. If for example they are finding it difficult to talk about a particular problem, you can ask whether they would like mum or dad to help out. Similarly, the basic areas of the interview can be mapped and the child given the opportunity to choose the order in which they are discussed. The key issue is to make sure that the child's anxiety and distress is contained so that discussions about anxiety-provoking situations and events can be undertaken and are not avoided.

Structured diagnostic interviews

General interviews can be supplemented by focused diagnostic interviews. These semi-structured interviews provide a systematic way of assessing the presence of symptoms against diagnostic criteria, typically DSM-IV (APA, 2000). For some clinicians the question of whether or not a child fulfils specific diagnostic criteria is less important than a more functional analysis that provides a good understanding of the onset and maintenance of the child's difficulties. Diagnostic interviews do, nonetheless, provide the clinician with a useful and systematic way of comprehensively assessing a range of anxiety disorders and symptoms. This does not preclude the development of a more functional analysis, or a problem formulation. Similarly, while interviews may help clarify whether a child meets diagnostic criteria, it is important to use such methods flexibly. Children may not, for example, fulfil all diagnostic criteria but nonetheless present with sub-threshold symptoms that still generate significant impairment and indicate that treatment is required.

A number of diagnostic interviews are available, although many are generic and assess a wide range of mental health disorders.

The Anxiety Disorders Interview Schedule (ADIS-C/P: Silverman and Albano, 1996; Silverman et al., 2001)

Based on DSM-IV diagnostic criteria, the ADIS was specifically designed to assess a range of anxiety disorders. It has been used extensively and is generally viewed as the gold-standard interview for assessing anxiety in children. There are parallel child (C) and parent (P) completed versions and it can be used with children aged 6–18 years. The ADIS-C/P is developmentally sensitive and assesses cognitive, physiological and behavioural responding across a range of situations that could be perceived as potentially threatening (e.g. peer situations, separation). In addition to identifying the specific symptoms associated with particular anxiety disorders, the degree of impairment is assessed. The interviewer rates the severity of symptoms and degree of interference with everyday life using an eight-point Likert scale (0 = none; 8 = very severely disabling). A clinician rating of 4 or more (definitely disturbing/impairing) is considered clinically significant, with lower scores suggesting sub-threshold symptoms.

The ADIS-C/P has good test–retest and inter-rater reliability and has been shown to be sensitive to treatment change (Barrett *et al.*, 1996a; Kendall *et al.*, 1997; Silverman *et al.*, 2001). However, while having many strengths, the ADIS is time consuming and can take 1.5 hours to complete.

Diagnostic Interview for Children and Adolescents (DICA-R: Herjanic and Reich, 1982)

The DICA was modelled on the highly structured Diagnostic Interview Schedule for adults that was developed for use in epidemiological studies (Robins *et al.*, 1982). It was designed for use by lay interviewers and can be used with children and young people aged 6–18 years to assess either DSM-III-R or DSM-IV diagnoses. There are versions for parents, children (6–12 years) and adolescents (13–18 years) and a computerised method of administration is also available. The DICA takes between one and two hours to complete and covers a range of mental health disorders including anxiety disorders. Each general item is read as written and rated as yes (1) or no (0). If answered affirmatively, detailed probe questions are used to gain further information which is then used to make a lifetime diagnoses. This can be particularly useful in genetic studies, where the reliability and validity of the DICA is generally good (see Reich, 2000). However, initial studies show poor parent–child agreement. Adolescent girls, for example, reported more internalising disorders than their mothers (Herjanic and Reich, 1982).

NIMH Diagnostic Interview Schedule for Children (NIMH DISC: Shaffer et al., 1996, 2000)

The NIMH DISC is a structured diagnostic interview that, like the DICA, was originally developed for use by lay researchers in large-scale epidemiological surveys. It is a structured interview that has evolved through different versions since its development in the early 1980s. The current version, DISC IV, can be used with children and young people aged 6–17 years and has parallel versions for parent and child to complete. It is an extensive interview, containing approximately 3000 questions, assessing over 30 DSM and ICD disorders. The interview first assesses whether specific symptoms have been present during the past year, and if positively endorsed, follow-up questions check their presence over the past four weeks. The responses to most of the DISC questions are coded as No (0), Yes (1), Not Applicable (8), or Don't Know (9). In order to assess the impairment criteria of DSM-IV, a series of questions are included at the end of each diagnostic section. These assess possible impairment in terms of getting along with parents/caretakers; participating in family activities; participating in peer activities; academic/occupational functioning; relationships with teachers, and distress attributable to symptoms. Once the presence of any impairment is ascertained, the severity is assessed.

Kiddie-Schedule for Affective Disorders and Schizophrenia (K-SADS: Kaufman et al., 1997)

K-SADS was developed from an adult scale and has undergone a number of revisions over the years to ensure compatibility with evolving diagnostic systems. The current version, K-SADS-P-IVR, is compatible with DSM-III-R/IV and can be used with children aged 6–18 to provide lifetime (over the past 12 months) and current (past week) diagnoses. There are parent- and child-completed versions which take between 1 and 1.5 hours to complete. During the interview, the various symptoms for each DSM diagnosis are rated on a 0–4 or 0–6 scale of symptom severity/frequency, e.g. not at all; slight (occasional); mild (sometimes); moderate (often); severe (most of the time); and extreme (all of the time).

- Structured diagnostic interviews tend to assess a range of mental health disorders and are extensively based on DSM criteria.
- Diagnostic interviews are thorough but time-consuming.
- ADIS-C/P focuses more on anxiety disorders and is generally considered to be the "gold standard" for assessing anxiety disorders in children.

Self-report questionnaires

An alternative approach to the diagnostic interview is to assess and quantify systematically the nature and extent of the young person's anxiety by the use of self-report questionnaires. The co-morbidity within specific anxiety disorders, and between anxiety and depression, poses particular problems for the valid and reliable assessment of anxiety in children. Weems and Stickle (2005) highlight that there is generally poor agreement between child, parent, teacher and clinician assessments. They note that this could be due to situational differences in behaviour, difference between assessment methods, inadequate assessment procedures or poor construct validity. They conclude that more research is required "detailing the characteristics of individual measures of anxiety and an accounting of how different modalities of assessment (e.g. self-report, parent report, interviews, behavioural observation, physiological measures) relate to each other" (p. 110).

The complexity of anxiety suggests the need to assess cognitions, behaviour and physiological responses across different contexts using a range of methods from multiple informants (Greco and Morris, 2002). Stallings and March (1995) recommend that assessment instruments should:

- be valid and reliable across multiple domains
- discriminate between symptom clusters
- evaluate both frequency and severity of symptoms
- incorporate multiple observations
- be sensitive to treatment effects.

Many of the earlier self-assessment measures of anxiety were downward extensions of adult measures of anxiety (e.g. Revised Children's Manifest Anxiety Scale; Fear Survey Scale for Children – Revised; State–Trait Anxiety Inventory for Children). While there is considerable overlap between the presentation of anxiety symptoms in adults and children, there are developmental considerations in both the nature (e.g. separation anxiety disorder) and the presentation of symptoms (Spence, 1998). A second limitation is the failure of many measures to distinguish between specific anxiety disorders. Thus, while total scores may suggest the presence of a significant anxiety reaction, the nature of that reaction, and the situations in which it is evoked, are often not specified. Finally, earlier scales do not relate to the current diagnostic classifications of anxiety disorders, resulting in their clinical utility being questioned (Muris *et al.*, 2002).

While anxiety scales may not be able to distinguish reliably between specific anxiety disorders and may overlap with depressive disorders, they are nonetheless helpful in the clinical setting by providing a quick and useful way of quantifying anxiety symptoms. The following are some of the more commonly used scales.

Revised Children's Manifest Anxiety Scale (RCMAS: Reynolds and Richmond, 1978)

The RCMAS, also known as the "What I Think and Feel" scale, is widely used to assess global anxiety. It consists of 37 items assessing the dimensions of worry/oversensitivity, physiological anxiety symptoms and fear/concentration problems (Reynolds and Paget, 1981). For each item the child decides whether the statement is true for them (Yes = 1, No = 0). Every fourth question constitutes a lie scale (eight items) and these items are excluded from the overall scoring system. An overall cut-off of 19 is used to identify children with anxiety disorders.

The RCMAS provides a good measure of general anxiety and has good concurrent validity with other trait anxiety scales such as the State–Trait Anxiety Inventory for Children (Dierker *et al.*, 2001). Limitations include poorer performance compared to newer scales; limited factor structure; and the fact that the dichotomous scoring system may decrease its power and sensitivity to treatment effects (Myers and Winters, 2002). The discriminative ability of the RCMAS is also poor, and it is not able adequately to differentiate children with anxiety from other internalising and externalising disorders (Perin and Last, 1992). Therefore despite its widespread use, the RCMAS may not be a pure measure of anxiety but more a measure of general distress.

Fear Survey Schedule for Children – Revised (FSSC-R: Ollendick, 1983)

The initial Fear Survey Schedule for Children was adapted from an adult scale and revised by Ollendick (1983) for use with children aged 7–18 years. The FSSC-R is an 80-item self-report scale that assesses a range of childhood phobias. Children rate their level of fear for each item on a three-point scale (1 = none; 2 = some; 3 = a lot), with scores being summed to produce a total score. Five main areas are assessed: fear of failure and criticism (e.g. getting poor marks for school work); fear of the unknown (e.g. getting lost in a strange place); fear of minor injury and small animals (e.g. spiders); fear of danger and death (e.g. falling from high places); and medical fears (e.g. getting an injection from the doctor or nurse). All items are highly intercorrelated, thereby questioning the utility of the different subscales.

The psychometric properties of the scale are good, it being shown to have good reliability and concurrent and discriminant validity (King and Ollendick, 1992). The FSSC-R has been shown to discriminate phobic children from controls and between specific phobias (Last *et al.*, 1989: Weems *et al.*, 1999).

Multidimensional Anxiety Scale for Children (MASC: March et al., 1997)

The MASC is an empirically derived self-report measure consisting of 39 items assessing the affective, physical, cognitive and behavioural domains of anxiety. An additional six items form an inconsistency index that assesses careless or inconsistent completion. The MASC can be used with young people aged 8–19. Each item is rated on a four-point scale (0 = never; 1 = almost never; 2 = sometimes; 3 = often). The questionnaire is summed to produce a total anxiety disorder index and scores on four sub-scales assessing physical symptoms (tense/restless and somatic autonomic, e.g. "my heart races or skips beat"), social anxiety (humiliation/rejection and public performance fears, e.g. "I wonder what other people think about me"), separation anxiety (e.g. "the idea of going away to camp scares me") and harm avoidance (perfectionism and anxious coping, e.g. "I stay away from things that upset me"). Two of these sub-scales match the DSM-IV diagnoses of social phobia and separation anxiety disorder, while the total score matches generalised anxiety disorder.

Internal and test–retest reliability is good and holds across gender and age (Baldwin and Dadds, 2007; March *et al.*, 1997; Rynn *et al.*, 2006). The scale has acceptable convergent and divergent validity. MASC correlates significantly with the Revised Manifest Anxiety Scale and has a low correlation with depression (Dierker *et al.*, 2001). The sub-scales and total scores can differentiate between children with and without anxiety disorders with up to 88% accuracy (March *et al.*, 1997; Myers and Winters, 2002; Rynn *et al.*, 2006).

Screen for Child Anxiety Related Emotional Disorders – Revised (SCARED-R: Birmaher et al., 1997; Muris et al., 1999)

This 41-item self-report scale measures symptoms of panic disorder (e.g. going to faint) generalised anxiety disorder (e.g. worry about the future), separation anxiety disorder (e.g. worry about sleeping alone), social phobia (e.g. nervous with strangers), and school phobia (e.g. afraid to go to school). Each item is endorsed on a three-point scale of frequency (0 = almost never; 1 = sometimes; 2 = often) which are summed to produce a total score, and five sub-scale scores.

There are parallel parent and child versions of the SCARED-R which have good psychometric properties, internal consistency and test–retest reliability, and moderate levels of parent–child agreement. SCARED-R differentiates between children with and without anxiety disorders and correlates strongly with other measures of anxiety including the RCMAS, STAIC and FSSC-R (Birmaher *et al.*, 1997; Muris *et al.*, 1999). However, the ability of SCARED-R to discriminate between specific anxiety disorders is limited (Muris *et al.*, 2004).

Spence Children's Anxiety Scale (SCAS: Spence 1997, 1998)

This was developed for completion by children and consists of 45 items; 38 assess anxiety and seven social desirability. The anxiety items assess the six DSM-IV categories of generalised anxiety (e.g. "I worry about things"), social phobia (e.g. "I feel afraid that I will make a fool of myself in front of people"), separation anxiety (e.g. "I worry about being away from my parents"), panic disorder/agoraphobia (e.g. "I suddenly feel as if I can't breathe when there is no reason for this"), obsessive-compulsive disorder (e.g. "I have to think of special thoughts (like numbers or words) to stop bad things from happening") and fear of physical injury (e.g. "I am scared of dogs"). Each item is rated on a four-point scale assessing frequency (0 = never; 1 = sometimes; 2 = often; 3 = always).

The SCAS was standardised on children aged 8–12 and has demonstrated good internal consistency and test–retest reliability; total scores are strongly correlated with RCMAS and there is a high correspondence between anxiety symptoms and the DSM-IV anxiety criteria (Spence, 1997). Finally, total SCAS scores distinguish anxious children from non-clinical children.

State–Trait Anxiety Inventory for Children (STAI-C: Spielberger et al., 1973)

The STAI-C was adapted from an adult scale and is also known as the "How I Feel Questionnaire". It comprises separate self-report scales for measuring two distinct anxiety concepts: state anxiety (S-anxiety) and trait anxiety (T-anxiety). The 20-item scale assesses a number of symptoms of anxiety such as "I get a funny feeling in my stomach" and "I am scared". Individuals respond to each item on a three-point rating scale, checking one of three alternatives that describes him or her best or indicates frequency of occurrence (1 = almost never; 2 = sometimes; 3 = often). While specially constructed to measure anxiety in nine- to 12-year old children, the STAI-C may also be used with younger children with average or above reading ability and with older children who are below average in ability.

The STAI-C has largely been used with community samples and the psychometric properties of the scale are generally weak. Internal and test–retest reliabilities are higher for the State sub-scale and for girls (Myers and Winters, 2002).

- Traditional measures of anxiety – SSRC, RCMAS and STAI-C – tend to assess general levels of distress not specific anxiety disorders.

- Newer measures – MASC, SCARED and SCAS – relate better to current DSM diagnostic criteria.

- Anxiety questionnaires are generally poor at distinguishing between specific anxiety disorders.

Problem formulations

Diagnostic interviews and structured questionnaires may confirm the presence of anxiety disorders and lead the clinician to suggest the use of a standardised anxiety treatment programme. There will however be other occasions where it is more appropriate to tailor the intervention specifically to the particular needs/problems of the young person. On these occasions the clinician needs to establish a clear CBT problem formulation.

The problem formulation underpins and informs the intervention and provides the explicit, shared, working hypothesis that determines the specific content of the treatment plan. If a formulation is not developed, therapy may become disjointed as sessions shift and the focus moves around in an incoherent and uncoordinated way. The formulation therefore provides a structure on which the individual cognitions and emotions associated with specific events can be arranged. Drinkwater (2004) suggests that formulations should be parsimonious, providing a good understanding that is easy to explain and is helpful for both the child and the clinician.

Problem formulations emerge from the assessment and are developed in partnership. The content is therefore obtained during the assessment interview and is provided by the child and their carers. It typically consists of their descriptions of feelings, physiological symptoms, cognitions and the meanings they ascribe to the events that occur. It is therefore important to use the child's words and terminology.

The clinician provides the cognitive model that is used as the structure for detailing and highlighting the relationships between cognitions, feelings and behaviour. Diagrams and drawings provide powerful ways of sharing formulations with children and young people. The diagram becomes a permanent visual representation that can be referred to during each session and revised accordingly. This maintains the therapeutic focus and momentum. The formulation also has an important psycho-educational function that helps the child to recognise the role of their dysfunctional cognitions in the development and maintenance of their problems. Providing children and young people with a copy of the formulation facilitates the development of self-efficacy. It provides the child with opportunities to reflect on the formulation in order to consider how current unhelpful patterns can be changed.

Maintenance formulations

As a general rule formulations should be kept simple and the clinician needs to avoid including too much information. Overly inclusive formulations often result in visual representations that become very complicated. Rather than facilitating understanding, overly inclusive formulations can overwhelm and confuse the child and their parents.

For the inexperienced clinician, maintenance formulations are the easiest. They should focus on key and recurrent cognitions and should not attempt to include all the cognitions that the child expresses during the assessment interview. There is a tendency to try to be overly inclusive, resulting in the formulation becoming cluttered, unfocused and overwhelming. The clinician needs to ensure that it is kept simple so that the formulation aids, rather than hinders, understanding. It is therefore important to include only information that is directly relevant to the anxiety problem. This could include: experiences or events that led directly to the onset of the anxiety; events or behaviours that specifically maintain it; specific cognitions that arise when the child becomes anxious; the feelings and physiological symptoms the child notices.

Maintenance formulations such as that described below are the simplest, and provide a way of demonstrating that triggering events produce cognitions that generate feelings that affect behaviour.

Mike (7) was referred with a longstanding problem of separation anxiety. During the initial assessment a recent situation was discussed where his mother had planned to go out one evening. As she walked out the door she could recall Mike crying and before she had got into the car he had run out of the house and clung tightly to her. He complained of feeling ill, and when asked by his mother how he was unwell, identified a number of symptoms. During the session Mike was asked to cast his mind back to that event and to imagine his mother going out of the house and shutting the door behind her. He was helped to identify what was racing through his head (Figure 5.1).

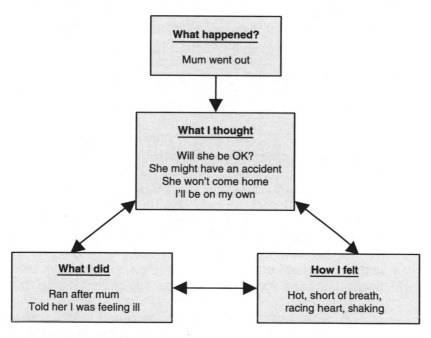

Figure 5.1   The case of Mike

This formulation was particularly helpful in highlighting the link between thoughts and feelings, and helped to begin the process of educating Mike and his mother into the physiological symptoms of anxiety.

Onset formulations

Depending on the degree of understanding that is required, different levels of cognitions such as core beliefs/schemas, assumptions or automatic thoughts can be specified in the formulation. For many, a maintenance formulation will provide sufficient information to aid understanding and to begin the process of experimentation and change. Others will want to understand how these problems came about; for them, a more detailed onset formulation specifying core experiences, and different levels of cognitions, will be helpful.

Problem formulations underpin individual interventions although initially they can be difficult for inexperienced clinicians to develop. It is therefore important to remain cognisant of the theoretical cognitive model and dysfunctional cognitions and processes that have been identified as important in the onset and maintenance of anxiety disorders. These are the cognitions that are assumed to drive emotions and behaviours and which will be the primary focus of the cognitive intervention.

A second difficulty for inexperienced clinicians is the problem of unravelling the different levels of cognitions. Padesky and Greenberger (1995) highlight that this is important since different interventions will be required for each cognitive level. Of these cognitions, automatic thoughts are the most accessible and represent the stream of consciousness that floods through the child's mind. Many of these are descriptive and relate to thoughts about the self (e.g. "no one likes me"), the world (e.g. "people are out to hurt me") and the future (e.g. "I will never have any friends"). With children, automatic thoughts are often referred to as "self-talk" and can be either positive (helpful and functional) or negative (unhelpful and dysfunctional).

Cognitive assumptions are the "rules for life" and represent the cognitive framework that an individual uses to make sense of their world and predict what will happen. These typically take two main forms: "if/then" statements, e.g. "if I want to be successful then I must study hard" or "if I have friends then they will always leave me", and "should" statements, e.g. "I should be popular". Assumptions are seldom directly verbalised but can be identified by giving children situations and asking them to identify what they think will happen. A useful way of challenging and changing cognitive assumptions is through behavioural experiments. These are designed to test the child's assumptions and provide an objective way of challenging and reappraising their cognitions.

The deepest cognitions are core beliefs and schemas. These are strong, simple, general and enduring cognitions, developed during childhood and shaped by significant events or recurrent experiences. Negative and critical parenting could for example lead a child to develop a core belief such as "no one loves me". Similarly, a child who has spent long periods of time being looked after in hospital might develop a belief that "I need other people to get by".

Core beliefs may not be directly vocalised but can be identified through the downward arrow technique. With this method, one of the child's common automatic negative thoughts is identified and then repeatedly challenged by the question, "so what would happen?" until the underlying core belief emerges. This is undertaken in the form of a gentle discussion, but it is useful to write each step down as it emerges.

Alice was 11 and had many worries about separating from her mother. One of the common worries Alice often verbalised was that "I get really worried when mum has to go out in the car on her own". The "so what" method was used to discuss this thought and help Alice vocalise what was at the heart of her worry, her core belief (Figure 5.2).

Core beliefs and schemas are strong, and resistant to change and to new or conflicting information. Interventions with these cognitions are designed to build alternative beliefs, rather than attempting to directly disprove or counter them. The emerging belief therefore highlights the limitations of the existing belief. For example, a strong belief that "I always fail at my school work" might be limited by developing a new belief that "I am OK at maths". This indirectly challenges the existing belief by building a new set of cognitions that recognises the exception to this rule.

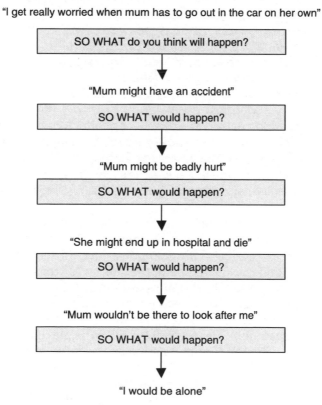

Figure 5.2 Downward arrow technique for Alice

Incorporating family factors

In addition to specifying different levels of cognitions, significant events and family factors can be incorporated into more sophisticated onset formulations. These can prove very helpful in highlighting the range of important factors and events that may have contributed to the development of the child's cognitions. In the example below the formulation provides an objective, no-blame approach, which identified how understandable and well-meaning parental behaviour contributed to the development and maintenance of their child's problems. The formulation is also enabling and provides a way for parent and child to begin to think about what may need to be different in order to bring about change.

> *James (9) lived with his mother and younger brother. He was referred by his GP with severe anxiety symptoms which prevented him from going out with his friends. James always seemed to be ill on the day of a trip and often ended up crying, complaining of headaches with a funny feeling in his tummy. His early life had been very difficult, with frequent domestic violence between his parents, some of which he had witnessed. His parents separated when he was four and it was during this time that his mother became very depressed and withdrawn. James and his mother were looked after by his maternal grandmother for the next three years. When James was seven an electric fire overheated and set fire to the house. The following year his mother was involved in a bad road traffic collision, although fortunately she was not physically injured.*
>
> *During the interview James's mother was keen to explore her role in the development and maintenance of her son's difficulties. She felt very guilty about past events and blamed herself for James's anxiety. She described a need to make things better for James and to make sure that he didn't miss out on any treats. If he felt unable to go out with his friends then she would take him. The formulation in Figure 5.3 was developed to explain this situation and helped James's mother to understand that her caring behaviour was contributing to her son's problems.*

The emerging formulation is discussed, tested and revised until a mutually agreed explanation is obtained. The formulation should be shared as soon as possible. This emphasises the collaborative nature of the intervention and maximises the opportunities for the child to contribute to and shape the model. When information is not known, question marks can be used to highlight that something important is missing. The evolving formulation becomes the working hypothesis which is the rationale and informs the intervention. The formulation is dynamic and will evolve and change over the course of the intervention as new information is assimilated into the model. Formulations are therefore a useful alternative to static diagnostic classifications and provide a functional, coherent and testable way of bringing together important variables that explain the onset of the child's difficulties and/or current maintaining factors.

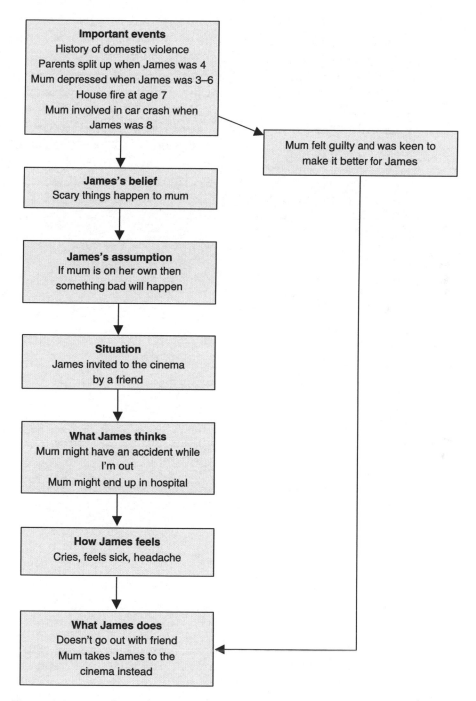

Figure 5.3   Formulation for James

- Formulations provide a shared understanding of the child's problems.
- The formulation is developed collaboratively and provides a shared understanding of the onset or maintenance of the anxiety.
- Maintenance formulations are the simplest and highlight the relationship between events, thoughts, feelings and behaviour.
- Onset formulations provide an understanding of significant events that have contributed to the development of the anxiety disorder and may identify different levels of cognitions.

6

Psycho-education, goal-setting and problem formulations

The anxiety response is complex and involves physiological reactions, behavioural responses and cognitive elements. The perception of danger triggers a number of physiological changes as the body prepares for a "flight" or "fight" reaction. Common physiological symptoms include sweaty palms, butterflies in the stomach, tummy aches, difficulty concentrating, irritability, racing heart, shallow breathing, dry throat, jelly legs, shaky voice, going red in the face, feeling faint, blurred vision and an urge to go to the toilet. Physiological symptoms such as these can be misperceived by the child or their parents as evidence that the child is unwell or ill. However, irrespective of whether they are associated with beliefs related to illness, these symptoms are unpleasant and result in the child engaging in behaviours designed to minimize their intensity. A common behavioural response is avoidance, whereby situations and events that trigger strong physiological responses are avoided. The specific expression of avoidance will depend on the stressor. With separation anxiety this may result in the child refusing to go to school, go out on their own, or sleep over with family or friends. They might present as being overly clingy, constantly wanting to stay and be with their parent, or display tantrums if separation is enforced. With simple phobias the avoidance is specific to the feared objects, events, places and stimuli associated with them. Thus a child who is fearful of dogs may avoid parks or walking past houses where dogs are housed. With social anxiety the fear is related to meeting, talking and being with people, resulting in the child avoiding social situations. Finally, children with generalised anxiety disorder may constantly seek reassurance about their worries and avoid many difficult activities or situations.

Underpinning these physiological and behavioural responses are important cognitive processes. These determine the way the child attends to, and perceives, events and the judgements they make as to the possible threat or danger that might arise. Cognitive models of anxiety suggest that the way information is selected, attended to and processed is subject to some degree of bias and that it is these distortions that contribute to the onset and maintenance of emotional disorders (Beck *et al.*, 1985).

Cognitive behavioural interventions for children with anxiety disorders tend to involve a number of elements that target each of the three core domains, i.e. cognitive, emotional and behavioural. These key elements are summarised in Figure 6.1.

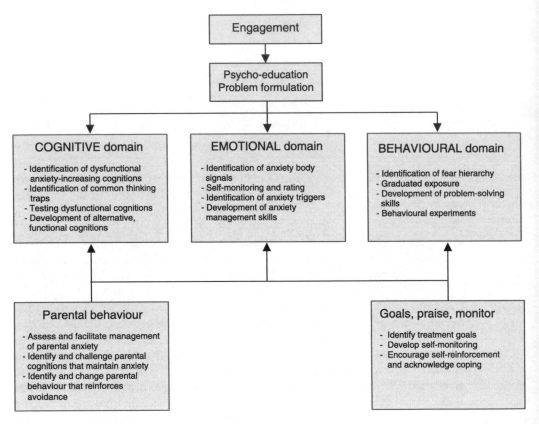

Figure 6.1 Elements of cognitive behavioural interventions for children

Once the child and their parents have ***engaged*** with the process of CBT, and are committed to exploring the possibility of change, it is then possible to begin the intervention. The order, specific content, and therapeutic emphasis will be informed by the problem ***formulation***. This is developed in partnership with the child and their parent, provides the rationale for the intervention and informs the content and focus. The intervention will inevitably involve some form of ***psycho-education*** in which the child and their family are provided with a cognitive explanation of the presenting symptoms and the intervention. This will highlight the three core domains of CBT (i.e. cognitive, emotional and behavioural) and will emphasise the important relationship between them. The process of CBT will be described and in particular the collaborative and active participatory aspects will be stressed. The intervention typically moves into the *emotional domain* as the child is helped to identify their different emotions and the signals their bodies use to indicate anxiety. Once the child can identify their anxiety signals they are encouraged to *monitor their occurrence and rate their strength*. This facilitates the child's understanding of situations and events that trigger their anxiety. Finally, children are helped to identify new relaxation skills to help them *manage* their anxious feelings.

The intervention will then major on the *cognitive domain* as the child is helped to identify the relationship between thoughts and feelings. Common anxiety-increasing thoughts are identified and the underpinning *cognitive traps* that pervade them highlighted. The child is then helped to actively experiment *to test* the reality of their anxiety-increasing thoughts. Through this process they begin to *challenge* their anxiety-increasing thoughts and develop alternative, *balanced* and more helpful ways of thinking.

Focusing on the *behavioural domain* allows the child to practise their new cognitive and emotional skills and to explore whether they are helpful in addressing their problems. A *hierarchy* of feared situations is developed and, starting with the least anxiety-provoking, the child *systematically confronts* each in turn. *Problem-solving skills* may also be taught to prepare the child for resolving future difficulties. Throughout, the child will be encouraged to identify, *praise and reward* themselves for attempting to use their new skills.

Although the particular benefits and optimum role of parents in CBT with anxious children have yet to be documented, there continues to be a widespread belief among clinicians that they should be involved in the intervention. At the very least, this might be *psycho-educational*, so that they, like their children, are educated into the cognitive model and are able to understand fully and support the intervention. In a number of situations the parents may themselves have significant *anxiety-related problems* which contribute to the maintenance or onset of their child's difficulties. If significant, the parents may need to be encouraged to seek specialist help in their own right. Alternatively they might be invited to *practise and use* the ideas their child is developing to manage their own anxiety.

Parental beliefs that might interfere with or impede the child's progress need to be addressed and challenged. These might relate to the parent's expectations about negative things happening or their child's readiness and ability to cope. Similarly, *parental behaviours* that maintain the child's anxiety, such as rehearsal of worries, limited opportunities to practise or over-protectiveness, need to be addressed.

The intervention occurs within a therapeutic framework that encourages *self-monitoring* as a way of increasing understanding and quantifying symptoms. *Goals and targets* are regularly identified and reviewed in order to demonstrate change and progress. Finally, the child and their parents are encouraged to acknowledge and *reward* attempts to cope and face anxiety-provoking situations.

Engagement

The initial task is concerned with developing the therapeutic relationship, with particular attention being paid to the process of engagement and psycho-education.

Many children initially appear ambivalent or anxious about attending therapy sessions. In many respects this is not surprising.

- Children typically do not refer themselves for help and often attend due to concerns from other professionals or their parents.
- They may not perceive themselves as having any worries or significant anxiety symptoms and thus do not see the need for any specialist help.
- They may perceive the reason for any identified anxieties as residing in someone else, e.g. a strict teacher.
- They may have lived with their anxieties and worries for such a long time that they have become a central part of their life. It is therefore difficult to consider how things could ever be different.
- They may be anxious about what will happen during therapy and fear that their worries will not be understood, or that they will be asked to do things that frighten them.

Initially children may not have any ownership of the difficulties, play down their significance or severity, or appear apprehensive, disinterested or unmotivated in securing change. Attending to the process of engagement allows these issues to be discussed and is a precursor to the active process of change that occurs through CBT. Failure to address these issues will result in the child continuing to be ambivalent, or unmotivated, with their preparedness and commitment to participate in an active process of change being compromised.

Identify a potential area of change

The first step of engagement requires the child to acknowledge that they have a problem. The clinician therefore needs to emphasise the importance of understanding the child's perspective and to encourage them to express their views:

- "Are you happy with your life or is there anything you would like to be different?"
- "What could be different at school to make you feel less anxious?"
- "What is the one thing that worries you most?"
- "Is there anything you would like to do but can't because of your anxiety?"
- "What would have to happen to make you feel that your worries had become so big that you had to do something about them?"

- "Have your worries ever stopped you from doing things you would really like to?"

> Secure recognition of a problem.

Assess readiness to change

Questions such as these help the child to recognise that there may be areas of their life that they would like to change. After the child has been able to recognise this, their views about embarking on an active process of change need to be explored. Recognition of a difficulty does not necessarily imply that the child wants to do something about it. They may feel ambivalent, or unsure, about how difficult it will be to change. In order to assess this, the "costs of change" and potential barriers need to be explored.

- "What would be the hardest thing about trying to change this?"
- "What might go wrong?"
- "What would be the worst thing that could happen?"
- "Is this the right time to try?"
- "What help would you need to be successful?"

The clinician needs to establish a safe relationship in which the child can begin to identify and acknowledge their problems, and to identify the potential goals and areas of change that they would like to secure. Engagement is developed through the basic counselling skills of warmth, empathy, reflective listening and respect. These skills convey to the child that they are important, they make useful contributions, their views are heard and their experiences, thoughts and feelings are acknowledged and validated. Through this developing relationship the child is encouraged to explore and identify those aspects of their life that are problematic and that they may like to change. The clinician attempts to increase motivation and interest in change by highlighting the difference between the current situation and the child's aspirations. The potential difficulties and barriers to engaging in a process of active change need to be discussed and acknowledged. Securing change will require some additional input and work from the child. There is the danger of failure: that they try but are unsuccessful. Similarly, timing may be an important issue so that while change is desirable this may not be the right time to try. These issues need to be carefully discussed and resolved before the child is ready to participate actively in a process of change.

> Establish a commitment to change.

Explain the basic cognitive model of anxiety

Acknowledging a problem and identifying a need for change are important, although the process of engagement also requires the child to believe both that the form of help that is being offered can bring about change and that the clinician is able to facilitate the development of the skills the child requires. Initially, this can be developed through the provision of information in which the child and their family are:

- introduced to the basic cognitive model of anxiety
- informed about the effectiveness of CBT for the treatment of anxiety
- made aware that the child will have a central and active role in the process of securing change.

Psycho-education provides the child and their carer with an explanatory model of anxiety within a CBT framework. Typically this highlights a number of issues, including:

- normalising anxiety as a common and normal response
- understanding the "fight or flight" responses to perceived danger
- outlining the common physiological bodily changes that accompany anxiety
- highlighting the link between cognitions and anxious bodily signals
- raising awareness of cognitive distortions and biases associated with anxiety
- specifying the effects on behaviour in terms of avoidance, loss of motivation and anxious performance.

This understanding will initially be at a general level and can be shared with the child, and parent, in different ways. The "anxiety trap" in Figure 6.2 provides a basic visualisation of the link between thoughts, feelings and behaviour and highlights how they are related.

At other times, the clinician may want to emphasise the potential role of cognitions in more detail. The "avoidance cycle" (Figure 6.3) shows the simple relationship between anxiety-increasing and anxiety-reducing cognitions. This can introduce the child and parent to the importance of thinking in different ways. While avoidance may bring temporary relief, it does not help the child to "reclaim their life". The cycle will repeat whenever they have to face a new or challenging situation.

These general models will be individualised over time as the child's difficulties and specific thoughts, feelings, and behaviours are elicited and incorporated into the model.

The early provision of information such as this is very important. It validates and acknowledges the child's difficulties; provides a way of understanding and making sense of their anxiety; and educates them into the CBT model. It also begins to highlight at an early stage how the anxiety cycle

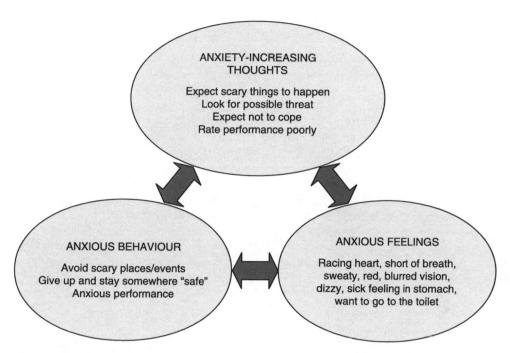

Figure 6.2   The anxiety trap

could be changed, and to dispel myths such as "I must be going mad", "I am ill" or "I am the only one who ever feels like this".

Provide information about CBT and likely effectiveness.

The hopeful and optimistic clinician

The final part of the engagement process requires the child to have confidence in both the proposed intervention and the clinician. The clinician needs to present as optimistic and hopeful, and convey a sense that there is a good chance that the child's anxiety will reduce. This message is important and will serve to facilitate engagement, to increase the child's and parent's commitment to attending meetings and their motivation to try new ideas. This optimistic ethos is achieved by providing information, such as that the clinician has seen a number of children with similar problems who have learned to face and overcome their anxiety. Similarly, the child and family need to know that there is good evidence to suggest that CBT is an effective intervention with anxiety problems.

The enthusiasm of the clinician needs to be balanced so that the child is aware that while CBT is effective, it does not work for everyone. In order to monitor this possibility, progress needs to be regularly reviewed thereby

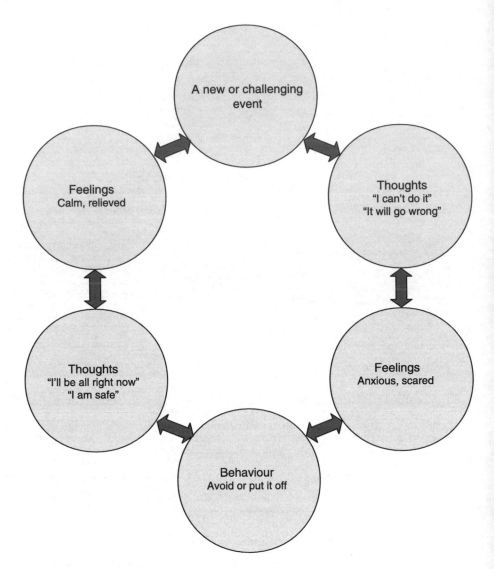

Figure 6.3   The avoidance cycle

allowing potential difficulties to be identified and discussed at an early stage. If, after an agreed period of time, the intervention proves unsuccessful then referral for an alternative intervention may be required.

> Instil hopefulness and confidence in the clinician.

Explain the process of CBT

Cognitive behaviour therapy is based on a number of guiding principles that inform the therapeutic process. Emphasising the key features of the process during the initial meeting is important and prepares the child and their carer for their active role in subsequent sessions. Similarly, as identified above, the therapeutic process provides a medium through which the clinician instils a sense of hopefulness and promotes self-efficacy. This is particularly important for children, who are typically referred for help by others and may have only partial ownership of the presenting problems and thus limited investment in, or understanding of, their role in securing change. Similarly, some children have lived with their problems for a number of years and will find it difficult to consider even the possibility of change, let alone their central role in bringing it about.

While the principles on which CBT is based are firmly embedded in the professional literature, children and parents will undoubtedly be unfamiliar with them unless they are made explicit.

Collaboration

CBT is a collaborative partnership between the clinician, the child and their parents. It is therefore very different to the "expert/professional" relationship that many children and families may have experienced. This needs to be acknowledged as the clinician differentiates themselves from other professionals and adults whom the child and their family may have encountered. It needs to be clearly stated that the child, parent and clinician are equal partners in the therapeutic relationship. Each brings their own experiences, knowledge and ideas that can be used to inform, develop and evaluate the use of alternative skills and behaviours. The child is the expert on their own experiences and interests. The parents provide an alternative perspective, and information about what may or may not help, while the clinician provides a framework in which the child's anxieties can be organised and understood. Collaboration requires the creation of a therapeutic process in which the child feels important and in which their ideas are encouraged, heard and valued. This may feel unusual for many children and it is not uncommon to find that there is some initial apprehension or suspicion.

Active

Implicit in the concept of collaboration is the expectation that each partner will have important contributions to make. The child and their parents will therefore have an active role in therapy. Rather than passively receiving advice and suggestions from the clinician, the child and their carers are actively involved in generating, identifying, developing, testing and evaluating new strategies and skills. For many children this will be a new concept.

Empowering

CBT is an empowering therapy designed to build on the child's strengths, and to facilitate self-development and efficacy. Undoubtedly there will be occasions when the child has been able to cope better with their difficulties, or has used strategies that have provided some degree of help. Self-reflection and problem-solving are used to help the child and their carers discover the skills and ideas that have previously been helpful. These are then developed and used to promote more adaptive cognitive processes and behaviours.

Openness

In order to develop a collaborative partnership, the relationship must be open, with information being freely shared in an accessible way. Sessions need to be pitched at the right developmental level for the child to access, and with younger children, this may involve more non-verbal methods and materials. Care needs to be paid to the use of language to ensure that it is simple but not patronising, understandable and jargon-free. The amount of information provided needs to be sufficient to secure a clear understanding but must not become unnecessarily detailed so that the child and their carers become overwhelmed.

Self-discovery

An open therapeutic stance needs to be adopted whereby an ethos of curiosity and experimentation is promoted. This reinforces the important message that there is no "one right or wrong" answer and also challenges some of the dichotomous thinking that is particularly common with adolescents. Through this process children discover that there are many different ways of thinking and coping with problems, and that single methods may not always be effective. The task is therefore to experiment with methods to identify those that are useful.

The initial meetings provide the child and their carer with considerable information. It is therefore useful to provide written summaries and hand-outs that can be taken home and read at leisure, or shared with those who were unable to attend the meeting. Examples of psycho-educational materials for children and carers are provided in Chapter 12. ***Learning to Beat Anxiety*** is a handout for parents, which provides introductory information about anxiety, the rationale for CBT and what parents can do to support their children during, and after, the intervention. A similar handout designed for children provides a basic understanding of anxiety, introduces the child to the nature and focus of CBT and, in particular, highlights the active and collaborative process.

> Highlight the collaborative and active nature of CBT with the child and clinician working in partnership.

Agree treatment goals

The initial process of engagement and psycho-education will clarify the readiness of the child and their family to embark on an active process of change. The next task is to seek a clear understanding of the goals towards which the child and clinician will work. Clarifying these at the outset of therapy is important. These goals will provide an explicit and shared set of expectations about what CBT can and cannot achieve. Goals should therefore be selected carefully, since overly ambitious or poorly defined goals may result in a lack of measurable success. This can be demoralising and may reinforce negative cognitions in the child or family about powerlessness, hopelessness or helplessness, a situation that needs to be avoided.

There are a number of factors to consider when agreeing good treatment goals, which are captured by the acronym SMART. This highlights that goals should be specific, measurable, achievable, realistic and time-oriented.

Specific

Good goals should be both positive and specific. Treatment goals need to emphasise positively what will be achieved, rather than what will be stopped. Goals such as to "not to feel anxious" or "not to worry so much" need to be phrased positively. A positive emphasis is more enabling and, by being action-oriented, highlights what the child is working towards, i.e. "to go to school on my own" or "to sleep over at my friend's birthday party".

Treatment goals also need to be specific so that they are clear and understandable to all involved. Clarity and specificity help to reduce potential ambiguity and define the context, or circumstances, in which the goal will be achieved. For example, a young person's goal of going into town with a friend is very different from going into town on their own.

Measurable

Although not always possible, it is often helpful to agree goals that can be objectively evaluated. For example, it is very clear whether a child "goes to school on their own", but a goal such as "feeling more confident in the playground" is more difficult to evaluate independently. In this situation the clinician will need to discuss what others would notice, or how the child would behave differently if they felt more confident.

In many instances the intervention will bring about changes in the frequency, duration or intensity of anxious thoughts and feelings, rather than their total eradication. In order to quantify this relative change it is important to use self-monitoring regularly so that any changes can be monitored over time. This is particularly important if goals are about sub-jective states such as "to feel calmer before school", where regular use of rating scales should always be encouraged.

Achievable

Achievement of the goals needs to be under the control or influence of the young person. Goals over which the young person has no control, such as "for all the family to be more relaxed" or "mum to be less stressed", need to be avoided. Successful achievement of these will depend on many factors outside the control of the young person and often beyond the specific focus of the intervention.

Treatment goals also need to be agreed by all involved. This "sign-up" emphasises the collaborative nature of CBT and once again highlights the central and important role of the child and their parents. There will, however, inevitably be times when parents and children identify different goals. These differences have to be acknowledged and prioritised, with larger or longer term goals being "parked" until easier or more immediate goals have been secured.

Realistic

As already mentioned, to have "no more worries" would be both unrealistic and unachievable. Worries or anxious feelings will continue, and as such the goal of therapy is to ensure that they occur less often, are less intense, and less troublesome. The child and their family therefore need to have realistic and achievable expectations about what treatment can achieve, and what it cannot.

Time oriented

The timeframe over which the treatment goals will be achieved needs to be specified. Inevitably this will involve some degree of prediction which will need to be reassessed. However, it does provide the young person with a "best guess" timeframe that indicates the possible length of treatment, and the goals that may be achieved in the short, medium and longer terms. Providing such a framework also helps to counter any unrealistic expect-ations about immediate change, and provides a target against which progress can be monitored.

Agree goals that are positive, achievable, clear, and measurable.

Break goals into targets

For each goal there will be a number of steps or targets that can be identified. The child who wants to achieve the goal of going to school on their own may identify the following targets.

- Walk to school at the weekend with mum.
- Walk to school on Tuesday in the afternoon with mum.
- Walk to school on Thursday morning with mum.
- Walk to school with mum and go into reception.
- Walk to school gates with mum and go into reception on my own.
- Walk to bottom of the road with mum and then go into reception on my own.
- Walk to school on my own.

The process of developing targets and forming a hierarchy of difficulty will be discussed in more detail in a later chapter. However, it is helpful for the clinician to be clear as to which targets might be short-term and the timeframe over which these might be achieved.

Agreeing clear goals and targets provides a way of assessing change and ensuring that clinician and child are working towards achieving the agreed outcome.

> Goals need to be broken down into targets that are ordered in terms of difficulty.

The formulation

The initial assessment typically ends with the development of a problem formulation. The formulation is developed and agreed collaboratively, and provides a shared understanding of the child's anxiety within a CBT framework. The formulation provides a visual summary of the relationship between important events, thoughts and feelings, and as such can be a very powerful way of helping the child and their parents to understand their anxiety. Formulations are also very enabling, since once the relationship between key aspects is understood, the child and their parents can begin to consider what they might need to do to bring about change.

As a general rule, formulations should be kept simple. They need to provide the information the child and their parents require to understand their problems and should not be overly detailed or inclusive. The formulation developed and shared with the child will be different from the formulation the clinician requires. The clinician's formulation will need to specify the nature and type of the child's cognitions in more detail and will need to be compared against explanatory theoretical models and reviewed during supervision. This level of detail is not required by the child or their parents.

Maintenance formulations

Formulations are dynamic, developing and evolving over time as new information is identified and assimilated. There are different types of formulations, the most accessible and easiest to develop being maintenance formulations. These simply serve to highlight the relationship between triggering events, automatic thoughts, feelings and behaviour.

> *Jane (8) had a fear of germs and diseases. The onset of the fear coincided with an incident where she discovered a dead bird in the garden which was covered in flies. Jane told her mother, who told her not to go near or touch it in case she caught germs. Jane then became very worried about flies and birds, fearing that she would become infected with germs if they came near her. Jane started to stay in the house and although it was summer would keep the windows and doors shut. If a bird came near her in the garden or a fly came in the house, Jane would cry, panic and hyperventilate. Figure 6.4 represents a simple maintenance formulation which highlights what happens when Jane sees a bird or fly.*

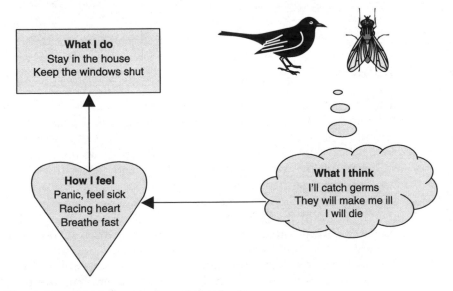

Figure 6.4   A maintenance formulation for Jane

> Maintenance formulations capture the relationship between thoughts, feelings and behaviour.

Onset formulations

On other occasions, the child and their parents may wish to develop a better understanding of how and why the anxieties developed. Key events that influenced the development of deeper seated beliefs that provide the child's framework for filtering and understanding their world may need to be developed. In this respect, onset formulations often include the specification of deeper rooted cognitions, such as core beliefs or schemas, and the cognitive assumptions through which these beliefs are operationalised.

Core beliefs are the rigid and fixed beliefs we develop about ourselves (e.g. "I am a failure"; "no one will love me"), our world (e.g. "people are out to hurt me") or the future ("I need people to help me get by"). These are developed during childhood by important events and provide the framework for interpreting the events that occur. Core beliefs are the deepest and least accessible cognitions. They are pervasive and underpin the way the child thinks about many situations and events.

Core beliefs are operationalised through cognitive assumptions or predictions. These are the rules for living that people adopt, and are often characterised through "if/then" statements. The child who has a core belief that he is "a failure" may assume that "if he tries then he will fail". The belief that "no one will love me" may be operationalised by the assumption that "if I get close to someone then they will leave me". Assumptions are therefore the child's predictions about what will happen, and in turn these will influence and shape the child's automatic thoughts.

Automatic thoughts are the most accessible cognitions and are often referred to as "self-talk". These are the thoughts that constantly go round and round in our heads. Many are descriptive, a number are about ourselves ("everyone will think I look an idiot in these jeans"), our performance ("oh no, I wish I hadn't said that to Mike") and the future ("I bet my teacher will have a go at me tomorrow"). The thoughts that are of particular interest are the biases and distortions that have been found to be associated with anxiety disorders.

Joe (11) had always been a sensitive boy, although over the last year his worries had become more frequent. On a number of occasions these worries had resulted in extreme anxiety, and he seemed to be increasingly worried about being on his own. Joe developed worries about health – his own, but particularly his mother's – resulting in her having to spend considerable time reassuring her son that they she was not ill. The family did not understand Joe's concerns about health.

They were all in good health and there were no major health problems. However, during the discussion Joe's mother recalled an event, one year previously, when she suddenly passed out and had to go to hospital to be checked and monitored. This event was initially seen as comparatively unimportant by Joe's mother, who was pronounced fit and well and had been ever since. However, the discussion revealed how this event suddenly shattered Joe's beliefs about his world. The security that his parents would always be there for him was challenged. Joe increasingly started to believe that his parents, particularly his mother, would die. This belief led him to develop a number of assumptions or predictions, and to think that if he stayed with his mother he would be able to prevent this from happening. These beliefs and assumptions were activated at times when Joe had to leave his mother, such as going to school. He then engaged in considerable reassurance-seeking and complained of being unwell, so that he would have to stay at home with his mother. This was captured in the onset formulation in Figure 6.5.

> Onset formulations identify important events that lead to the development of cognitive beliefs and assumptions that underpin an anxiety.

Four system formulations

The basic CBT model tends to concentrate on the three core domains of thoughts, feelings and behaviour. It is sometimes useful to break this into four systems, where bodily symptoms and feelings are separated. Clinical experience with anxious children suggests that separating feelings and symptoms is not always necessary, and indeed can prove difficult. However, it is particularly useful when children are misperceiving their anxiety symptoms as signs of serious physical illness. Identifying physiological symptoms, and providing an alternative anxiety response explanation for their occurrence, can prove very reassuring.

Sara had many health-related worries, believing that she was seriously ill. She had undergone many physical investigations and the paediatricans were confident that there was no physical reason for her symptoms. Self-monitoring records identified a clear relationship between certain situations (school), times of the day (first thing in the morning on week-days), her thoughts and the presence of her symptoms. In particular, Sara was concerned about her racing heart and rapid breathing, which she perceived as signs of a serious physical illness.

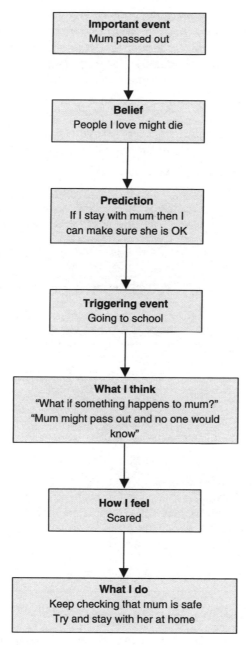

Figure 6.5 An onset formulation for Joe

Figure 6.6 represents one of the CBT formulations that were developed to help Sara understand that her symptoms were anxiety-based, influenced by her thoughts. Other situations were tracked through in a similar way to identify this repeated pattern, which helped Sara to reappraise her belief that she was unwell.

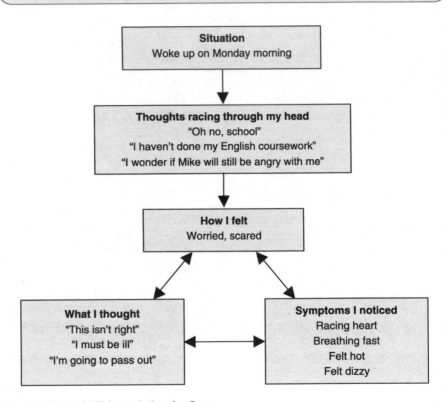

Figure 6.6   A CBT formulation for Sara

Incorporating parental factors

On other occasions important parental behaviours or cognitions may need to be included in the formulation. This helps to highlight how the problems developed, and what might need to change in both the child and parent if the situation is to improve.

Anna (12) was referred with a generalised anxiety disorder. She had always been a worrier but this had become particularly difficult since she moved to secondary school. It was now affecting her ability to complete her school work and to hand in homework assignments. When Anna was set some work she would immediately think that she would be unable to cope or to complete the task. Anna described her mind going blank and being unable to decide where to start. She recalls panicking, feeling hot and lightheaded with a racing heart. She constantly sought reassurance from her teacher/mother that she was doing the right thing and that her work was correct.

In terms of early development, Anna was born with a blood clot and spent the first six weeks in hospital. This was a difficult time for Anna's mother, who did not know whether her daughter would survive. Fortunately this did not result in any significant cognitive impairment, but it led to a very close relationship with her mother. Anna's mother described how Anna had become a very precious girl and how she had become over-protective of her. Anna's mother also suffered from an anxiety disorder and was very sensitive to any signs of distress in her daughter. This appeared to have encouraged a sense of dependency on the past Anna, who at present felt unable to attempt anything without her mother (Figure 6.7).

> Important parental cognitions and beliefs can be included in formulations.

Formulations should be developed in an open and objective way, taking care to avoid negative and unhelpful issues such as "blame". Over-protective or controlling parental behaviours, for example, could be discussed as "caring" in which the parent attempts to minimise their child's distress. The process of psycho-education will, however, help the parent to recognise that such "caring" behaviour may no longer be helpful as the child needs to develop independence and autonomy.

In order to facilitate the open and collaborative process of CBT, it is helpful to share the formulation as soon as possible. The clinician does not need to have all the information before they start this process but can provide a framework to which information can be added. Missing or unknown information can be highlighted with an empty box or a question mark, which can then become the focus for future meetings. Formulations therefore need to be seen as dynamic and evolving, and as such should be regularly reviewed and updated.

The formulation provides a helpful summary of the current situation, which in turn informs the nature and focus of the intervention and the skills the child and their parents may need to develop.

> Formulations are dynamic and provide a visual summary that informs the intervention.

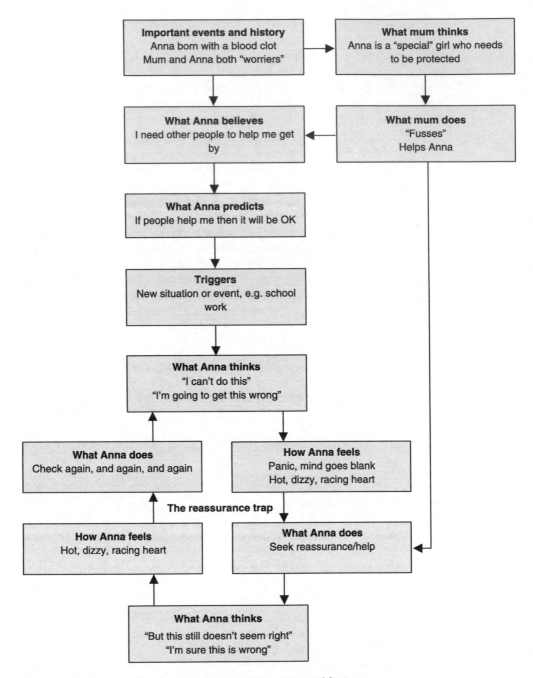

Figure 6.7   Formulation for Anna incorporating parental factors

7

Involving parents

The additional benefits of involving parents in CBT programmes with children have not been consistently demonstrated. However, the dominant clinical view, which is endorsed in the practice parameters produced by the American Academy of Child and Adolescent Psychiatry (2007), is that parents should be involved in the treatment programme. Their involvement provides opportunities to address parental behaviours that have been found to be associated with anxiety in children. Although these associations may not be specific to anxiety it has been found that parents of anxious children:

1   are overly intrusive and controlling, thereby limiting their child's opportunities to learn to face, and overcome, challenges
2   encourage their child's avoidance of fearful situations
3   may be more negative and critical of their child's performance
4   may model anxious behaviour.

Involving parents in the intervention therefore provides opportunities to reduce parental anxiety, facilitate appropriate child autonomy and coping, and develop parenting skills that reinforce courageous coping behaviour while minimising the attention received for anxious and avoidant behaviour. The focus and outcomes of work with parents are summarised in Figure 7.1.

Assessing parental motivation and readiness for change

There are two factors that need to be assessed before parents are able to be actively involved in the intervention. The first is their motivation and readiness to change. The second is the nature and extent of their own anxiety problems, and in particular the extent to which these might interfere with, or

95

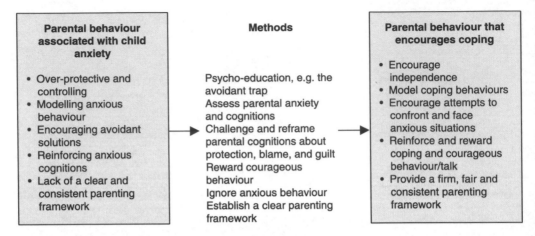

Figure 7.1   Focus and outcomes of work with parents

impede, their child's treatment. Parents who are not ready, willing or able to engage in the process of CBT will be unable to support their child. If the parent suffers from significant anxiety then this may interfere with their ability to encourage exposure and practise tasks or to model courageous coping behaviour. Similarly, parental anxiety may restrict opportunities for the child to learn to cope with anxiety-provoking situations.

Motivation and readiness to change

During the initial assessment it is important to pay attention to parental cognitions that might be contributing to their child's anxiety or affect the parent's commitment to embarking on an active treatment programme. Parental cognitions may indicate possible blame/guilt ("I shouldn't have started him at nursery so early"), hopelessness ("he has had this problem for such a long time I'm not sure whether it can change"), unrealistic expectations ("I tell him it would be OK if he just relaxed"), helplessness ("we have tried lots of things but nothing ever works") or a lack of commitment to pursuing CBT ("we have talked about this and I think that medication would be really helpful").

As previously mentioned, the clinician needs to counter ambivalence and uncertainty by presenting as optimistic and hopeful. New information for the parents relating to the clinician's knowledge about working with children with anxiety problems needs to be shared to counter cognitions relating to hopelessness and helplessness. The clinician needs to highlight that many children learn to manage their anxiety successfully and that CBT has been shown to be an effective intervention for anxiety problems. The clinician can also counter issues of blame and guilt by providing information about how anxiety develops and is maintained. Through this process the clinician can highlight that while past events cannot be undone, change is still possible.

The provision of new information through psycho-education can help parents to challenge some of their beliefs, assumptions and behaviours. Information about the avoidance cycle can, for example, help parents recognise that while avoidance may offer short-term relief, their child's anxiety persists and continues to affect everyday life, with situations or events being avoided. This can help parents understand that for their child to reclaim their life they need to be helped to confront and face their fears and learn to cope with anxious situations.

The parent's beliefs and assumptions about their child's ability to cope, and the meaning they attribute to their child's distress, may also need to be explored. Questions such as "do you think your son will be able to overcome his anxiety?"; "how do you cope when he gets distressed?"; "when he does get so upset, what does that say about you?" may provide useful information. They may identify cognitions about the need to protect their child from possible harm (e.g. "he is so sensitive and can't cope without a lot of help from me"), highlight the parent's ability to manage distress (e.g. "I just can't stand seeing him become so stressed"), or that distress is an indication of being a "bad" or "uncaring" parent. Cognitions such as these need to be discussed, acknowledged, challenged and reframed. Parents need to be helped to understand that they can't always protect their child from possible danger. As the child grows older they will naturally need to become increasingly independent and learn to do things without their parents. They will need to go on sleepovers, to school, socialise with friends, cope with teasing and learn to cope with worrying or fearful situations and events. Allowing the child to learn to face and overcome challenges in a controlled way (i.e. through exposure and practice) is therefore positive, and helps them to develop essential life skills.

Similarly, parents need to recognise and accept that their child's attempts at mastery may not always be as skilful or effective as they would like. However, it is through this trial-and-error learning that the child's coping skills will develop. Parents may also need to be helped to understand that performance does not always need to be excellent. In many instances a good enough performance is all that is required.

Finally, important underpinning parental assumptions such as "if I let my child become distressed then I am a bad parent" or "if my child is distressed then they will develop problems later in life" need to be explored. Through this discussion the parents need to be helped to question and challenge such assumptions and to recognise that children will quite happily avoid difficult or challenging, situations unless encouraged and supported to confront them. In these situations the child may display some degree of distress, but this will be short-lived and is not an indication of significant or lasting distress. Through these discussions parents can be helped to recognise that supporting their child to confront and cope, rather than encouraging them to avoid any distress, is a positive and helpful approach to parenting.

> Parental cognitions that may impact on the process of therapy need to be identified, discussed and reappraised.

The extent and nature of parental anxiety

In view of the association between parent and child anxiety, the clinician needs to assess the possible extent and influence of parental anxiety on the treatment programme. If the parent has a significant and incapacitating anxiety disorder then they may need to be referred for treatment before they are able to be actively involved in helping their child. If this is not possible, or the parent is unwilling, then the clinician should consider whether another significant adult figure can be involved in the programme. This is particularly important when considering practice tasks involving exposure. The adult helper needs to be able to encourage the child to face and confront feared situations rather than possibly condoning or inadvertently reinforcing avoidance. The adult helper therefore needs to be able to model courageous behaviour rather than mirroring or amplifying the child's anxiety.

> *Josh (9) was afraid of travelling in cars. He would avoid going in the car, and on occasions when he had to travel would be very anxious throughout the journey, fearing that they would have an accident. Josh was asked whether anyone else had similar worries and immediately replied, "Yes, Mum, she's much worse than me". It subsequently emerged that Josh's mother had been involved in a road traffic collision and since that time she had avoided cars. If forced to travel in a car she became acutely anxious and hypervigilant, constantly making comments to the driver about potential hazards. Understandably, this increased Josh's anxiety about the possibility of being involved in an accident. It also emerged that Josh's avoidance was reinforced by his mother. When Josh voiced his anxieties about going on trips in the car, his mother would immediately volunteer to stay at home with her son.*

If parental anxiety is mild then the child and parent can learn to face and overcome their fears together. Although most of the intervention will be focused on the child, the parent can be encouraged to adapt the ideas and apply them to their own problems. Thus parents can be helped to become aware of their own anxiety signals and to model coping and problem-solving in which they learn to approach feared situations. It can be very reassuring for children to learn that their parents also have worries and to discover that they can perform as well as, or perhaps even better than, their parents.

> *Wayne (12) had agreed to practise his mental imagery ("my relaxing place") at least twice over the coming week. His mother was also a worrier: she decided that she would also benefit from developing her*

relaxation skills and also agreed to practise these twice. During the next meeting Wayne was delighted to discover that he had practised on five occasions while his mother had only managed one.

> Parental anxiety that may be contributing to the onset or maintenance of the child's anxiety need to be assessed.

Challenge parental beliefs that avoidance is helpful

During the intervention children will need to confront situations that make them anxious. It is at these times that parents are likely to revert to their previous way of responding and will attempt to minimise their child's distress by taking control or by encouraging avoidance. The parent therefore needs to be prepared for this possibility. Catastrophic beliefs about the child hyperventilating, passing out or becoming ill need to be discussed. Ambivalence about encouraging the child to cope needs to be acknowledged. Parental beliefs about the need to minimise their child's immediate distress should be challenged as the short-term gains versus long-term costs are emphasised.

Through these discussions, parents can be reassured that encouraging their child to confront and face their worries is helpful: that their child will become worried, and feel unsure about facing their fears, but that this is understandable. Thoughts that they may be contributing to their child's distress by encouraging exposure need to be positively reframed. Parents need to be reassured that distress is short-lived and that by encouraging and supporting their child to face their fear they are helping them to reclaim their life.

> Help parents to encourage their children to confront and learn to cope with fearful situations.

Assess parental management

During the course of the assessment it may emerge that the parents' management of the child's behaviour may also be contributing to the child's anxiety.

- Important parental rules and boundaries may be lacking. This may result in the child failing to learn the limits of their world, which can make them feel unsafe or insecure.

- Rules may be unclear or inconsistently applied. This may contribute to the child's beliefs that their world is uncontrollable and unpredictable.
- Parents may attend overly to their child's worries. This rehearsal and repetition of anxious thoughts and feelings signals to the child that their worries are important, and may result in their anxiety being validated and heightened.
- Parents may protect their children and encourage avoidant responses. This may maintain the child's beliefs that their world is frightening and that they will be unable to cope.

Parental management that is unclear, inconsistent or results in anxious behaviour being reinforced needs to be addressed and replaced with an approach that is firm, fair, consistent and helpful. This involves developing parenting practices where there are clear rules and boundaries that are firmly and consistently enforced. Anxious thoughts and behaviour receive minimal parental attention, while attempts at coping and trying to face anxious situations are rewarded.

Parenting based on these principles will be beneficial. Boundaries provide security and, by helping the child to understand their limits, create a sense of safety. With anxious children this is particularly important, since it is worries about uncertainty and the unknown that contribute significantly to their distress. Consistency reduces uncertainty while maximising transparency and fairness. A firm, consistent and objective approach therefore helps to challenge common cognitive biases that the child may have, particularly personalisation such as "it's only me who ever gets told off" or "you always pick on me". Similarly, ensuring that the child's anxious behaviour receives minimal attention sends a clear message that challenges, rather than validates, the importance and significance they ascribe to their worries and anxious feelings.

In order to establish helpful parenting, the meaning that parents ascribe to the notion of firm, fair and consistent parental management will need to be elicited and discussed. For some parents the idea of being firm may equate with harsh, punitive or uncaring practice. These beliefs will inevitably be influenced by their own experiences as children and may be very firmly established and resistant to change. These beliefs need to be explored and the events and situations that influenced their development understood. Once the parent's meaning has been identified the clinician can help the parent to begin to question and challenge their beliefs. For example:

- clear boundaries do not require the introduction of numerous rules
- consistency does not require mechanistic precision
- "firm" does not imply that the household becomes a cold and uncaring environment
- enforcing boundaries does not mean that the parent is harsh or uncaring.

Discussions such as these may bring new information to the parent's attention and help them understand that parenting is complex, and is based on a continuum of practice rather than a simple dichotomous dimension, e.g. "we have rules or we don't". Important meanings that shape parental beliefs can be unravelled and challenged, e.g. being firm and clear is different from being punitive or authoritarian.

Once important parental cognitions have been acknowledged and reappraised, the practicalities of establishing firm, fair and consistent parenting can be discussed. The approach will require the establishment of a few important rules that are fair, simple and clearly understood by everyone involved. Consistency can be facilitated by developing good supportive communication between parents. Initially this may require daily discussions and reviews where parents can talk openly about their parenting practice in an honest but non-threatening way. Parenting practice can be further developed through learning new problem-solving skills which can be used to deal with future problems and challenges.

> Establish a positive, firm and consistent parenting framework.

Reinforce coping behaviour

Once the parent has been able to introduce a positive and consistent framework, the next element involves ensuring that the child's inappropriate or anxious behaviour receives minimal attention, while their appropriate and courageous behaviour receives maximum attention and reinforcement.

Parental behaviour that focuses on and attends to anxiety signals, or that may be reinforcing the child's avoidance, needs to be addressed. In particular, parents may need to shift the balance of their attention so that positive courageous behaviour is reinforced and anxious inappropriate behaviour is ignored.

Attend to courageous behaviour

Anxious parents may inadvertently increase their child's anxiety by attending to and commenting on early signs of anxiety. Seemingly innocent comments such as "you look very pale Mike, are you sure you are OK?" or "Claire, I know that you are going to get really worried about this" tend to draw the child's attention to their anxiety signals and increase their anxiety. The tendency for anxious parents to criticise their children, to emphasise their anxiety signals and to encourage avoidance can be addressed by asking the parents to look for, and attend to, positive and courageous behaviour. Initially this may need to be undertaken in a structured way in which the parents are asked to keep a "being brave diary". They are instructed to write down at least one example per day of a situation where their child has made some attempt to face their fears. Examples could involve the child:

- successfully managing their anxiety
- undertaking a new or courageous task
- practising new skills
- talking positively about a future challenge.

Diaries such as this aim to redirect parental attention away from their child's anxiety signals and worries by encouraging parents to look for coping behaviour. Parental beliefs about their child's inability to cope are directly challenged. Early signs of anxiety are responded to in a caring way but are then ignored and played down as parents focus on their child's coping. This may not, however, initially be easy for some parents and so they may need preparatory training.

> *Julie (11) had social anxiety, with many worries about what the other children thought about her and whether she would be able to join in with discussions. She was due to start secondary school the next week and her mother Mary was talking about how Julie was really worried and wouldn't be able to cope. Mary talked about how the school would be big, how easy it was to get lost, that there were four times as many children as at Julie's last school, and how there would be lots of noisy rough boys in her year group. Julie quietly mentioned that Anna, a girl from her old school, was also starting in her class and that she was someone she had spoken with before. However, this was not heard by Julie's mother, who continued to explain how she had planned to take time off next week so that she could fetch her daughter from school if (when) she panicked.*

Encourage parents to notice courageous and coping behaviour.

Positive reinforcement

Once parents are able to recognise their child's attempts at facing and overcoming their fears, they need to ensure that these attempts and the use of new skills are reinforced. The process of reinforcement serves to increase the child's motivation to make future attempts to confront feared situations and events. Reinforcement should be contingent on attempts at coping rather than the achievement of a successful outcome. This provides a way of countering overly high expectations by emphasising that irrespective of the outcome, it is trying rather than success that should be rewarded.

Reinforcement can take many forms, including verbal and non-verbal comments (saying "well done", hug, smile), material rewards (DVD, sweets, extra money), physical activities (swimming, bowling, bike rides), outings (cinema, going to the special park, watching a football game), special time (extra time with a parent, staying up late) or treats (such as a long bath, a takeaway or dinner while watching the TV). Rewards do not have to cost money, and indeed some of the best involve parents and children spending time together engaging in activities such as playing a game, reading or cooking a special cake. If material reinforcers are used then parents need to decide on their value, and to decide what is and is not appropriate. Typically material reinforcers should be small, and should follow fairly closely the challenge the child is facing.

> *Mike was worried about going into college to pick up an application form. This was the first big step on his ladder to get him in to college and he was worried. He had put this off a few times already and so decided that he needed something to encourage him. He wanted a new CD from the music shop close to college and so decided that buying this would be his treat. He would go and buy this after he had gone into college to collect the prospectus*

Externally provided rewards are very helpful in the early stages of the programme and can provide the extra incentive to encourage the child to face their fears. However, it is important that alongside this the child acknowledges and praises themselves, and learns to focus on their strengths. This process can be encouraged by asking the child/young person to keep a positive diary in which they write one or two things each day that have been positive. These can be:

- nice things that others have said about them, e.g. "you are a really nice and understanding person to talk with"
- activities or tasks in which they feel they have performed well, e.g. "I think I played well in that match"
- a challenge they have faced, e.g. "I am really pleased that I went up and spoke with Mike at school today"
- nice thoughts about themselves, e.g. "I look good in these jeans"
- nice feedback from someone else, e.g. "Mary said I did well with that maths homework".

The diary helps the child to focus on their strengths and provides a good way of helping them to acknowledge their successes. It is also a permanent reminder that can be an objective way of countering any negative biases and doubts. However, this may initially be difficult for some children and young people, who may not be used to recognising and acknowledging their strengths. In the early stages it may therefore be important to involve parents or close friends to facilitate this process. Similarly, children often fail to recognise the importance or significance of what they have achieved. This may be the result of cognitive biases such as selective abstraction or unrealistic expectations, resulting in small positive achievements being negated or overlooked.

> *Judy had managed to get out of the house and walk to the garden gate for the first time in five weeks. When this was discussed during the next meeting, Judy was very dismissive of her achievements, saying "It wasn't long ago that I could go out whenever I wanted. I could go to town, get a bus or see my friends, so going to the gate is nothing to celebrate."*

On these occasions it is useful to acknowledge the frustrations of change and how it can take time to regain life and overcome problems. A useful method for helping children to note their current achievements is to distinguish between the past and the present. Thus, while in the past Judy could do all these things, she has not been able to do them for the past five weeks. Going to the gate for the first time in five weeks was an important step forward.

Praise and reward courageous behaviour and attempts to change.

Ignore anxious behaviour

Parental attention needs to be redistributed so that the reduced attention paid to anxious behaviour is offset by an increase in attention towards courageous behaviour. Parents therefore need to learn to ignore their child's anxiety talk, symptoms, avoidance and complaining.

Many parents become trapped in responding to their child's anxious behaviour and may initially find this difficult to change. Preparation requires the provision of a clear rationale that challenges parental beliefs that unconditionally attending to their child is helpful. Instead parents need to understand that attending to anxious behaviour reinforces and encourages it. Openly asking parents whether providing reassurance reduces their child's anxiety or anxious symptoms will often result in a negative reply. This can then lead into a discussion about how actively attending to such behaviours and talk may actually increase their anxiety. Parental attention towards a low-level anxiety symptom, "I've got that funny feeling in my tummy again", may increase the child's internal focus and make the symptoms feel stronger or worse. This is often done innocently by remarks such as "have you got that hot shaky feeling as well?" or "come and have a cuddle and tell me if it gets worse". Focusing on such behaviours also signals to the child that what they are feeling, or thinking, is important. Busy parents wouldn't talk about such things unless they were important, and this may therefore increase the potency of their worries.

Planned ignoring is a way of reducing this possibility and involves the parent responding to the child's anxious behaviours with minimal attention.

Parents are instructed to listen and respond empathically to their child's complaints the first time, but are encouraged to direct their child to an alternative coping strategy, and withdraw their attention, if the complaining continues. Thus complaints of symptoms are met with positive reassurance, e.g. "oh dear, I am sure it will get better". If the child continues to talk about their symptoms or worries then the parent is instructed not to respond but instead directs them towards neutral, external stimuli. This can be achieved in a gentle yet firm way, by comments such "come and help me do some cooking" or "can you go and find your reading book for me?". Comments such as these provide the child with a task that helps to refocus their attention outwardly and away from their worries or anxious feelings.

There will be occasions when this strategy is very successful, while at other times the child will persist and may become distressed. The parent needs to be prepared for this possibility by prompting their child to try some of the new anxiety-coping techniques they have learned. Once again the parent needs to remain calm and in control and to covey a sense of optimism that the techniques will work and the anxiety will reduce. Finally, parents need to be prepared for the worse possible case and to understand that comments such as "you don't care" or "you don't love me" are understandable, angry protests rather than genuine, deep-seated beliefs.

> Minimise attention for anxious behaviour by planned ignoring and externally focusing attention.

How should parents be involved in the programme?

This initial process will help to clarify the extent and nature of parental involvement in treatment sessions. As indicated earlier, parents may have a limited or substantive role, and may be involved in supporting their child or as a target for treatment in their own right. In making this decision, the clinician needs to consider the type and level of parental involvement required to maximise the success of the treatment outcome. As a general guide, the following factors may indicate different levels of involvement.

The facilitator

This is the most limited involvement and typically requires parents to attend treatment sessions at the start, midpoint and end of treatment. The purpose is primarily psycho-educational, with the parents being helped to understand the CBT model of anxiety and the skills the child has learned. This level of involvement is often indicated when:

- working with adolescents who are keen to participate on their own
- parents' own psychological needs are substantive and run the risk of dominating treatment sessions and detracting from the needs of the child
- parental engagement is limited and they are unwilling or unable to attend treatment sessions.

The co-clinician

Typically the majority of sessions are conducted jointly with parent and child. The child's problems are the focus of the treatment sessions with parental attendance ensuring a full understanding of the issues discussed and skills being developed. The parent is better able to understand the intervention and to prompt and support their child's use of new skills and out-of-session assignments. Parents may be involved as co-clinicians if:

- the parent is interested, able to support their child, and positively disposed to CBT
- the parent does not have any particularly significant psychological problems that would impact adversely on the child's problems
- the parent does not have a significant anxiety disorder that might require treatment in its own right
- the child feels comfortable, able to talk freely and wants their parent present.

As a co-client

Parents are involved in this capacity if they, or their family, have specific problems that impact directly on the child's anxiety. Treatment sessions will involve direct work with the child (with or without parental involvement) plus additional parent or family sessions where these issues are addressed. Co-client involvement is more likely to be indicated when:

- a parent has a mild/moderate anxiety disorder that the clinician feels competent to treat
- there are parental or family management issues that have contributed, or are contributing, to the onset or maintenance of the child's anxiety
- parents may need sessions without their child to think about how they can resolve important adult issues such as financial, work or relationship problems.

> Clarify and agree the extent and role of parents in the intervention.

8

Emotional recognition and management

The initial therapeutic focus of many CBT anxiety programmes is on the emotional domain. This is different to the initial focus of CBT interventions for other disorders. For example, with depression the initial focus is in the behavioural domain, an early task being that of behavioural activation. With PTSD the intervention may start in the cognitive domain, as the clinician attempts to discover the meanings the child has assigned to their traumatic experiences. With anxiety disorders, the initial key tasks are to help children and young people develop skills to:

1 understand the anxiety reaction and the "flight or fight" response
2 identify their specific body signals associated with anxiety
3 recognise that anxious feelings are associated with situations and thoughts
4 learn a range of methods for managing anxious feelings.

Many children are not aware of the anxiety response or their physiological symptoms, which in some instances can be misperceived by the child and/or their parents as signs of being ill or seriously unwell. A greater understanding and recognition of these symptoms challenges such illness beliefs and allows the child to intervene, and actively manage their anxiety response. The primary aims and methods of work in the emotional domain are summarised in Figure 8.1.

Psycho-education: The flight–fight response

Children who are particularly aware of, and sensitive to, their anxiety signals may misperceive their physiological stress response as signs of being ill. In

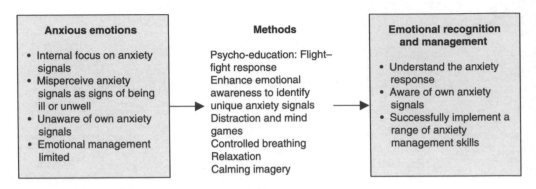

Figure 8.1   CBT intervention in the emotional domain

these situations it can be useful to educate the child about the anxiety or stress response, often called the "flight or fight" response. Understanding this can help children normalise their symptoms, thereby challenging any illness beliefs.

The explanation needs to be kept simple, while providing the child with an understanding of the different physiological symptoms they might experience. This might, for example, involve a story about Stone Age man going out hunting and being confronted by a large dinosaur. Stone Age man has two choices: either run away (flight) or stay and defend himself (fight). Whatever he chooses, his body needs to prepare itself for some form of action.

When a potentially dangerous situation arises, the body produces chemicals (adrenalin and cortisol). These produce physical changes that help it prepare to fight or run away. These chemicals make the heart beat faster, so that blood can be pumped round the body to the muscles. The muscles need oxygen, and so breathing becomes faster in order to provide the muscles with the fuel they need. People may feel very alert and focused as they concentrate on the threat.

As the blood supply to the muscles increases, blood gets diverted away from those parts of the body that aren't being used, and from the vessels running around the outside of the body. When this happens people often notice a churning or sick feeling in the stomach and may go pale. As the body focuses on fuelling the muscles, other bodily functions are shut down. We don't need to eat at times like this, and so some people notice their mouth becoming dry and a difficulty in swallowing.

The body is now working very hard and starts to become hot. In order to cool down, the body starts to sweat and pushes the blood vessels to the body surface, resulting in some people becoming flushed or red in the face. Sometimes the body may take in too much oxygen, resulting in people feeling faint, lightheaded, or feeling as if they have wobbly, or "jelly", legs. Muscles that continue to be prepared for action (tensed) start to ache and people may notice headaches and stiffness.

All these bodily changes are designed to help us cope with dangerous situations. Although we don't have dinosaurs anymore we continue to experience this stress response. The dinosaurs have become our worries and our fears. This information is summarised in ***The Flight–Fight Response*** worksheet in Chapter 12.

> Understanding the flight–fight response helps to make sense of the physiological changes that occur when one is stressed or frightened.

Emotional awareness

Children are often poor at distinguishing between their emotions and at identifying the specific body signals associated with them. Helping children to recognise and understand their own anxiety body signals is therefore an early and important goal of CBT programmes.

"Hot" situations

A common approach to increasing emotional awareness is to identify a recent "hot" situation in which the child felt very frightened or scared. The clinician initiates a detailed and focused discussion in which the child is guided through their "hot" situation and helped to identify the physiological anxiety signals they noticed before, during and after the situation. For example, a child who was anxious about going to school might be encouraged to mentally scan and check their body and describe their body signals on waking in the morning, as they closed the front door and left home, arrived at the school gates, walked into the classroom, and as they left school at the end of the day. The discussion aims to help the child attend to possible anxiety symptoms and highlights changes in body signals (i.e. their anxiety build-up) as they approach their feared situation. Tracking the event provides an opportunity to contrast "before" and "after" body signals and serves to highlight that while anxiety is unpleasant, it does reduce.

In Vivo

There may be occasions when the child becomes anxious during a therapy session. This provides a real-life opportunity to help the child check and identify their anxiety body signals. If this occurs, the clinician needs to feed back to the child that they appear to be becoming uptight or anxious, thereby acknowledging and validating their emotional reaction. The child is then encouraged to hold on to the anxiety, and is reassured that although these feelings are unpleasant, they will pass. The clinician then guides the child in scanning their body to identify their unique anxiety signals and to rate the strength of the various signals.

> *Marcus (16 years) had many worries about germs and was particularly concerned about contamination from bodily fluids and the possibility of developing AIDS. During an initial meeting in a hospital clinic, Marcus appeared very anxious and uncomfortable and appeared to be pre-occupied with something on the floor. This was commented on and Marcus expressed concern about a wet patch on the carpet. Further questioning revealed that Marcus was worried that this patch was caused by a spillage of bodily fluids. The opportunity was taken to systematically guide Marcus to scan his body and identify and rate his anxiety signals. The exercise proved useful in identifying his key signals (racing heart, difficulty in breathing and feeling hot). Marcus was reassured that this patch was caused by a cup of coffee that had been knocked over earlier in the day. Throughout the session he was periodic-ally asked to rate the strength of his anxiety, an exercise that helped him recognise that anxiety reduces over time. This experience also provided a useful way of emphasising the relationship between his thoughts (stain caused by spillage of bodily fluids) and anxious feelings (scared).*

Anxiety signal worksheets

While many children will be able to volunteer some of their anxiety signals, the use of body signal "menus" provides a more systematic way of checking the presence of important, but possibly overlooked, signals. The worksheet in Figure 8.2 was completed by Millie (9) and provided a structured way of talking about some of the more common anxiety signals.

Focusing on anxiety signals helps children to recognise their own specific anxiety reaction. The child can then map out their anxiety pro-gression, identifying the signals that are particularly important at different levels of anxiety. The overall aim is to increase awareness so that the child can implement effective anxiety management strategies at the earliest opportunity. Intervening early prevents anxiety from escalating. An example of an anxiety signal worksheet, *My Anxiety Body Signals*, is included in Chapter 12.

> Emotional recognition can be facilitated through discussing "hot" situations and the use of symptom worksheets.

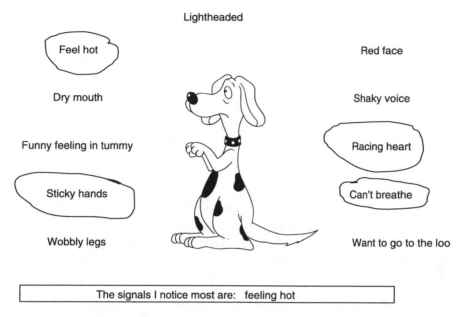

Figure 8.2 Anxiety signal worksheet

Emotion rating

An important part of emotional monitoring is to help children recognise that the strength of their anxiety varies over time and in different situations. This can be achieved through the use of emotional rating scales, anxiety thermometers or SUDS (subjective units of distress). These provide a way of quantifying feelings as the child is encouraged to rate the strength of their feelings on a scale that ranges from calm/no anxiety to really scared/strong anxiety. This can simply involve a numerical rating (1–10 or 1–100), or for younger children could be a more visual scale like that provided in Figure 8.3.

Figure 8.3 Anxiety rating scale

Rating scales are used regularly in CBT as a way of quantifying subjective states such as anxiety, or strength of belief in cognitions, and provide a way of assessing progress over time.

Emotional monitoring

In addition to recognising the specific bodily signals associated with different emotional states, a second goal of emotional awareness is to increase the child's understanding of factors associated with their emotions. Emotional monitoring helps children understand that:

- feelings change throughout the day
- specific events or situations trigger different feelings
- thoughts and feelings are linked
- the strength of feelings varies over time.

In turn, this increased awareness helps children:

- become better at recognising the range of feelings they experience
- prepare and plan how to cope successfully with situations that produce strong emotional reactions
- understand that they can change how they feel by changing the way they think
- realise that although strong anxiety feelings are unpleasant, they do reduce over time.

Emotional monitoring can take many different forms, with the specific focus and format being tailored to the particular needs of the child. Emotional monitoring is therefore preceded by a discussion designed to ensure that the child both understands the importance of monitoring and feels able to engage with the process. The potential advantages of monitoring need to be highlighted, e.g. better understanding of how they feel, identification of difficult or "hot" situations, opportunity to explore possible anxiety-increasing thoughts. This needs to occur alongside an open discussion about the possible difficulties of monitoring. Many children may for example be reluctant to use paper and pencil diaries; others will forget to fill them out; some may worry that others might see their diary; while others may not have enough time to undertake such a task.

Potential barriers such as these need to be discussed openly and possible solutions explored. For children who are reluctant to use paper and pencil diaries, other formats such as computer logs, email or tape-recording may be more attractive options. For those who might forget, ways of reminding them such as involving someone else or visual prompts can be explored. Ways of maintaining privacy need to be discussed. For example, a mood diary may be completed at home at the end of the school day rather than at school. If the time commitment involved in self-monitoring appears too great, this can be reduced by asking the child to record one, or two, days. Potential barriers need to be identified and solutions agreed so that the child is able to undertake the task successfully in a way that is appealing and practical for them.

> Explain the rationale for self-monitoring and explore potential barriers.

"Hot" feelings diary

A common method of helping the child recognise the relationship between situations, thoughts and feelings is to use a "hot" feelings diary. The child is asked to record any "hot" situations where they notice a strong anxiety response. They briefly describe the situation, how they felt and the thoughts that were racing through their mind as this occurred. This can be achieved through the use of a standard diary sheet such as that given in Table 8.1, or the child can design their own.

Table 8.1 My "hot" feelings diary

Day and time	What was happening	How did you feel?	What were you thinking?
Monday morning	School assembly	Faint, nervous	I can't breathe I need to get out of here
Saturday afternoon	In town with friends	Shaking, faint, felt hot	There are so many people about. I need to go home, I can't handle this
Tuesday afternoon	Dance class	Sweating, faint	I keep messing up. I am not feeling well and so will have to leave early and go home

Having asked the child to complete the diary, it is essential that this is reviewed during the next meeting. When reviewing the diary it is important to encourage the child and parent to reflect on what they have written. The task of the clinician is to help them attend to key aspects of their diary and to look for any patterns or themes.

- "Are there any particular times this seems to happen?" (e.g. mornings, school days)
- "Does it tend to occur in certain places or situations?" (e.g. away from home, crowded places)

- "What are the important emotional reactions and body signals that have been identified?" (the child's feelings and body signals)
- "Have you noticed anything about the way you are thinking when you feel like this?" (bias to threat, focus on bodily symptoms, need to escape)

This form of questioning embraces the collaborative process of the therapeutic partnership. The clinician uses their expertise to provide the child with a framework in which they can explore their cognitions, emotions and behaviours. The questioning is designed to facilitate the process of guided discovery in which the child is helped to focus on, and discover, important and/or new information and relationships.

Computer logs

Motivation to self-monitor can be increased if the monitoring diary is based around the child's interests. Written diary monitoring sheets will be attractive for some children, whereas others might be more interested in constructing their own.

The worksheet in Figure 8.4 is an example of a feelings log completed on a computer by a 10-year-old boy. The objective of the log was to gain a better understanding of how the child felt throughout the week. He dragged and dropped his dominant feeling into each part of the day and then rated how strong the feeling had been. In this case the parent and child worked together to produce the diary, although the degree and extent of parental assistance needs to be negotiated and agreed.

This format was very engaging for this computer-literate boy and the diary served to highlight that:

- although the child's dominant negative emotion was anxiety, there were also a number of times when he felt happy, particularly in the evenings
- anxious feelings occurred each school-day morning but not at the weekend
- anxious feelings were particularly strong on Wednesday.

Worksheets

With older children it may be possible to engage in a focused discussion to help them identify how they feel in different situations and which are the most anxiety-provoking. The main purpose at this stage is not necessarily to develop an anxiety hierarchy but to increase the child's awareness of the relationship between anxiety and specific situations. It is also helpful to focus on situations that make the child feel calm or reduce anxiety, as this may provide useful ideas about how the child can manage their anxiety symptoms.

With younger children the use of worksheets such as those in Chapter 12 can be helpful. In the *Things That Make Me Feel Anxious* worksheet the child simply selects those events/situations that generate anxiety and then

Choose the feeling that you notice most for each part of the day.

Choose a number to rate how strong it is

1 (Not very strong)   2   3   4   5 (really strong)

Day	Morning	Afternoon	Evening
Monday	4	2	3
Tuesday	4	2	5
Wednesday	4	5	1
Thursday	2	2	3
Friday	1	3	4
Saturday	2	3	2
Sunday	3	3	2

Figure 8.4   My feelings log

draws a line to the anxious face. It is always helpful to leave a couple of blank boxes so that the child can add any of their own important worries.

> Explore which form of self-monitoring is attractive, engaging and achievable.

Anxiety management

Once the child is able to identify their anxiety signals they can then explore ways in which their feelings can be managed. The aim is to equip the child with a toolbox of strategies that they can draw on in different situations. The need to develop and use a range of skills is stressed, and it is highlighted that no one strategy will work all the time. The child is therefore encouraged to experiment and discover what works for them. Similarly, if they encounter a situation where their preferred method fails, the child is encouraged to actively move on and to try using another strategy.

Immediate relief

There will be occasions when the child may suddenly become anxious and need to quickly calm down and regain control. At these times they need immediate relief, and controlled breathing and distraction may be helpful.

Controlled breathing

This simple method helps the child to regain control of their body by concentrating on controlling their breathing. It is a quick method that can be done anywhere, and often people are not aware of what the child is doing. As soon as the child becomes anxious they are instructed to slowly draw in a deep breath and to hold it. They then count to 5, slowly let the breath out, and as they do so, think to themselves "relax", "calm down" or "chill out". This is repeated three or four times or until the child feels calmer and more in control.

Controlled breathing can be taught to younger children in a fun way by asking them to blow bubbles. If the child does not control their breathing and blows too hard or too quickly then they will not be able to blow any bubbles. Encouraging the child to blow calmly and steadily in order to blow big bubbles teaches them the principles of controlled breathing. Similarly, the analogy of blowing out candles on a birthday cake can be used. The child is instructed to imagine a birthday cake with candles and to blow each candle out in turn. To be successful they need to take a breath, hold it, aim at the candle and then slowly let the breath out in a controlled way. They are then instructed to repeat this and blow out the rest of the candles.

The ***Controlled Breathing Diary Sheet*** in Chapter 12 provides a simple worksheet that can be used to develop and practise this technique.

Distraction

When some children become anxious they focus internally and become fixated on their physiological anxiety signals. The more they focus on them, the worse the physiological symptoms become and this increases anxiety-increasing cognitions relating to feeling ill, being unable to cope, or losing control. At these times the child may find it helpful to refocus their attention away from their internal bodily signals to external stimuli.

In distraction the child is taught to redirect their attention and to focus on external events. A simple way of doing this is to describe in detail what is going on around them. The description has to be very detailed and in order to develop a good picture the child is instructed to describe the scene as if they are talking with a blind person. The clinician helps the child attend to a range of dimensions including size, shape, colour, textures, noises, sounds and smells. The task can be made more demanding by asking them to do this as quickly as possible. The idea is to keep the child busy and focused on external stimuli, thereby reducing the attention paid to possible anxiety-increasing internal signals.

Mind games

Mind games or thinking puzzles are another way of redirecting and refocusing attention on neutral tasks. A mind game is anything that is moderately challenging, and could involve:

- spelling their name backwards
- counting backwards from 51 in 3s
- naming all the people they know whose name begins with the letter S
- naming all the characters from their favourite TV show
- spotting the car number plates with the letter K.

The puzzle needs to be sufficiently hard to be challenging, but not so difficult that it feels impossible. It also needs to be sufficiently long to sustain the child's attention and thus reduce their anxiety build-up.

> Immediate relief from anxiety symptoms can be obtained through controlled breathing and distraction tasks.

Longer term relief

In addition to strategies that provide more immediate relief, it is helpful for children to learn how to disperse anxiety that builds up throughout the day. In order to maximise success and the likelihood of skills being used, the child needs to explore ways of unwinding that can readily be incorporated into their everyday life.

Physical activity

A natural way of tensing and unwinding is through physical activity. Sports and other vigorous activities provide ways of tensing muscles that can help children to relax. For some, this may simply require a rescheduling of the activity they already undertake so that it occurs at the time they feel most stressed. Other children may be less physical and so require help to identify possible strenuous activities such as a brisk walk, practising a dance routine or re-arranging their room. Once the child has identified a range of unwinding activities, they are then encouraged to try to use them at the times they feel most tense.

> Sam (14) enjoyed running and went for a short run each day before going to school. He found that running helped him to unwind and clear his mind. He only ran in the morning. This was discussed and Sam agreed to explore running at other times, particularly when he noticed himself becoming stressed, to see if this helped him to calm down.

The **My Physical Activities** worksheet in Chapter 12 provides a summary of some of the physical activities that children may find enjoyable. Blank boxes are left for the child to add their own additional activities.

Relaxing activities

A similar idea is activity rescheduling, where the child is encouraged to use activities they already find relaxing at the times they become tense. These relaxing activities could be anything such as:

- reading a book or magazine
- watching TV or a DVD
- listening to music
- playing a computer game
- talking to a friend
- baking a cake.

So instead of:

- sitting around on their own worrying about tomorrow, they could try reading a magazine

- sitting in their bedroom feeling anxious, they could try watching TV
- lying in bed feeling uptight, they could try listening to their MP3 player
- feeling stressed, they could try playing on the computer.

Progressive muscle relaxation

Progressive muscle relaxation is a way of systematically helping children to tense and relax their bodies. The child is guided through a series of exercises in which each major muscle group is tensed and then relaxed. This process increases the child's awareness of their body signal, identifies those parts of their bodies in which stress particularly manifests itself, and provides ways in which these feelings can be dissipated.

Progressive muscle relaxation is best taught sitting or lying down, and can often be practised at home and included as part of the child's bedtime routine. In terms of preparation, a time needs to be chosen that is free from noise and distractions; the room needs to be warm and quiet with the child sitting or lying comfortably. The child is guided to identify and check each major muscle group, which are then, through a series of exercises, tensed and relaxed. The clinician focuses the child's attention on the difference between tension and relaxation and so helps them to become more aware of their anxiety signals. By the end of the session the child will have tensed all their major muscle groups and will be encouraged to enjoy the relaxed state they have induced. The child is urged to practise their relaxation exercises at home and informed that the more they practise the better they will become at relaxing. It can be useful to do this at the times they feel particularly stressed or at bedtime as part of their routine which may also help the child to fall asleep.

Many commercial relaxation tapes and CDs are available, although often these are targeted at adults. They tend to vary in length, the exercises they use, number of muscle groups they focus on, and whether or not they include music. It is a matter of personal taste as to which are used, although clinical experience suggests that children usually enjoy those that are relatively brief and are accompanied by music.

When undertaking progressive muscle relaxation children may initially appear very self-conscious and fidgety and may want to keep their eyes open. Do not worry. The clinician needs to reassure the child that they can do whatever they wish as long as they are comfortable and able to listen to the instructions. The clinician should also explain that he or she will also follow the instructions but will remain seated in the chair, which should be positioned so that they are not looking directly at the child.

With younger children progressive muscle relaxation can be made fun through a game of "Simon Says". The child is instructed to engage in various activities such as those below, designed to tense their muscle groups:

- walking around the room stiff and upright like a soldier
- stretching up to the sky

- running on the spot
- making a scary face
- puffing themselves out to become a big balloon.

After engaging in the tensing exercises the child is helped to relax by imagining themselves to be a big, heavy, slow-moving animal and then a sleeping lion that has to stay as still and quiet as it can.

Calming imagery

Children may prefer to use calming or relaxing imagery as a way of unwinding. Imagery is a method that works well for some children, particularly those with good imaginations.

The child is asked to think about a special relaxing place which could be somewhere they have visited (e.g. on holiday), somewhere they have seen, or an imaginary place (e.g. floating in space or swimming with dolphins). By asking the child to draw a picture of their special place, the image can be developed. The child is encouraged to develop a multisensory image in which they attend to colours, shapes, sizes, noises, smells, and tactile sensations. Once the child has drawn and described their relaxing place in detail, they are asked to conjure up their image and to imagine being there. The clinician helps to create the visual scene and will incorporate some of the other sensory sensations the child produced:

- the smell of the hamburger stand
- the sound of the stream gently trickling past
- the breeze blowing gently through their hair
- the cold of the snow on their face
- the feeling of floating in space.

The child will be encouraged to practise developing their special place and instructed to transport themselves there when they feel tense and need to relax. The development of imaginal relaxation is summarised in the **My Special Relaxing Place** worksheet in Chapter 12.

> *Julie (12) was asthmatic and suffered from panic attacks which had recently resulted in her being admitted to hospital on a number of occasions. Julie was asked to describe her relaxing place and immediately identified a beach she had gone to on holiday a couple of years previously. Through discussion Julie was helped to create a multisensory image. She described the beach in detail and was then helped to focus on specific details: the colour of the golden sand, the white rocks reaching out into the crystal-clear blue water. The sound of the waves crashing on the rocks and the birds screaming high in the sky. The taste of the salty water as it dried in the hot sun on her face. The smell of the hamburger stand at the end of the beach.*

The anxiety management skills the child finds helpful can be summarised on the *My Feelings Toolbox* worksheet in Chapter 12. This provides a permanent record of the different ideas they could call on if they become anxious.

> Children need to be encouraged to use a range of methods to manage their anxiety.

9

Cognitive enhancement

Once the child has begun to understand and manage their anxious feelings the primary focus of the intervention shifts to the cognitive domain. It is during this stage that the child and their carers are helped to become aware of the importance of their thoughts and the relationship between these, their anxious feelings and what they do. In particular, sessions are designed to address the important dysfunctional cognitions and biases identified in Chapter 3. The overall aim is to identity and test anxiety-increasing cognitions and to develop alternative cognitions that are functional, balanced and helpful. Key targets, methods and outcomes of this work are summarised in Figure 9.1.

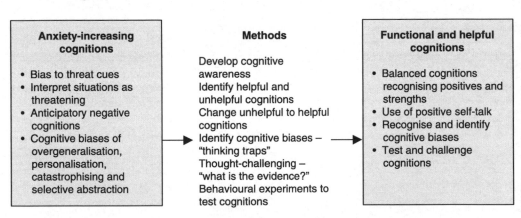

Figure 9.1 Key targets, methods and outcomes

Once aware of the relationship between their cognitions and anxious feelings, children are helped to assess systematically the evidence underpinning their thoughts and to attend to new or overlooked information that might challenge them. This encourages the child to test and reappraise their cognitions and, through this, to develop a more balanced cognitive style where strengths and achievements, which may previously have been over-looked or negated, are recognised.

Work in the cognitive domain therefore helps children and young people to:

1 develop cognitive awareness – this involves learning to identify and communicate thoughts and to become aware of these when preparing to confront, or during, anxiety-provoking situations
2 recognise that some thoughts are helpful, enabling and make them feel good while others are unhelpful, disempowering and make them feel anxious
3 change unhelpful thoughts to those that are more helpful and empowering
4 identify common cognitive distortions and biases associated with anxiety, particularly overgeneralisation, personalisation, catastrophising and selective abstraction
5 test and challenge their thoughts and develop more balanced and help-ful ways of thinking.

Developing cognitive awareness: identifying and communicating thoughts

A fundamental requirement of CBT is that children are able to identify and communicate their thoughts or "self-talk". The most common method of identifying anxiety-increasing negative thoughts, particularly with older children, is the direct approach whereby they are simply asked to describe a worrying or fearful situation and the accompanying thoughts. As the event unfolds, the clinician regularly asks the child "what were you thinking?", "what was rushing through your head?" or "what was going round in your mind?". Through direct questioning such as this the clinician is able to build up an understanding of the child's cognitions and to identify any anxiety-increasing attributions, assumptions and biases.

The clinician's questioning may not need to focus directly on the child's cognitions. Children's descriptions are often littered with numerous examples of their cognitions. The clinician therefore needs to attend care-fully to the child's comments and to become a "thought catcher" in which the child's cognitions are noted, collected, and fed back at an appropriate time.

Some children initially find the task of identifying their thoughts very difficult. They may need more guided help in order to tune into the idea that they do have "self-talk" and to identify their automatic thoughts. In these situations it can be useful to ask the child to think about the first time they came to meet you. Through a series of prompts they can be guided to think about issues such as what they thought would happen, what the room would be like, what they thought would be talked about. This provides a way of demonstrating to the child the idea of automatic thoughts, and that at any one time, although they may not be aware of it, they have lots of thoughts racing through their mind.

However, it is not uncommon for questions such as "what were you thinking?" to be met by a brief answer of "nothing" or "I don't know", particularly with younger children. On these occasions more detailed psycho-education may be required in order to help the child find a way to communicate their thoughts.

A readily understood and effective way that is often used to communicate self-talk is through the use of thought bubbles. These are familiar to most children, with those as young as six and seven being able to understand that thought bubbles represent what a person is thinking and that this might be different to what they are doing. The clinician can prepare some worksheets, such as that in Figure 9.2, in order to help the child grasp this concept. The child is shown the picture and asked to write or draw in the thought bubble what the character might be thinking.

The task can be developed to help children recognise that there are many possible ways of thinking about the same situation. Thus, in the

Figure 9.2   Use of thought bubbles

example shown in Figure 9.3, the child would be encouraged to identify three different thoughts that the cat might have. In later sessions the generation of multiple thoughts such as this will be used to challenge the child's initial anxiety-increasing thoughts in order to highlight that there is more than one way of thinking about situations.

Figure 9.3 Generating different thoughts

Once the child has demonstrated that they are able to use thought bubbles as a way of communicating inner thoughts, they can then apply this to their own problems. For example:

- "What would you put in your thought bubbles when you see that dog running towards you?"
- "Fill out your thought bubbles when you have to show your work to the class"
- "Use the thought bubble to show me what races through your head when you step off the bus in town".

A worksheet that can be used to explore some of the thoughts a child might have in particular situations, *My Worrying Thoughts*, is included in

Chapter 12. Similarly, for children with generalised anxiety disorders where there are multiple worrying thoughts, the ***Tumbling Thoughts*** worksheets might be helpful. ***Tumbling Thoughts*** provides a helpful metaphor for the child to visualise the way worrying thoughts keep tumbling round and round in their heads.

> Identity the best way for the child to communicate their thoughts.

Identify helpful and unhelpful thoughts

Once children are able to identify and share their thoughts, the next step is to encourage the child to appraise them. The aim of this task is to recognise that some ways of thinking are helpful while others are unhelpful. Unhelpful ways of thinking are typically biased and critical and serve to increase anxiety, such as:

- "I bet there will be lots of people in town and I won't be able to cope"
- "I know I will get this work wrong"
- "I am always ill when I sleep over at my friend's house".

These ways of thinking not only make the child feel unpleasant but are also de-activating. They are unhelpful and increase the likelihood that the young person will avoid situations: instead of going to town or sleeping over they may stay at home where they feel "safe". Thoughts such as these can also be demotivating and, in the above example, may result in the child giving up, or not trying with their school work.

Helpful ways of thinking are more balanced and serve the purpose of reducing or moderating the child's anxiety. More helpful ways of thinking about the previous situations could be:

- "There may be lots of people in town but my friend could help if I felt uptight"
- "This work is new so I expect everyone will get some questions wrong"
- "I am sure we would have a great time and I could always phone mum to collect me if I didn't feel well".

These ways of thinking are more enabling, and encourage the child to face and confront challenging situations.

Activities and worksheets can be used to help children identify helpful and unhelpful thoughts, and the relationship between these and how they feel. The ***Cool Cat*** and ***How Would They Feel?*** worksheets in Chapter 12 highlight different ways of thinking about events and can be used to engage the child in a discussion about the effect of different ways of thinking on their feelings and behaviour.

Similarly, quizzes can be a fun way of helping children to distinguish between helpful and unhelpful thoughts. The quiz in Figure 9.4 provides some examples and the clinician can add some of the child's thoughts which they have identified during their meetings.

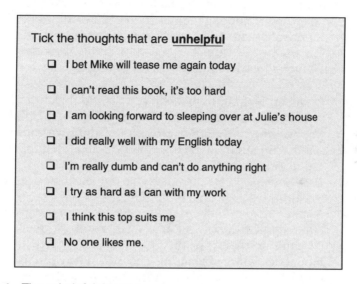

Figure 9.4 The unhelpful thoughts quiz

Changing unhelpful thoughts to helpful thoughts

Understanding that there is more than one way to think about an event or situation and that some ways of thinking are unhelpful leads into the next stage: changing unhelpful thoughts to more helpful thoughts.

While helping children to develop a more enabling and helpful thinking style is an important objective, it is also important for the clinician to maintain a balanced perspective and to ensure a sense of reality. The tendency to become overly positive and optimistic, as a way of countering the child's negative biases, needs to be resisted. The aim of the clinician is not simply to encourage children to think positively – that everything is OK and that they will successful. Instead the aim is to help the child to discover information that will help them to develop alternative cognitions. This is achieved through encouraging the child to attend to new or overlooked information. This helps them to discover evidence that allows them to challenge their unhelpful thoughts and to develop a more balanced way of thinking.

Prepared worksheets provide a useful way of introducing the child to this concept before focusing on their own specific cognitions. When undertaking this process it is important to highlight that there is no one answer but many possible ways of thinking. This will help children to feel more comfortable about volunteering their ideas and will counter any preconceived ideas that there is "an answer". In turn this will help the child to feel more relaxed and reduce possible performance anxiety about "getting it right". Similarly, the third-party perspective can be less anxiety-provoking, particularly for very anxious or young children. It provides safe opportunities to practise developing alternative thoughts before moving on to challenge their own.

The examples in Figure 9.5 can be discussed with children to highlight the following four features of helpful thoughts.

- *Enabling:* Helpful thoughts motivate and direct the child to a course of action. In the examples in Figure 9.5 the unhelpful thoughts are dis-empowering and do not provide the child with ideas about what they can do differently to change the situation. Helpful thoughts tend to be action-oriented.
- *Reduce anxiety:* Helpful thoughts reduce anxiety and other unpleasant emotions whereas unhelpful thoughts increase these feelings.
- *Balanced focus:* Unhelpful thoughts focus on negative aspects. These are often about themselves ("no one ever talks to me"), their performance ("I can't do these") or the future ("she'll never be my friend"). Helpful thoughts are more balanced. They are more open in content and serve to counter this immediate negative bias by directing the child's attention towards overlooked or new information.
- *Reduce uncertainty:* Anxiety is associated with uncertainty. Helpful thoughts reduce uncertainty by providing the child with an action plan that increases their sense of control over situations and events.

> Develop alternative, helpful, and enabling ways of thinking.

Positive self-talk

The modification of "self-talk" is a commonly used strategy in many CBT anxiety programmes. Anxious children tend to have higher rates of negative cognitions in anticipation of, rather than during, exposure to feared situations. If children are to be taught to use positive "self-talk" then this would suggest that this strategy should be encouraged while preparing for, rather than during, anxious situations.

The child can be helped to replace anticipatory negative anxiety-increasing cognitions such as "this is going to be dreadful" with more

Figure 9.5 Examples of unhelpful and helpful thoughts

positive anxiety-reducing cognitions such as "I have done this before and it wasn't too bad". Similarly, they can be encouraged to replace anticipatory cognitions that predict failure such as "I will get this wrong" with more helpful "self-talk" such as "I will try so I can only do my best". Typically, positive "self-talk" involves the use of short enabling statements that the child repeats to themselves at stressful times. The statement therefore counters their negative anticipatory cognitions and, by repeating it, focuses their attention and drowns out their negative thoughts.

The development of positive "self-talk" will take time. The child's natural tendency towards anxiety-increasing negative cognitions will be strong, particularly in anxiety-provoking situations. Countering this will therefore require practice, and it is important that any attempts are reinforced.

> Counter negative anticipatory cognitions by promoting positive self-talk during the preparatory period.

Coping bias

In addition to reporting more anticipatory negative cognitions, anxious children tend to have lower expectations about their ability to cope with challenging and threatening situations.

Expectations about being unable to cope can be countered through preparatory problem-solving and successful imagery. Children can be helped to imagine their anxiety-provoking or challenging situation and to verbalise what they think will happen so that each potential difficulty can be identified. Once identified, the clinician guides the child through each problem and systematically explores possible solutions and ways of coping. This prepares the child with potentially useful strategies which they can then incorporate into their image. The situation is replayed in the child's imagination, using the strategies that have been discussed, as the child now imagines themselves coping. This needs to be practised and provides a way of countering and challenging the child's tendency to anticipate failure rather than success.

Finally, the "successful outcome" needs to be agreed at the outset, and may be that the child copes or gets through the challenge rather than an exceptional performance.

> Counter coping bias by preparatory problem-solving and imaging success.

Identify common cognitive distortions and biases – the "thinking traps"

It is important to highlight that there are times when everyone thinks in unhelpful ways. This is normal, and everyone has doubts and worries at some stage. However, for some these unhelpful ways of thinking take over. As we found previously, those with anxiety problems are more likely to:

- attend selectively to threat, or negative stimuli, and interpret ambiguous situations as threatening
- expect to be unsuccessful
- perceive themselves as less able to cope with challenging situations
- display cognitive distortions involving overgeneralisation and catastrophising.

It is therefore useful to help anxious children identify and understand potential cognitive distortions and biases. These ways of thinking develop over time, become pervasive and affect many situations and events. These are thinking traps, and there are six common traps that anxious children need to watch out for.

The negative glasses

The selective bias towards threat can be conveyed to children through the metaphor of "negative glasses". These glasses only allow the wearer to see the negative or scary parts of what goes on. The negative glasses never see the whole picture and never seem to find the good or helpful things that happen.

> *Lucy invited Mary (10) and four other friends to her birthday party at the local bowling alley. Mary won the first game and was the only one of the group to get a strike, so she won a special prize. They ate Mary's favourite ice cream, she sat next to Lucy in the car, and they had a wonderful party. When they got back to Lucy's house. When her mum came to collect Mary she asked if she enjoyed herself. Mary replied "We got lost on the way to the bowling alley. Lucy's dad didn't know where he was."*

Positive doesn't count

The expectation that the child will be unsuccessful and unable to cope can be conveyed through the "positive doesn't count" thinking trap. Any positive events and successes are negated or dismissed as unimportant, lucky or irrelevant, as the child attempts to confirm their belief that they fail, and are unable to cope. This trap may also serve to reinforce the child's beliefs that events are uncontrollable as their positive attempts at exerting control are dismissed as unsuccessful.

Linda (11) didn't like maths and was always telling people that she didn't understand it and was rubbish at maths. During a class test she got 15/20. When her friends told Linda how well she had done, Linda dismissed her success and said "That work isn't important. We did that ages ago. I can't do this new work."

The Fortune Teller

The tendency for anxious children to expect things to go wrong or to be unable to cope can be conveyed through the "Fortune Teller" and the "Mind Reader". The Fortune Teller makes negative predictions about future events and highlights potential problems and difficulties rather than success. The child therefore expects to fail and to be unable to cope.

Robbie (14) had been invited into town with his friends. When his dad asked Robbie what time he would be going, he replied "I'm not. They always go to the same music store, talk about their favourite bands and just leave me out."

The Mind Reader

Similarly, the "Mind Reader" knows what everyone else is thinking, and once again anxious children tend to think that others are going to be critical, intimidating or threatening. Thinking like this increases anticipatory anxiety.

Joshua (15) was wearing his new trainers to school. As he walked across the school yard he saw a group of young people looking at them and found himself thinking "Oh no, you don't like these. I've brought the wrong ones. You must think I am a real dork."

Snowballing

The tendency for anxious children to extrapolate a single negative event or outcome to other current or future situations can be captured by the concept of snowballing. With this form of overgeneralisation, a single event becomes bigger and bigger as it pervades many aspects of the child's life and takes over.

Liz (14) had a bad hockey training session and as she got changed she thought "This is awful. I can't play hockey, my friends will think I'm a loser and nobody will want to hang out with me anymore."

Blowing things up

With this thinking trap, comparatively small events are blown up into something very big. By so doing, events become more frightening or scary than they really are.

Sam (15) forgot his sports kit and got told off by his sports teacher. Most of the class were busy getting changed and weren't listening to what was going on, but Sam thought "That is so embarrassing, everybody is listening and laughing at me. I am not going to do sports again."

Disaster thinking

This way of thinking is particularly common with children who experience panic attacks. The normal physiological anxiety signals are perceived as signs of some impending disaster, which typically result in the child thinking that they will die or will need to be taken to hospital.

Mary (14) got off the bus in town and started to feel anxious. She noticed her heart beginning to race and found herself thinking "Oh no, this can't be right. This must be a heart attack like granddad had."

A handout of some of the common cognitive biases is provided in Chapter 12. ***Thinking Traps*** summarises some of the more common thinking traps such as selective abstraction, discounting positives, overgeneralisation, predicting failure and catastrophisation.

> Identify common and pervasive cognitive biases and distortions.

Test and challenge cognitions and biases

Once children are aware of their unhelpful thoughts and thinking traps, the next stage is to help them objectively test their reality. This is particularly important since the majority of negative thoughts are never shared or discussed with others. They tumble around in the child's head, are rarely challenged, and the more they are heard the more they are believed. The thought-testing process therefore provides the child with a structured, powerful and objective way of countering their thinking traps and for assessing the evidence that supports or challenges their way of thinking. There are a number of ways in which this can be achieved.

"Stop, Find, Think"

In challenging situations anxious children have a tendency to attend to threat cues or to interpret neutral stimuli or events as threatening. The child needs to be aware of potentially important thinking traps. The negative glasses find and focus overly on possible "danger signals"; the Mind Reader may increase the child's tendency to "jump to conclusions" and expect negative things to occur. Once aware of this tendency children can be encouraged to refocus their attention by searching for the non-threatening features of the situation. This can be done through a three-step process: Stop, Find, Think.

Step 1: Stop. As the child approaches or interprets a situation they have perceived as dangerous, they can be encouraged to "stop". Visualising a traffic stop sign or a traffic light can act as a useful visual cue which can be accompanied by controlled breathing to control any physiological symptoms of anxiety.

Step 2: Find. Once the child has stopped the cognitive and physiological anxiety escalation, the bias towards threat cues can be countered by actively encouraging the child to find "safety" or helpful information. The child's attention is therefore diverted away from internal anxiety-increasing cognitions and physiological symptoms, towards more neutral external stimuli. The child is encouraged to attend to neutral or positive stimuli such as familiar people, friends, or smiling faces.

Step 3: Think. After the child has attended to neutral or anxiety-reducing stimuli they are encouraged to reappraise the situation by "thinking again". Unhelpful, anxiety-increasing cognitions are challenged and replaced with more helpful and positive cognitions.

The natural tendency to attend to threatening stimuli will be dominant. As such, the child will need to be coached through these steps and this process rehearsed, and practised, during clinical sessions.

Counter threat bias and the tendency to jump to negative
conclusions by:

STOP unhelpful thoughts and anxious feelings

FIND safety and helpful information

THINK positive coping thoughts

Thought-challenging

Children with anxiety tend to demonstrate attentional bias towards threat-related stimuli. This is often reflected in their negative cognitions in which they expect bad things to happen ("people stare and laugh at me"), things to go wrong ("no one will sit with me") or to perform poorly ("I can't do this; I won't be able to cope"). Thought-challenging aims to counter this bias by helping the child attend to a wider range of cues by bringing overlooked or new information to their attention.

Thought-challenging is typically a verbal process and begins by identifying one of the child's frequent or strong unhelpful thoughts. The child is then asked to rate how strongly they believe it on a 1–100 scale. The next step involves asking the child to identify the evidence that would support that thought. The process is then repeated, but this time the child is asked to identify the evidence that would *not* support this way of thinking. They are therefore being asked to find, and attend, to information that they might have overlooked or negated. After this, the child is asked to rate how strongly they now believe their original thought and whether there is a more balanced and helpful way of thinking.

> *Stephen (11) was very anxious about being with his peers and often thought the other children ganged up against him. This made Stephen feel very anxious during school breaks and he would often avoid going out, preferring to stay in the classroom on his own. One of Stephen's common thoughts was that "other people always look at me and want to start trouble": a thought he believed very strongly, scoring 90/100.*
>
> *Stephen was asked to list the evidence that supported this thought. Whenever he went outside at break time there was a group of six or seven young people who sat on the wall and watched him walk out. A couple of these were people who had called Stephen names in the past, and one had taken his school bag and emptied it out on the playing field.*
>
> *Stephen was now asked to look for any evidence that would not support this thought. Initially Stephen could not find any: a common response from children who are strongly focused on the negative and threat cues in their environment. However, Stephen was helped to question some of his assumptions and biases. It emerged that this wall was a popular place for young people to hang out and many different groups sat there. The wall was opposite the school doors and so anyone sitting on the wall would be facing and looking at all the children who came out. They weren't just looking at Stephen. This group of young people did mess around a lot but they were laughing and joking rather than being angry and threatening. They hadn't been involved in any trouble recently and Stephen hadn't heard of them being aggressive or threatening to anyone. They hadn't said anything to Stephen for a number of weeks and the incident with the bag had happened last year. This was information that Stephen had overlooked, ignored or downplayed. Bringing this to his attention helped Stephen to question this thought, which had now reduced to 55/100. During other meetings Stephen was helped to continue to challenge this thought, resulting in a more balanced and helpful way of thinking about this situation: "Lots of people like to sit on the wall and hang out".*

Check out the evidence

While a number of young people can engage in a verbal thought-challenging process, a powerful and more concrete alternative is to involve children in actively checking out the evidence for their thoughts. Children are therefore encouraged to find the evidence from their everyday life that supports or challenges the reality and strength of their predictions.

This involves behavioural experiments, which are discussed in more detail in Chapter 10. The process begins by identifying dominant or frequent unhelpful thoughts and rating their strength. The child and clinician then engage in a discussion to identify what evidence they need to obtain to check out their thought. For example, a young person who thought:

- they were "rubbish at school work" might be asked to record their marks for their next few assignments
- that "my teachers always pick on me" might be asked to log all the times this happens
- that "nobody ever calls me on the telephone" might be asked to keep a record of any telephone calls they receive.

Once the required evidence has been identified, the timeframe needs to be agreed and then the young person is asked to clarify what they expect to find:

- if they were "rubbish at school work" then they would not get any grades better than D for their next five assignments
- if "my teachers always pick on me" then we might expect at least one example every day
- if "nobody ever calls me on the telephone" then they should not receive any calls over a one-week period.

The evidence is then collected and reviewed to explore whether it supported or questioned their original thought. The young person's strength of belief in the original thought is then rated and a more balanced alternative developed.

- results showed that three out of five assignments were rated D, E and E, and these were all in maths. The other two assignments achieved C grades. This helped to develop a more balanced and contained thought: "I find maths difficult but I do OK with my other school work".
- The diary showed two examples of being picked on by a teacher, and in both cases this was the PE teacher. This helped to develop a more helpful and contained thought: "most of the teachers are OK but I need to be more careful in PE".
- the telephone log showed that there were no calls over the one-week period. This provided some support for the thought that "nobody ever calls me on the telephone" and also suggested that perhaps a more proactive approach was required.

There will be occasions when although the evidence may not support the child's initial unhelpful thoughts, they may nonetheless appear unprepared to accept the results of the experiment. Often children are strongly hooked into their unhelpful thoughts and beliefs and may dismiss and discredit any contradictory evidence as unusual or lucky. The child's cognitive distortions and biases may inhibit their ability to think about, and process, this new information. In these situations it is important that the clinician maintains a sense of objectivity and suggests that the evidence collection is repeated. Adopting such an empirical and objective position continues to encourage self-discovery and reflection and avoids the clinician attempting to impose their view on the child.

In addition to encouraging reflection it is important that the clinician promotes a sense of curiosity and keeps an open mind. The purpose of the evidence collection is not to prove to the child that their way of thinking is "wrong"; it is to check out the evidence that supports or challenges their belief. There will therefore be occasions when the child's unhelpful or negative thoughts appear to be supported, as in the example above, where the young person did not receive any calls during the agreed monitoring period. This in itself is important information. In this case, if the young person is not receiving any calls, then perhaps they need to become more proactive and set themselves a target such as calling two people every week.

> Promote objectivity and use experiments to test and reappraise common, or strong, cognitions.

10

Problem-solving, exposure and relapse prevention

The final part of the intervention focuses on the behavioural domain and is primarily concerned with practice and exposure. During this stage the child learns to apply their new skills to successfully face and overcome the situations they find challenging and anxiety-provoking. The child is encouraged to systematically approach and confront situations they previously avoided in a stepped way that maximises the likelihood of success. This may involve a number of methods including problem-solving, the development of graded hierarchies, *in vivo* and imaginal practice, behavioural experiments and positive reinforcement (Figure 10.1).

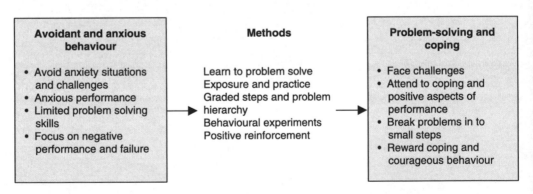

Avoidant and anxious behaviour	Methods	Problem-solving and coping
• Avoid anxiety situations and challenges • Anxious performance • Limited problem solving skills • Focus on negative performance and failure	Learn to problem solve Exposure and practice Graded steps and problem hierarchy Behavioural experiments Positive reinforcement	• Face challenges • Attend to coping and positive aspects of performance • Break problems in to small steps • Reward coping and courageous behaviour

Figure 10.1 Problem-solving and other skills

The key tasks during this stage are to help children and young people:

1 develop problem-solving skills
2 systematically face and cope with feared and avoided situations
3 undertake behavioural experiments to test their assumptions and beliefs
4 acknowledge and praise new attempts at coping.

Problem-solving

Avoidance is a common way of dealing with situations or events that generate anxiety. While avoidance might bring short-term relief, the child does not learn effective ways to cope with anxiety-provoking situations. On these occasions it is helpful to provide children with a six-step framework for solving problems, as follows.

> Step 1: What do I want to achieve?
>
> Step 2: What are the possible solutions?
>
> Step 3: What are the consequences of each solution?
>
> Step 4: On balance, what is the best solution?
>
> Step 5: Try it
>
> Step 6: Evaluate it

The first step is to define the problem the child wants to overcome. It is important to focus on the positive outcomes they wish to achieve. Instead of stating "can't talk with people" or "can't go out" these need to be phrased as positive goals such as "to feel OK talking with two people" or "to be able go to the local shops". This has both an enabling and a positive effect as the child attends to securing their goal rather than becoming immersed in, and overwhelmed by, their current limitations.

The second step involves option generation in which the young person is encouraged to think through as many ways as possible to secure their goal. Judgement needs to be suspended. The task is to identify possible options, not to evaluate them. The child is therefore encouraged to think of as many alternative solutions as possible and not to worry if some may seem silly or unrealistic. If the child is unable to generate any ideas then they could be encouraged to ask a friend what they might do. Alternatively they could be asked to identify a successful model – someone who they feel is able to cope successfully with this challenge – and to watch what they do. The clinician needs to encourage and praise the child for identifying options, since many children may find this step difficult. A worksheet is included in Chapter 12, ***Possible Solutions***, which can be used to generate solutions to problems. The worksheet encourages the child to keep asking themselves the "or" question, i.e. "or I could do. . . ." until a number of possibilities have been identified.

Step 3 is that of option appraisal, whereby the possible consequences of each solution are identified. The child may need to be prompted to consider both the short- and long-term consequences and the outcomes for both themselves and others. As mentioned earlier, some solutions (e.g. avoidance) may bring short-term benefits but are unhelpful in the longer term. Similarly, while some solutions may appear helpful to the child (e.g. "ask mum to telephone my friend and invite them over") the consequences for the mother in terms of increased work and responsibility may be less positive.

This leads to the fourth step of choosing a solution. On the basis of this information the child is asked to decide which would be their preferred solution. Like all decisions, the child will need to make this on the basis of the information that is available. It will be the best option at the time of choice but there is no guarantee that it will be successful. The worksheet ***Which Solution Should I Choose***, included in Chapter 12, provides a summary of steps 3 and 4.

The fifth step is that of implementation. A time and day needs to be agreed to try the plan and any necessary support needs to be arranged. The child can be helped to imagine practising the task. They can be encouraged to imagine the situation in detail and talked through the application of their solution before trying it in real life. Similarly, the need to acknowledge and praise attempts, irrespective of whether or not they were successful, needs to be highlighted. Attempts at exploring ways of confronting and facing challenges need to be reinforced, not the outcome.

The final step involves evaluation and reflecting on the usefulness of the plan. Once again the child will need to be guided through this, since their immediate feedback may be negative. They may simply focus on the strength of their anxious feelings or report their cognitive biases, which might emphasise the negative aspects of their performance. The child needs to be helped to attend to new or overlooked information in order to develop a more balanced perspective.

> *Tracey's group at school had been doing a project about the environment and everybody had to take turns to present their work to the class. Tracey was very worried about talking to people and so completed the worksheet opposite to explore how she could cope with this challenge.*
>
> *Tracey asked Louise to help her and over the next two days they worked out what they were going to say and practised. Tracey was very anxious before her talk but as she started she became less nervous. She knew lots about the environment, Louise helped and the class were very interested in what she had to say. After the presentation Tracey felt very pleased with herself. When this was reviewed Tracey was able to identify three new pieces of information. First she learned that she did have things to say that her classmates found interesting. Second, they didn't laugh and tease her as she had predicted. Finally, and perhaps most importantly, Tracey discovered that she could find ways to face and deal with her worrying situations rather than avoid them.*

Which solution should I choose?

Once you have a list of possible ideas the next step is to think about the negatives (–) and positives (+) of each solution. You may want to ask someone to help you.

When you have finished look at your list and choose the best solution for your challenge.

My challenge is: Standing up in front of the class and talking about my project

Possible solution	Positives (+)	Negatives (–)
1. Do it on my own	There aren't any! I <u>can't</u> do it.	I will get nervous and stop talking. I will forget things and make a fool of myself.
2. Ask Louise to do it with me	Share the presentation Louise is better than me at talking. We can help each other out if we get stuck.	People will think that I can't do this on my own. They will laugh at us.
3. Ask my teacher to help	It would be a good presentation. He would help me if I got stuck or stopped talking.	No one else has asked our teacher to help. They will all think I'm weird.
4. Say I'm not feeling well and so can't do it	Wouldn't have to do it so wouldn't be worried.	Would be disappointed. It is a good project.

My best solution is: To ask Louise to help me.

> Generate and evaluate alternative solutions to problems and worries.

Facing and coping with anxiety-provoking situations

Exposure

A key element of anxiety treatment programmes is exposure, in which the child confronts and learns to cope with feared situations or events. Through exposure the child learns that by facing feared situations the associated anxiety becomes less. The concept of learning through doing is therefore central to the treatment of anxiety disorders and will also have an effect on the child's cognitions. Dominant anxiety-increasing cognitions and fears about being unable to cope are directly challenged during exposure tasks, facilitating the development of alternative cognitions.

For the child, the idea of exposure – facing the thing that they are most afraid of – will be threatening and will generate anxiety. Similarly, parents may be keen to protect their child from possible distress and may be reluctant to encourage and support their child through such a task. The rationale for exposure therefore needs to be explicit and the following key points emphasised.

- The child is currently managing their anxiety by avoidance.
- Avoidance brings short-term relief but does not provide a long-term solution.
- The child needs to face feared and worrying situations in order to learn how to master and overcome them.
- The child will feel anxious but this will reduce the more they face and confront worrying situations.
- The child will be involved in all decisions and will start off by learning to cope with easier situations first.
- They will only try to tackle more difficult situations when they feel ready to do so.

The actual process of exposure needs careful planning, since in order for it to be effective the child needs to experience and overcome high levels of arousal. If exposure is not of a sufficient duration, anxiety will not reduce (habituate). Treatment sessions should be sufficiently long to allow the feared situation to be mastered rather than simply rehearsed, and should result in the child being successful and feeling relaxed and in control.

In order to demonstrate to the child changes in the strength of their anxiety, regular self-monitoring is an integral part of exposure. This provides a way of quantifying the strength of the anxiety while demonstrating that levels of anxiety reduce over time.

Before undertaking exposure it is important that the child and their parents have a clear understanding:

- of their anxiety within a CBT framework and the importance of their anxious cognitions
- that exposure is a way of learning to cope with, and master, worrying situations rather than avoiding them
- that anxiety decreases over time, and by staying in the fearful situation their anxiety will reduce
- that anxiety may initially increase but will eventually go down.

After completing exposure tasks the child needs to reflect on the experience. In particular the young person's attention needs to be drawn to what happened to their anxiety, whether their anxious cognitions and expectations about being unable to cope came true, the most difficult part of the task and whether they would build on this in the future.

Finally, if exposure is undertaken outside of treatment sessions with the support of parents, it is important to discuss how the parents will cope with the task and manage their child's distress. They need:

- to be reassured that they are helping their child and are not being unkind or uncaring
- to understand that they are helping their child to face and overcome their worries so that their child can reclaim their life
- to acknowledge that their child will feel anxious but that this feeling will reduce the more they face and learn to cope with the feared situation
- to model courageous coping behaviour and not to reinforce avoidance.

The clinician needs to engage in an open discussion with the parents about whether or not they are able to support their child through exposure tasks. If a parent is unsure then another supporter should be identified and involved in the programme.

> Exposure is an important way of proving to the child that they can cope with their anxiety.

Graded steps and hierarchy development

For a number of anxious children the worrying situation they wish to overcome, or the overall goal they wish to achieve, may appear large and unobtainable. Attempting to tackle such a large goal increases the possibility of failure, which in turn would serve to reinforce any negative cognitions about the impossibility of change. In order to avoid the possibility of failure the overall goal needs to be broken down into a series of small, achievable steps.

The process of hierarchy development involves the child first clarifying their overall goal. This can be placed at the top of a picture of a ladder, as the child is then helped to identify some of the intervening steps that would lead to their ultimate goal. The steps at the bottom of the ladder are the easiest and generate the least anxiety. As the steps go up the ladder the tasks become more difficult and the associated anxiety increases. Writing each step on sticky post-it labels can be helpful, as these can be repositioned in different places on the ladder as new steps emerge. It is also useful to rate the degree of anxiety presented by each step, since this provides another way of checking that the steps are in ascending order.

The number of steps will depend on the size of the overall goal and the child's current abilities. The clinician needs to ensure that the steps are achievable and if in doubt, steps should be made smaller. It is better for the child to succeed with a small step than fail in attempting something too large. It is also preferable to start with relatively easy steps in order to boost the child's confidence and to nurture the belief that change is possible and that worries and difficulties can be overcome. Finally, it may be necessary to repeat a step a few times in order for the child to feel confident in their new abilities before moving to the next step.

The hierarchy should be clear, concrete and specific and for any exposure task a detailed plan should be agreed. This will involve clearly specifying the task, when and where it will be undertaken, what coping methods the child will use (e.g. positive thinking, distraction, deep breathing), who will support the child and how their performance will be reinforced. This degree of preparation and planning is an important element of all behavioural tasks and serves to increase the possibility of success. Similarly practice, either role-play or imaginal, can be helpful in preparing the child for their challenge and allowing them to practise using their new skills.

Mike (16) had experienced panic attacks at school for the past six months. These had become so bad that Mike had stopped going to school and was planning to transfer to the local college. In order to do this, Mike had to go into college and be interviewed by the head teacher. Mike was really worried about this. He feared that he wouldn't cope and would have a panic attack.

Going for an interview was too big a task, so Mike drew up a ladder for success identifying the steps he would need to take in order to reach his goal.

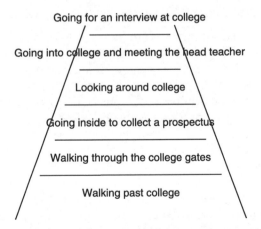

My Ladder to Success in Chapter 12 provides a visual way of helping the child to identify, and organise in increasing difficulty, the smaller steps they need to accomplish in order to achieve their goal.

> Breaking challenges into smaller steps increases the chance of success.

Behavioural experiments

The process of challenging assumptions and beliefs and developing alternative, more balanced and helpful cognitions is a key aspect of CBT. However, for some children, engaging in this verbal and potentially abstract process can be difficult.

- The child may have limited cognitive skills and be unable to engage in a reflective, abstract process.
- The young person may be able to engage in a process of cognitive reappraisal but do so in an artificial and detached way that does not transfer to everyday situations.
- The young person may be fixed in their own beliefs and be unreceptive to new or overlooked information.

In situations such as these, learning by doing, through behavioural experiments, can be a powerful way of helping the child to test objectively the validity of their cognitions. Through experiments the child has a chance to test their beliefs and assumptions independently and objectively. The abstract and artificial discussion is replaced with a concrete test in everyday life. Objective information obtained from real-life experiments is harder to dismiss or ignore.

Bennet-Levy *et al.* (2004) suggest that behavioural experiments result in information that can serve two main purposes.

- *Hypothesis-testing experiments.* These are concerned with testing the child's cognitions about certain events or situations. For example, a child who has panic attacks might think that a racing heart is a sign of an impending heart attack. This cognition could be tested by a simple behavioural experiment in which the child is asked to run on the spot for a few minutes. The child is asked to note their increased heart rate and to reflect on possible reasons for it. The experiment demonstrates that:
    - there is an alternative explanation for an increased heart rate
    - a raised heart rate will return to normal
    - a raised heart rate does not necessarily have serious consequences.
- *Discovery experiments.* These are investigative experiments designed to test the relationship between different aspects of the CBT cycle or to test specific cognitions. They are designed to provide the child with new information and are genuinely open in the sense that the outcome of the experiment is unknown.

When developing behavioural experiments with children and young people it is important to do the following:

1   *Ensure that they are helpful:* The experiment needs to be constructive and result in the discovery of useful information. Since the outcome of behavioural experiments cannot be predicted, the possibility of an outcome that confirms negative cognitions needs to be considered.

2   *Ensure that they are safe:* It is important to ensure that the experiment will not be detrimental to the well-being of the child. Experiments involving particularly unpredictable situations should therefore be avoided.

3   *Ensure that they have clear aims:* The purpose of the experiment should be explicitly shared with the child and their carers, i.e. to discover new information or to test and challenge a specific cognition.

4   *Ensure that they are developed collaboratively:* The experiment needs to be devised and constructed in a collaborative manner. This ensures that it fits with the child's life and maximises the possibility that it will be achievable.

5   *Ensure that they have a defined target:* The target cognition, emotion or behaviours that are the focus of the experiment should be clearly defined.

6   *Ensure that they have a clear and, wherever possible, objective way of recording outcome:* If the experiment is assessing subjective variables such as the degree of emotional intensity or strength of belief in cognitions, this needs to be quantified by use of rating scales.

7   *Agree when the experiment will occur:* Agree with the child and their carer when and where the experiment will take place and support help may be required. With younger children it will be particularly important to ensure that their carers/parents are involved. With older children it may be helpful to enlist the support of a friend.

8   *Reflect on the outcome:* The experiment is a way of obtaining new information that can help the child challenge and reassess their cognitions or develop a better understanding of the relationship between elements of the cognitive model. The child therefore needs to be encouraged to reflect on the outcome with questions such as "so what does that tell us?", "what have you learned from that experiment?" or "in the light of what has happened, how strongly do you now rate your belief?"

My Experiment in Chapter 12 provides a framework that can be used to structure and detail the steps involved in planning and assessing a behavioural experiment.

When she was seven, Linda became stuck in a lift in a shop for 30 minutes, an experience which resulted in her having a major panic attack. Subsequently Linda had avoided lifts but now, at the age of 12, was keen to face and overcome this difficulty. This led Linda to think that "lifts always break down", a thought she rated as believing 96/100. The clinician and Linda discussed this and devised an experiment to find out if this was the case. Linda and her mother went to a shopping centre where there was a glass lift. The task was to watch the lift for 30 minutes and to record how many times it went up and down and how many times it broke down. The lift moved up and down 24 times and did not break down during the period that Linda watched, resulting in her revising the strength of her belief to 88/100. The experiment was summarised under a number of headings on the worksheet below.

Linda's Experiment

1. What do I want to find out?
Check out how often lifts break down

2. What experiment could I do to check this out?
Watch the lift at the shopping centre for 30 minutes

3. How can I measure what happens?
Record how many times it goes up and down and how many times it breaks down

4. When will I do this experiment and who will help?
Saturday morning with mum

5. What do I think will happen?
The lift will break down while I watch (96/100)

6. What happened?
Lift went up and down 24 times and did not break down

7. What have I learned?
Lifts don't <u>always</u> break down (88/100)

While this experiment challenged Linda's thought that lifts always break down, the change was small and she still felt unable to enter a lift. Further questioning revealed that her concern about the lift related to her fear that she would become trapped inside and that no one would know she was there. The glass-sided lift was discussed with Linda and it was highlighted how the lift was clearly visible to everyone in the shopping centre. Her parents suggested that one of them could go inside the lift with her while the other waited outside and watched, thereby being able to seek help if required. This resulted in Linda feeling able to face her fear and she agreed to undertake an experiment in which she would go up one floor in the lift. A day and a time were chosen and she entered the lift with her mother while her father watched. They went up one floor to the café, where they celebrated with a drink and cake. Linda was so pleased with herself that she and her parents entered the lift together to return downstairs. The strength of Linda's belief that "lifts always break down" reduced to 55/100 after this experiment.

Behavioural experiments provide a powerful and objective way of testing and challenging cognitions.

Praise and acknowledge coping and achievements

An important aspect of CBT programmes is to change the focus of attention away from anxiety signals and rehearsing worries towards praising courageous and coping behaviour. It is therefore important for children and young people, as well as parents, to recognise and acknowledge their attempts at coping and managing their anxious feelings. Initially this can be difficult, since children and their carers may find it difficult to acknowledge any change or success. They may be preoccupied with future worries so that any success is negated through comments such as "it may have been OK today but I don't think this will happen again". Similarly, successful attempts at overcoming the first steps in a fear hierarchy may be dismissed as unimportant, or by statements such as "well, this isn't really a big deal. Everyone else can do this." These situations need to be challenged and the child's success celebrated. The future orientation needs to be countered by drawing attention back to the here and now: "well, we don't know what will happen next time but just look at how well he coped today". Comparisons with past achievements also need to be challenged: "you may have been able to do that last year but this is the first time you have done it for six months". Similarly, the tendency to minimise success can be addressed through clear statements such as "well, it might be easier for other people but for you this was a big step and you did really well".

In some situations children may have very strong negative biases and find it difficult to find any positive coping behaviours or thoughts. Their natural tendency to attend selectively to negative events and anxiety-increasing thoughts needs to be actively targeted through the establishment of a positive coping diary or a record of achievement. With this, children are required to focus on and record any attempts they make to cope with, and manage, their anxiety. The clinician will often need to spend time reviewing the past week as a way of helping the young person to recognise some of the positive attempts they have made. This may need to be repeated in subsequent meetings, but as the diary grows the young person will begin to recognise that while they may still become anxious, there are a number of occasions when they can use skills to help them cope.

On other occasions young people might be able to find some coping examples but continue to dismiss these as unimportant ("well, I might feel OK talking with Mike but that was never really a big problem anyway"), or fail to perceive these successes as possible indications of change ("I am not getting anywhere, I have been here before and it always goes wrong"). On these occasions the clinician's natural tendency to increase the degree to which they challenge and counter the young person's cognitions needs to be contained. Excessive enthusiasm or challenge may serve to alienate the young person. Instead the clinician needs to maintain an objective stance in which the young person's frustrations are acknowledged while continuing to highlight their achievements.

A way of recording progress is provided in *My Record of Achievement* in Chapter 12.

> Acknowledge and celebrate coping and courageous behaviour.

Relapse prevention

The final part of the intervention is concerned with consolidation and relapse prevention. The child needs to be encouraged to reflect on what they have learned, to identify the skills they have found useful and how these can be applied in the future.

The structure and content of the review is flexible, although typically it will involve three elements. The first is psycho-educational, in which the key features of the CBT intervention are highlighted. In the next the child is helped to consider the application of these principles to their own situation and to identify issues and skills that have proved particularly relevant. The final section involves considering how this information can be used to prepare and plan for dealing with any future setbacks and difficulties.

When reviewing key aspects of the intervention it is often useful to highlight:

- the central relationships between thoughts, feelings and behaviour
- the need to be aware of thinking traps
- the need to challenge anxiety-increasing cognitions and replace them with cognitions that are helpful and enabling
- the importance of confronting and facing anxiety-provoking situations rather than avoiding them.

This naturally leads into the second stage, in which the child is encouraged to reflect on the application of the above to their own particular problems.

- Pertinent information, important anxiety signals and skills found particularly helpful should be identified.
- The child's dominant thinking traps need to be discussed and the ways of identifying, challenging, and testing these rehearsed.
- The progress the child has made should be reviewed and contrasted with how they were at the start of the intervention.

While reviewing keys skills and progress, the clinician needs to take the opportunity to reinforce important cognitions that will contribute to the continuing success and use of these skills. These tend to emphasise cognitions that challenge three main themes.

- *Powerlessness:* it is important to highlight that success and change have been due to the child's efforts and the new skills they have acquired and implemented. This develops the belief of self-efficacy, which directly challenges beliefs that are deterministic or related to powerlessness. This emphasis clearly signals that the child is able to actively influence situations and events.
- *Failure:* documenting the child's achievements challenges potentially negative cognitions that the child can never be successful and always fails.
- *Unpredictable:* anxious children tend to perceive their world as unpredictable and it is this uncertainty that contributes to a great deal of their anxiety. The intervention has provided the child with a way of understanding their world and helps them to recognise that it is more predictable than they had imagined.

The final stage prepares the child for relapse prevention and coping with future challenges. Key elements of this discussion involve the following.

- *The identification of potentially difficult future events or situations.* Based on the child's previous problems, it would be expected that there might be situations or events that would increase the likelihood of their anxious feelings and thoughts returning. These might, for example, involve transitions that would demand more independence and require separation from parents, such as starting at secondary school. They could be about general periods of change or going somewhere new, which might increase the worries of a child with generalised anxiety disorder. Alternatively, if children with specific phobias are exposed to new events or situations associated with their phobia, their anxious feelings might increase.
- *Preparation for temporary setbacks.* Increased awareness prepares the child and their parents for the possibility that they might, at some time in the future, experience increased feelings of anxiety. Raising this expectation normalises any such episodes and prepares the child and their parents to expect them. It is important to emphasise that these are temporary setbacks. They do not imply permanent failure or that the previous difficulties have returned. Similarly, the child and their parents need to be reassured that this does not imply that their newly acquired skills are no longer working.
- *Encouraging early intervention.* Encouraging the child to be alert to potentially difficult situations also increases the likelihood that potentially helpful skills can be drawn on at an early stage. Intervening early helps to ensure that previous unhelpful anxiety-increasing patterns do not become firmly established, thereby increasing the likelihood that positive change can be quickly achieved.
- *Continue to practise.* The final message is to encourage the child to practise using their new skills and to persevere with their use. The message that the skills the child has acquired will not work all the time

needs to be emphasised. Similarly, the need to use a variety of methods rather than rely on a single strategy should be highlighted. Finally, the importance of practice needs to be stressed so that the child is fully aware that their new skills will become more effective the more they are used.

Relapse prevention involves reviewing key aspects of the CBT model, identifying their specific application to the child's problems, raising awareness about possible temporary setbacks and encouraging the continued use of a range of strategies.

11

Common problems

Despite careful planning, it is inevitable that a number of issues will arise during the course of the intervention that will affect progress. The clinician needs to be prepared for this eventuality. Adopting such an expectation acknowledges both the reality and the complexity of therapy. Problems are challenges to be overcome rather than indications that CBT has failed or is not working. While it is not possible to prepare for all eventualities, the following presents some of the more common problems that are encountered during the course of CBT.

1. Family context is not supportive

While CBT can be undertaken successfully with young people on their own, the support and involvement of at least one carer in the programme is desirable, and is indeed essential with younger children. Parental involvement is required for a variety of reasons, including:

- *psycho-educational* – to increase parental understanding of their child's anxiety, the treatment rationale and the skills their child will be developing and using
- *practical* – to facilitate arrangements such as arranging transportation to appointments and liaising with school
- *generalisation* – to encourage and prompt their child's use of new skills, thereby aiding transfer and practice of skills outside of clinical sessions
- *support* – to help their child undertake out-of-session assignments
- *motivational* – to encourage and support their child to face fearful situations or events.

Unfortunately family support is sometimes not available. This may be a temporary situation, caused by competing demands or changing circumstances. In these situations it may be advisable to delay the intervention until appropriate support is available.

On other occasions the child may be part of a severely dysfunctional family unit, with their problems being a manifestation of wider systemic issues.

> *Jess (10) was referred with chronic school refusal and had not been to school for 12 weeks. During the assessment Jess identified many worries about his parents and was concerned that his mother would have an accident. It also emerged that his father had a longstanding back problem from a work accident, resulting in constant untreatable pain. He had not worked for a number of years and this had created financial pressures which had come to a head following the initiation of court proceedings for debt. Recently the parents had been arguing, and during a recent row his mother had threatened to leave.*

The child's separation anxiety may, as in the example above, have a clear function in terms of ensuring the parent's safety. At these times individual CBT would be unlikely to be successful and instead consideration should be paid to other therapeutic approaches such as family therapy.

> Consider delaying intervention, or alternative therapeutic approaches.

2. Unmotivated or disinterested

Acknowledgement of a problem and a readiness to change are prerequisites for any active intervention. This is no different for CBT, which is based on a therapeutic process that is collaborative and involves active participation of the child and their parents. However, children and young people are often referred to specialist services by their parents, schools or other adults and may not necessarily recognise that they have any problems that need to be addressed. On other occasions children may have learned to cope with their anxiety through the use of inappropriate strategies such as avoidance or relying overly on others. They will inevitably feel fearful about the possibility of change and so deny, or play down, the extent of their worries or the impairment they cause. Children may therefore present as anxious, reluctant and unmotivated.

Engaging in any active therapeutic process at this stage would be inappropriate and unlikely to be successful. Instead, the clinician needs to attend carefully to the process of engagement and, through this, increase the child's commitment and motivation to change. Motivational interviewing can help to increase:

- the child's desire to pursue a particular outcome
- their readiness to embark on a process of change
- confidence in their ability to achieve this outcome.

The process of engagement may take time as the aims, goals and priorities of the intervention are elicited, negotiated and prioritised as an acceptable starting place for both the child and their carers.

The initial process of engagement is fundamental to the success of any intervention and, as identified by Graham (2005), requires the child to acknowledge that:

- there is a difficulty or problem
- this problem could be changed
- the form of help being offered could bring about this change
- the clinician is able to help the child develop the skills they require to secure this change.

When children and young people present as ambivalent, bored or disinterested, and are reluctant or not engaging in sessions, it is useful to reassess their readiness to change. Although developed for use with adults, and used extensively in drugs and alcohol services, the Stages of Change model developed by Prochaska *et al.* (1992) provides a helpful structure for conceptualising therapeutic readiness. The model identifies six different stages in the process of change and hypothesises that a different therapeutic focus is required for each. The stages are described as pre-contemplation, contemplation, preparation, action, maintenance and relapse.

During the pre-contemplation and contemplation stages the child will not have engaged fully in therapy. They will not have acknowledged that they have a problem, identified an agenda for change, or believe that the current situation could be different. The therapeutic tasks during these stages are primarily threefold.

Promoting ownership

First, there is a need to ensure that the child is actively engaged in discussions and to elicit their views about the current situation and their future and possible goals. Focusing on the child and encouraging their views and participation sends a clear signal to the child that they are important, and have something important to say which the clinician wants to hear.

- "I have heard what mum has to say but I want to know what *you* think about this."
- "Is there anything *you* would like to be different?"

- "Does this feel like something *you* would like to think about some more?"

This occurs within the context of a developing therapeutic relationship built on the core counselling skills of empathy, listening, reflection, validation and acknowledgement.

Promoting discrepancy

The second task is to promote discrepancy between the here and now and what the child wants in the future. Promoting discrepancy is assumed to increase the child's motivation to engage in an active process of change. Examples of promoting discrepancy are as follows.

- "I hear that you plan to go away on camp next year with your friends. If I have understood what you have told me, at the moment you have to sleep with mum every night. What will you need to do so that you able to go away on your own to camp?"
- "You tell me that you will have lots of friends when you start sixth-form college next term. That sounds very different from now. Didn't you say that you haven't any friends at school?"

Resolving ambivalence

The third task is to explore possible ambivalence about embarking on a plan of change. Children may feel worried about trying something new, unsure whether they will be successful, or concerned about the support or help they will receive. The child needs to be encouraged to voice their uncertainty so that each potential barrier can be heard and a plan made to overcome it. Potential questions might be:

- "What might stop you from trying this?"
- "What might go wrong?"
- "What has helped in the past?"

Focusing on these issues will hopefully increase engagement and commitment and prepare the child for active change as they move to the stages of preparation, action and maintenance. These are the stages when the child is assumed to be ready to engage in an active process of change such as cognitive behaviour therapy. During the preparation stage the child will attempt to make some small change. This success typically leads to the action stage, where more substantive change occurs. It is during this stage that the child acquires and practises new skills, with them becoming integrated into their everyday life during the maintenance stage. The final stage is that of relapse, where the previous problems and patterns may re-emerge.

There may be times when, despite the clinician's efforts, the child is not ready or committed to an active process of change. In these situations the clinician needs to acknowledge that the time is not right to pursue an intervention, but remains positive and optimistic. The child needs to know that the clinician is able to provide them with effective help and support whenever they feel ready to pursue this option.

> Assess readiness to change, increase motivation and identify goals.

3. Out-of-session assignments are not completed

CBT is an active process which is guided and informed by the child's experiences as they confront and attempt to address their challenges. Self-monitoring, graded exposure, behavioural experiments, target-setting and *in vivo* practice are important treatment components of anxiety treatment programmes. Often these are undertaken as out-of-session assignments with the outcome being reviewed, and built on, in the following treatment session. They are therefore important and provide the bridge between the clinical sessions and real-life practice and coping.

On some occasions the child may agree to complete a monitoring diary but will return with a blank sheet, or report that there was nothing to write down. The act of self-monitoring can in itself be therapeutic and may help to put the child's anxiety in perspective. This needs to be explored, but it may highlight that anxiety is less of a problem, or is less severe, than originally thought, or that the situation has begun to improve positively. However, for some children and young people the failure to complete an out-of-session assignment is less positive. Self-monitoring diaries may be forgotten, or not completed, with opportunities to practise skills mysteriously proving unavailable.

Out-of-session assignments are considered by many to be a central ingredient of CBT programmes for anxiety. In a meta-review, Kazantzis *et al*. (2000) found that homework assignments facilitated greater treatment effects, suggesting the central importance of this activity in treatment programmes. However, little research has investigated the effect of homework completion with children. In one of the few studies, Hughes and Kendall (2007) failed to find that homework completion resulted in any significant difference in the outcome of children with anxiety disorders. Indeed, these authors noted that the general therapeutic relationship was more important than the specific completion of homework tasks.

In situations where homework assignments are not completed, it is important for the clinician to address the issue directly and engage the child in an open and honest discussion. The rationale and importance of out-of-session assignments needs to be emphasised and potential barriers that prevent their achievement need to be explored. The clinician should ensure that the assignment is consistent with the child's overall treatment goals and that the child can fully understand both the relevance and the importance of the assignment. In some instances the task may be too onerous, and so a more limited and achievable target needs to be agreed. For example, a child may be asked to identify one or two particularly difficult situations rather than keeping a daily log. Alternatively, the method may be unattractive: for example, some children like keeping paper records while others do not. However, these children might be more interested in making their own computer log or emailing their thoughts after a particularly stressful event. At other times children may need some additional support to undertake the task, and attention needs to be paid to enlisting the help of others. This will be particularly important during exposure tasks, where the child is learning to face their fears and to cope with their anxiety. Avoidance is typically their coping strategy, and so failure to undertake an *in vivo* exposure task may suggest that the target is too big. The clinician may therefore need to negotiate a smaller and more achievable task with the child or to undertake more imaginal practice during clinical sessions before attempting *in vivo* exposure.

Inevitably, despite the provision of a clear and understandable rationale, there will be times when the child simply does not want to undertake any out-of-session tasks. In order to promote collaboration and maintain engagement, this view needs to be acknowledged and respected. During the earlier stages of the intervention much information can be obtained by discussing difficult situations during the clinical session so that home-based monitoring or the completion of any records or forms may not be required. Out-of-session assignments do become more important during the later stages of the intervention, where the child needs to experiment and practise their new skills. However, by this stage the relationship between the child and the clinician will have become more established and the child may be more willing to undertake out-of-session assignments.

> Assignments are less important early in therapy. Minimise the demands of assignments and explore different formats.

4. Passive and uncommunicative during sessions

Talking with an adult about personal problems and worries is an unusual experience for many children and young people. Adolescents may feel embarrassed and present as quiet and unforthcoming, fearful that the extent and nature of their worries may not be understood. Younger children may have more limited verbal skills and may struggle to find the words to describe their thoughts and feelings and to engage in verbal interactions with the clinician. Similarly, despite reassurances, anxious children might worry about how to answer questions and whether they have provided what they perceive to be the "right answer".

For children the therapeutic experience will be unfamiliar and the expectations of sessions may not be clear. Parents, professionals, television programmes and friends are some of the many potential sources of information that may result in the child developing an initial set of expectations about what will happen. In many respects the clinician may be perceived as an expert who will offer advice about what to do and how to cope while the child and their parents passively listen. This is at odds with the collaborative process of CBT, where the child is an active participant who, through the process of guided discovery and behavioural experiments, learns to cope with their difficulties.

When children appear uncommunicative and volunteer comparatively little information, it can be helpful to acknowledge this and to clarify and reiterate the expectations of CBT. In particular the clinician should emphasise and encourage:

- *participation* – you want to hear the child's views and ideas and what it is really like for them
- *learning through experimentation* – you will be working together to try to find out why problems happen and to experiment to see whether they can be changed
- *partnership working* – you as the clinician do not have the "answers"; these need to be discovered together
- *self-efficacy* – you are keen to hear about what the child has found helpful and which of the new skills they try are useful
- *openness* – sometimes you get things wrong or don't understand things properly, and therefore need the young person to tell you when this happens.

The clinician can also encourage and reinforce the importance of the child's contributions by exploring some of their interests. Websites, favourite bands, books, films can, for example, be followed up and discussed, thereby sending an important message to the young person that you listen and that they have important information you want to hear. Furthermore, exploring such information can provide the clinician with a wealth of material that can help to identify important cognitions.

CBT with children and young people often requires more direct input from the clinician. This is particularly apparent when a child is quiet and uncommunicative. A common tendency is for the clinician to try harder to engage the child by asking more and more questions. In turn this reinforces the child's expectations about treatment (e.g. the clinician talks and I listen) and unintentionally encourages the child to become more passive. Clinical sessions may be viewed as increasingly unpleasant and may increase the child's anxiety as they worry about the questions they will be asked. The clinician needs to be alert to this possibility and to resist this tendency.

Instead children need to be allowed space; the reason for their lack of communication needs to be understood; the child's silence needs to be directly acknowledged and alternative non-verbal means of communication explored.

Children and young people may sometimes feel overwhelmed and unable to answer general open questions. In these situations it is helpful to make the questioning more concrete and specific. The clinician may act as an "option provider" where they provide the child with a range of possibilities and enquire whether any of these might be similar for them.

> *Jenny (9) was very quiet in sessions, often responding to direct questions with a shrug of her shoulders or a quiet "don't know". When asked how she felt during playtimes at school Jenny shrugged her shoulders and stared at the floor. The clinician waited and then rephrased the question. "Some children have told me that they feel excited or happy at playtimes. Do you have any of those feelings at playtime"? Jenny shook her head. The clinician tried again: "I have also met some children who feel sad or worried at playtimes. Do you ever feel like this?" This time Jenny nodded and muttered quietly that she had no one to play with.*

The option provider therefore presents a range of possibilities for the child to accept or reject. It is important to ensure that the child feels able to reject the possibilities that are provided and that they don't simply acquiesce to the clinician's ideas. Once again this is particularly important for the anxious child. The child therefore needs to be empowered or given permission to say "no", and this can be highlighted by prefacing options with phrases such as "you may not feel like this but . . ." or " I don't know whether you feel like this but sometimes . . .".

> Discuss the importance of the child's contributions and how you will learn together. Use more direct questions and provide the young person with "options".

5. Limited cognitive or developmental ability

There will be occasions when the child or young person appears to struggle to access their cognitions or to engage in some of the cognitive demands of the intervention. It is generally accepted among clinicians that children aged seven years and over, of average ability, can engage in most of the cognitive tasks of CBT. Even younger children may be able to engage in a simpler, modified format of CBT. If uncertain, the clinician needs to check whether the child has a way of accessing and communicating their thoughts, and then to ensure that the cognitive demands are pitched at the correct level for the child to access.

Depending on the child's age and developmental level, the emphasis on the cognitive component will vary. Younger children may be able to access their thoughts, identify another perspective and engage in some structured tasks of thought evaluation and appraisal. However, they may struggle with more complex and abstract tasks such as distinguishing between different levels of cognitions and processes or different thinking traps. With younger children the intervention may therefore have a greater emphasis on behavioural experimentation, i.e. learning through doing. The child's cognitions are less directly addressed but are indirectly challenged through practice and experimentation. Simpler and less specific cognitive techniques may be used, such as positive "self-talk". Through the use of positive "self-talk", coping self-statements and successful practice, the child will be able to develop a more balanced set of cognitions.

In all instances it is important to ensure that language is simple, and that abstract concepts are presented in concrete ways. Metaphors can be particularly helpful. The idea of automatic thoughts can be likened to computer spam, or worrying thoughts to a washing machine in which things just go round and round. Metaphors such as these not only provide a concrete way to aid understanding but also can lead to the development of helpful analogies. Children can be helped to deal with their negative automatic thoughts by building a better firewall, or to turn off the washing machine to stop the thoughts tumbling round.

Memory problems can be overcome by the use of visual cues and prompts. A child, for example, can have a small cue-card (postcard) stuck to the inside of their pencil case. When they put their pencils away before going out to break they will see the card which could contain a few helpful statement or ways to stay calm. Colour strips can be useful, and can be wrapped around the child's pencil to remind them to watch out for the red (worrying) thoughts. Similarly, an empty thought bubble can be drawn on a book as a simple visual reminder to the child to check out their thoughts. Finally, tasks can be simplified so that the child, for example, has fewer decision choices, or develops and uses a few positive self-statements.

> Simplify language; use concrete metaphors and visual cues.

6. Difficulty accessing thoughts

It is not uncommon to find that children and young people are unable to identify and vocalise their thoughts, particularly to direct questions such as "when that happened what were you thinking?". The clinician needs to assess whether this is a true difficulty or perhaps anxiety, or reticence, on the part of the child. Direct questioning and focusing on thoughts is sometimes not required. Children often share a number of their beliefs, assumptions and appraisals as they talk. The clinician therefore needs to become what Turk (1998) described as a "thought catcher", noting the important and recurrent thoughts that emerge during the course of clinical sessions. These can be noted and then fed back to the child at a suitable time.

Another way of helping children to communicate their thoughts is through the use of thought bubbles, as discussed in Chapter 9. This can be established by the use of a few examples and then the thought bubble can be used as a vehicle for the child to communicate their thoughts. The clinician can have available some blank outlines of thought bubbles during sessions, which can be used as visual prompts. These can be used as the child is asked "what would we put in your thought bubble when this happens". The child can either say or be invited to draw a picture or write their thought in the bubble.

It is also not uncommon to find that children are unable to verbalise their own thoughts and feelings but are able to describe those of a third party such as a friend or someone of a similar age. Moving a discussion to the third party may make it less personal and threatening, while providing the clinician with a useful insight into the way the child perceives their world and events.

Alice (14) became very anxious in social situations but despite careful probing the clinician was unable to identify the thoughts that Alice had in such situations. During the discussion the clinician asked Alice to iden-tify someone who she thought was really good at talking with others. The clinician asked her to describe what that person might think if she saw a small group of school friends approaching her. This was one of the situations Alice found difficult. Alice quickly replied "Oh she would think something like great; I will talk with them about that rubbish supply teacher". Alice was then asked what a friend, more similar to her, might think in the same situation. Once again Alice was able to volunteer her thoughts: "I suppose she would be worried. She wouldn't know whether the girls wanted to talk with her or whether she would say something stupid.".

> Catch the cognitions that emerge during discussions: use visual methods such as thought bubbles or try a third-party perspective.

7. The child does not respond to verbal methods

A number of children will engage more readily with non-verbal methods. Often these provide a more familiar and less threatening focus which makes the child relaxed and more forthcoming. A variety of different methods have been described in the previous chapters, including the use of thought bubbles, worksheets, quizzes and games. Many of these materials are quick and easy to produce and require only basic computer skills. Over time the clinician will acquire a growing library of resources to draw on and adapt. These materials can be readily tailored to the specific interests of the child. In addition to being attractive and engaging they send an implicit message of the importance the clinician places on the child.

Another method that can be useful, particularly with younger children, is the use of puppets. The clinician can introduce the child to the puppet and describe a situation where the puppet has similar problems and worries as the child. The child can then be encouraged to talk with the puppet, and as they do so the clinician can structure the discussion in a variety of ways:

- *exploratory* – to identify possible thoughts – "I wonder what he might be thinking as he walks into the playground and sees the other children"
- *to generate alternative thoughts* – "I wonder if there is another way of thinking about this?"
- *to identify ways of coping* – "what could he do to make help him feel better?"
- *to coach someone through a problem* – "what could he do when he felt like this?".

Adolescents may be interested in drawing, composing poetry or writing songs, and each of these can be used as a medium to help the child convey their thoughts and feelings.

> Children may feel more comfortable engaging in non-verbal materials.

8. The parents are anxious

A number of researchers have demonstrated an association between child and parental anxiety. In clinical practice it is therefore not uncommon to be working with both a child and a parent with anxiety disorders. In many instances this may not be problematic, although the clinician needs to be aware of the extent and nature of the parent's anxiety. This will help them to decide whether the parent needs to be referred for specialist help in their own right, or whether they can provide some anxiety-management sessions.

The timing and sequencing of any possible parental anxiety work needs careful consideration. If the parent's anxiety is severe and significantly incapacitating, this may require specialist intervention before work with the child is undertaken. If it is less severe, the parent's own anxiety may be addressed simultaneously although they will probably need to learn to cope before they can help their child.

The clinician also needs to be aware of the possible implications of the parent's anxiety on the child's treatment programme. A parent with generalised anxiety disorder may for example find it hard to encourage and support their child through a graduated exposure task. Researchers have also highlighted how anxious parents are more likely to support their child's avoidance, and so they may not be able to positively encourage their child to face and learn to overcome their worries. These issues also apply to other mental health problems. Depressed parents may present as unmotivated and unable to enthuse and instil hope in their children. Parents with PTSD may experience anxiety and traumatic flashbacks which may interfere with their ability to support their child. Also, the parent will have their own expectations of treatment and the likelihood of success. If they have experienced previous unsuccessful attempts at change they might convey a sense of hopelessness to their child which will undermine the treatment programme.

In these situations the clinician needs to discuss openly the impact of the parent's cognitions and problems on the intervention. The parent's difficulties need to be directly acknowledged and the degree to which they will limit their ability to help their child highlighted. An alternative source of support that can model coping behaviour and participate in the programme needs to be identified and included in the intervention.

> Assess the extent of the parent's own anxiety and the degree to which they will be able to support their child throughout the intervention.

9. Attendance is erratic

Appointments may be missed and/or cancelled for very good reasons. Usually these are limited events and do not significantly interfere with the momentum of the intervention. In some instances this may occur regularly and become a repeated pattern that negatively interferes with the intervention. In these situations the clinician needs to note when attendance became problematic. Non-attendance may be a sign of ambivalence but can also be a very effective means of avoidance and may indicate that the young person has become anxious about clinical sessions.

Jo (14) was an uncommunicative girl who experienced significant anxiety in social situations, resulting in her having few friends and rarely going out. During an early session the clinician struggled to elicit from Jo some of the thoughts she might experience in social situations. The clinician decided to help Jo by becoming more concrete, and said "what would go through your head if I took you to school and asked to go up to a group of children and start a conversation?". Jo became very anxious at this question and repeatedly muttered that she "could not do it". Jo did not attend the next session. When next seen, the clinician discussed Jo's non-attendance and recalled the above incident and speculated whether this might have contributed to her non-attendance. Jo was able to acknowledge this and volunteered her fear that the clinician was going to take her to the situations she found difficult and "make" her cope.

Non-attendance needs to be directly acknowledged at the start of the next session. If a cancellation is caused by practical reasons such as an inconvenient day or regularly clashing with other priorities (e.g. dropping off or picking up other children from school), then appointments can be renegotiated. A series of appointments at mutually convenient times can be made in advance to aid planning. If a young person fails to attend an appointment they should be actively followed up. While sending another appointment by post is a simple option, telephone contact provides an opportunity to discuss possible barriers to attendance. Practical problems such as travel arrangements or permission to leave school can be resolved. Telephone contact provides the clinician with opportunities to reinforce the child's progress and to acknowledge their attempts at change, thereby challenging any ambivalence they might be feeling. The difficulty of attending sessions and attempting to change can be validated and reassurances provided that the young person will be fully involved in agreeing targets and that their views will be respected. A short telephone call can be a powerful and effective way of re-engaging with young people when they feel ambivalent.

> Non-attendance needs to be discussed actively and possible anxieties or barriers addressed.

10. Not acknowledging success

It is not uncommon to find children and young people discounting or failing to recognise evidence of change. There are many reasons why this occurs, some of the more common being unrealistically high standards, a negative bias in which success is overlooked, and attributing change to external events rather than personal efforts.

Perfectionism

Anxious children often set themselves very high standards and it is against these that they assess their performance. For many, these high standards are unrealistic and unobtainable, and in essence the young person is constantly setting themselves up to fail. In this situation the belief that performance is only acceptable if it is perfect is dysfunctional and will have the effect of any improvement being negated or overlooked.

Perfectionism can be directly challenged during sessions by first identifying and acknowledging their tendency to the all-or-nothing cognitive bias. With this thinking trap everything is assessed in extreme and absolute dichotomous terms. Performance is either "good" or "awful" and anything that falls short of perfect is dismissed as unsatisfactory. The anchor points are viewed as the only options by the young person, with the possibility of a continuum existing between them being something that they had not considered.

Once the bias has been identified, the clinician can help the young person recognise that there is a continuum of performance by the use of scaling techniques. The anchor points are assigned the values of 100 and 0 and then through discussion the young person is helped to identify different levels or standards of performances between these points. Visually, the developing scale can be a very powerful way of challenging dichotomous thinking. It helps the young person recognise that perfection is seldom achieved and provides opportunities to identify and discuss the cognitions underlying their perfectionism. In turn these assumptions may be directly tested through behavioural experiments.

Alex (13) was a very competent artist who spent many hours on her art homework. Most of the time was spent on minor alterations and finishes, since Alex assumed that she would only get good marks by spending as much time as possible on her artwork. However, this had recently become problematic, with Alex failing to meet the deadline for completing her course work. She felt unable to hand in her work, feeling that she had not spent enough time to secure a good grade. Alex had a piece of non-assessed artwork she had recently been assigned, and so agreed to try an experiment to test her belief about amount of time and good marks. She agreed to spend 20 hours on this assignment, less than half the time she usually spent. At the end of this time she handed her work to her mother, who took it to school. Alex was very anxious and predicted that she would get a low grade for this assignment. However, when the marks were returned she achieved an A grade. Reflecting on this experiment helped Alex to challenge her assumption linking amount of time and grades.

Perfectionist assumptions such as this are strong and well established, and will continue to be evident during treatment sessions. Continued use of scaling techniques and building up a catalogue of contradictory evidence from experiments are helpful ways of challenging these underlying cognitions. The repeated use of visual scales can help young people to identify that performance other than perfect is often all that is necessary.

Finally, the young person could be helped to identify ways of assessing performance other than by objective success. Alternative, equally important criteria such as personal accomplishment or enjoyment can be developed. Thus, although they did not win the race, they may be able to recognise that they trained hard, controlled their anxious feelings and enjoyed taking part.

Negative bias

The tendency to notice and attend to negative events is a common bias. It is therefore not surprising that some young people are unable to recognise their successes or some of the small changes they have made. In these situations the negative bias needs to be directly challenged by asking the young person to actively detail their successes. This process is an inherent part of treatment sessions whereby targets are reviewed and success and change are celebrated. However, when this negative bias is strong, it can be useful for the young person to keep their own record of achievement that can be periodically reviewed.

> *Sam (9) had identified the steps required to achieve his goal of sleeping over at his friend's house. After 6 weeks into the programme Sam was down, feeling that he had not got anywhere and that he would never be able to sleep over at his friends, Reviewing the ladder helped Sam to focus on his achievements and helped him to recognise the progress he had made.*

Not due to me

At other times the young person may recognise some change but not attribute this to their efforts. The reason for change is externalised and attributed to other factors. This tendency needs to be challenged and the importance of the young person's new skills in effectively coping with worrying and fearful situations emphasised. This reinforces the increasing control the child has in anxious situations, which in turn will help to counter any worries about uncertainty and unpredictability. The clinician therefore needs to identify and encourage the child to reflect on external attributions for positive outcomes and, through a process of Socratic questioning, help the child to recognise and acknowledge their role in achieving this success.

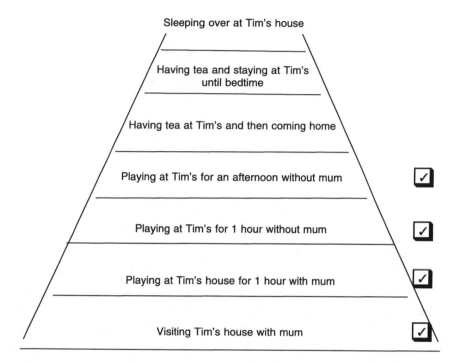

Figure 11.1 Sam's ladder to success

Cognitions of perfectionism, bias towards negativity and external attributions for successful outcomes need to be challenged.

12

Materials and worksheets

The materials included in this chapter provide examples of information and worksheets that can be used with children, young people and their parents. These materials are freely available to photocopy and can also be downloaded in colour from the following website: www.routledgementalhealth. com/cbt-with-children

The materials in this chapter are provided as examples and the clinician is encouraged to develop their own library of resources. Different versions of worksheets, tailored to the interests and developmental level of the child, can be developed. Personalised materials can be prepared relatively quickly and can serve to increase the child's interest, engagement, and commitment to cognitive behaviour therapy. Adapting materials to reflect the child's interests also signals the importance of the child in the therapeutic process and highlights that the clinician listens, responds to their interests, and hears what they say.

Entertaining worksheets can be produced with minimal computer skills. For personal use, attractive images can be freely downloaded from many computer programs and websites. Thought bubbles are relatively simple to create, with worksheets being enhanced by the use of colour and different types and sizes of font. Over time the clinician will develop a library of materials that can be readily modified and adapted for future use.

Worksheets involving images and colour are particularly appealing for younger children. It is important, however, that they are pitched at the right level and serve the purpose of facilitating, rather than detracting from, the therapeutic process. This is particularly important with adolescents, who may be less interested in such materials or may find them patronising or childish. This needs to be determined during the assessment process, and any materials that are used to supplement or reinforce the intervention modified accordingly.

Psycho-educational materials

Chapter 6 highlights that one of the early tasks of cognitive behaviour therapy (CBT) is to educate the child and their parents into the cognitive model of anxiety. This understanding provides the rationale for CBT, facilitates the process of engagement, and can increase motivation to embark on an active process of change. *Learning to Beat Anxiety* is a handout that introduces parents to anxiety and some of the common physiological symptoms. The connection between anxious feelings and worrying thoughts is highlighted and the behavioural consequences, in terms of avoidance, are emphasised. This provides the rationale for CBT and emphasises the aims of identifying and challenging anxiety-increasing thoughts and learning helpful ways of thinking and coping. Finally, parents are provided with some simple ideas about how they can SUPPORT their child during CBT. This involves parents showing their children how to be *successful* by modelling coping and courageous behaviour (S); adopting an *understanding* approach in which the child's problems are recognised and accepted (U); being *patient*, and understanding that change is gradual and takes time (P); *prompting* and encouraging children to use their newly acquired skills (P); *observing* children in order to highlight their strengths and success (O); *rewarding* and praising attempts at coping (R); and being available to *talk* with, and support, their child (T).

The second *Learning to Beat Anxiety* handout is for children and young people. This provides a simple understanding of anxiety and how worries and anxious feelings can sometimes take over and stop the child from doing the things they would really like to do. The need to fight back and to learn to beat anxiety is stressed, and the child is introduced to the key aims of CBT. Finally, the collaborative and active nature of CBT is noted and the importance of learning through doing and experimentation highlighted.

Emotional recognition and management

After psycho-education and the development of a CBT formulation, the intervention focuses on the emotional domain (see Chapter 8). The *Flight–Fight Response* provides a summary of the physiological changes that occur during the stress reaction. A number of the key bodily changes and symptoms are identified, and the purpose of these in preparing the body to run away from, or fight, potential danger is explained. The worksheet provides an opportunity for the child to begin to think about their "dinosaurs", i.e. the things that worry them and make them stressed. Understanding the stress reaction is particularly important for children who are sensitive to their anxiety signals or who are misperceiving them as signs of serious illness.

My Anxiety Body Signals builds on the introductory psycho-educational materials by focusing on the child, and identifying which of their own anxiety signals are the strongest and most noticeable. Increased awareness of anxiety signals can alert children to the need to intervene early and to take appropriate action to manage and reduce their anxious feelings. Similarly, the *Things That Make Me Feel Anxious* worksheet provides a way of helping children identify those situations or events that make them anxious. Spaces are left on the worksheet to include events or situations that are particularly relevant for the child. Finally, *My Hot Diary* provides a summary sheet for recording those times when the child notices strong feelings of anxiety. Once a feeling is noted, the child is instructed to write down the day and time it occurred, what was happening at the time, how they felt in terms of both strength of the anxiety and particularly strong anxiety signals, and any thoughts that were running through their head.

The remaining worksheets are designed to help develop a range of methods to manage anxious feelings. *My Physical Activities* aims to identify potential enjoyable physical activities that can then be used to counteract anxious feelings at the times children are feeling particularly stressed. The *Controlled Breathing Diary Sheet* provides instructions about how to regain control of breathing when feeling anxious or panicky. The technique is quick and easy to use, and can readily be used in many situations. *My Special Relaxing Place* provides instructions for imaginal relaxation. The child is encouraged to develop a detailed image of a special place, real or imaginary, that they find relaxing. This should be a detailed, multisensory image, as they are asked to attend to different features of their image including colour, sound and smell. The development of the image can be enhanced by asking the child to draw a picture of their special place. Once the image is developed, the child is encouraged to visualise their special place whenever they feel stressed, and to practise using this to relax at the end of the day as they lie in their bed. The final worksheet of this section, *My Feelings Toolbox*, provides a summary of the different methods the child has found helpful in managing their anxiety. Children are encouraged not to rely on one method but to develop a number of different techniques.

Cognitive enhancement

These materials accompany Chapter 9, and provide examples of worksheets that can be used to help identify anxious thoughts. In *My Worrying Thoughts* the child is asked to write or draw a situation that worries them in the box at the bottom of the page. They are then asked to think about the situation and to write some of the thoughts that race through their mind in the thought bubbles. Similarly, *Tumbling Thoughts* provides a simple metaphor which highlights the way worrying thoughts keep going round and round in our heads. This worksheet can be used in an exploratory way by asking the child to complete the thought bubbles by writing down the thoughts that often go round and round in their minds. ***Thinking Traps*** provides information about some of the common thinking traps. These include selective abstraction (negative glasses), discounting positives (positive doesn't count), overgeneralisation (blowing things up), predicting failure (Mind Readers and Fortune Tellers) and catastrophisation (disaster thinking). The ***Cool Cat*** and ***How Would They Feel?*** are worksheets that explore different ways of thinking about the same situation or event. These can be used to highlight that some ways of thinking are helpful and result in pleasant feelings, while others are unhelpful and result in unpleasant feelings.

Problem-solving

These worksheets relate to the behavioural domain, which is discussed in Chapter 10. ***Possible Solutions*** provides a way of helping the child to list a variety of options for dealing with a problem. Judgement is suspended since the task at this stage is to generate as many different ideas as possible. Appraisal of these possibilities is undertaken in ***Which Solution Should I Choose?***. After listing their challenge or problem and the solutions they have generated, the child is asked to identify the positive and negative consequences of each. On the basis of this evaluation, the child is then helped to make a decision about the best option. ***My Experiment*** provides a structured format for planning and undertaking behavioural experiments. The first step requires the identification of the worrying thought that is to be tested. In step 2 the child is helped to identify an experiment they could undertake to test this thought. The third step involves specifying how the experiment will be assessed, i.e. what will be measured. Agreeing the day and time of the experiment and who will be around to support the child is the fourth step. The child is then asked to state their prediction, i.e. what they think will happen, and in step 6, after the experiment, to specify what actually happened. The final step involves reflecting on the experiment and identifying what the child has learned, and how this may have challenged or altered their thought. ***My Record of Achievement*** provides a way of countering tendencies to dismiss or negate the positive things that occur. The child is asked to keep a list of the fears, worries and challenges they have faced, conquered and coped with. This can be periodically reviewed and provides a developing record of progress. Finally, ***My Ladder to Success*** provides a way of breaking challenges into smaller steps. This increases the likelihood that each step will be achievable and that the child will be successful.

Learning to Beat Anxiety

A parent's guide to anxiety and cognitive behavioural therapy

What is anxiety?

- Anxiety is a **NORMAL EMOTION** – it helps us cope with difficult, challenging or dangerous situations.
- Anxiety is **COMMON** – there are times when we all feel worried, anxious, uptight or stressed.
- But anxiety becomes a **PROBLEM WHEN IT STOPS YOUR** child from enjoying normal life by affecting their school, work, family relationships, friendships or social life.
- This is when **ANXIETY TAKES OVER** and your child has lost control.

Anxious feelings

When we become anxious our body prepares itself for some form of physical action, often called the "**FLIGHT–FIGHT**" reaction. As the body prepares itself we may notice a number of physical changes such as:

- shortness of breath
- tight chest
- dizziness or light-headedness
- palpitations
- muscle pain, especially head and neck pain
- wanting to go to the toilet
- shakiness
- sweating
- dry mouth
- difficulty swallowing
- blurred vision
- butterflies or feeling sick.

Often there is a reason for feeling anxious such as:

- facing a difficult exam
- saying something to someone they may not like
- having to go somewhere new or do something scary.

Once the unpleasant event is over our bodies return to normal and we usually end up feeling better.

Worrying THOUGHTS

Sometimes there may not be an obvious reason for feeling anxious. Another cause of anxiety is the **WAY WE THINK** about things. We may think that

- things will go wrong,
- we will be unsuccessful
- we will be unable to cope.

Life can seem like one big worry as minds become full of negative and worrying thoughts. We can't seem to stop them, we find it hard to concentrate and think straight, and the worrying and negative thoughts seem to make the physical feelings worse.

Stop DOING things

Anxiety is unpleasant and so we find ways of making ourselves feel better. Feared or difficult situations **MAY BE AVOIDED**. We may stop doing things that worry us. The more we stop or avoid things, the less we do and the harder it becomes to face our fears and overcome our worries.

What is COGNITIVE BEHAVIOUR THERAPY?

Cognitive Behaviour Therapy (CBT) is based on the idea that how we feel and what we do are due to the way we think. CBT is one of the most effective ways of helping children with anxiety problems, and looks at the link between

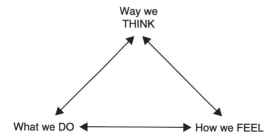

CBT assumes that a lot of anxiety problems are related to the way we think. Because we can change the way we think, we can learn to control our anxious feelings.

- Thinking in more positive ways can help us feel good.
- Thinking in more negative ways may make us feel fearful, tense, sad, angry or uncomfortable.

Teaching children to understand their thoughts is important. Children with anxiety tend to:

- think in negative and critical ways
- overestimate the likelihood of bad things happening
- focus on things that go wrong.
- underestimate their ability to cope
- expect to be unsuccessful.

CBT is a practical and fun way of helping children to:

- identify these negative ways of thinking
- discover the link between what they think, how they feel and what they do
- check out the evidence for their thoughts
- develop new skills to cope with their anxiety.

SUPPORT your child

During CBT it is important that you **SUPPORT** your child.

S – Show your child how to be successful

Show your child how to successfully approach and cope with anxious situations. Model success.

U – Understand that your child has a problem

Remember that your child is not being wilfully naughty or difficult. They have a problem and need your help.

P – Patient approach

Don't expect things to change quickly. Be patient and encourage your child to keep trying.

P – Prompt new skills

Encourage and remind your child to practise and use their new skills.

O – Observe your child

Watch your child and highlight the positive or successful things they do.

R – Reward and praise their efforts

Remember to praise and reward your child for using their new skills and for trying to face and overcome their problems.

T – Talk about it

Talking with your child shows them that you care and will help them feel supported,

      SUPPORT your child and help them to overcome their problems.

Learning to Beat Anxiety

There are times when we **ALL** feel worried, anxious, uptight or stressed. This is **NORMAL** and often there is a reason. It could be

- Going somewhere new or doing something different.
- Having an argument with a friend.
- Performing in a sports or music competition.

At other times anxious feelings can be very strong or come very often. It may be hard to know why you feel so anxious and you may find that these feelings stop you from doing things.

- If you feel worried about going to school, you may stop going and stay at home where you feel better.
- If you feel worried talking with others, you may avoid going out and stay at home on your own.

At these times the worry takes over and may you from doing the things you would really like to do.

When this happens you need to take control and learn how to beat your anxiety.

What can we do?

- Sometimes it is the way we **think** about things that makes us feel anxious. We:

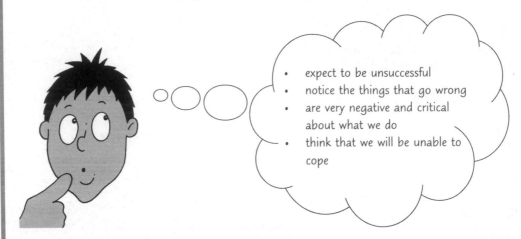

- expect to be unsuccessful
- notice the things that go wrong
- are very negative and critical about what we do
- think that we will be unable to cope

If we change the way we think then we can feel less anxious. We can learn to do this through something called cognitive behaviour therapy (CBT).

How will CBT help?

CBT will help you find:

- the anxious thoughts and feelings you have
- the link between what you think, how you feel and what you do
- more helpful ways of thinking that make you feel less anxious
- how to control anxious feelings
- how to face and overcome your problems.

What will happen?

We will work **together**. You have lots of useful ideas and important things to say, which we want to hear.

We will **experiment** with new ideas to find what helps you. You will:

- check out your thoughts and find more helpful ways of thinking
- discover ways of spotting and controlling your anxious feelings
- learn to overcome and beat your worries.

So let's have a go and see if it helps!!

Flight—Fight Response

When we see something scary or think frightening thoughts, our bodies prepare us to take some form of action.

This can either be to run away (**flight**) or to stay and defend yourself (**fight**).

To do this the body produces chemicals (adrenalin and cortisol).

These chemicals make the heart beat faster so that blood can be pumped around the body to the muscles.

The muscles need oxygen and so we start to breathe faster in order to provide the muscles with the fuel they need.

This helps us become very alert and able to focus on the threat.

Blood gets diverted away from those parts of the body that aren't being used (tummy) and from the vessels running around the outside of the body.

Other bodily functions shut down. We don't need to eat at times like this and so you may notice the mouth becoming dry and it being difficult to swallow.

 The body is now working very hard. It starts to become hot.

 In order to cool down the body starts to sweat and pushes the blood vessels to the surface of the body, resulting in some people becoming flushed or red in the face. Sometimes the body may take in too much oxygen, resulting in people feeling faint, light headed, or as if they have wobbly or jelly legs.

Muscles that continue to be prepared for action (tensed) start to ache and people may notice headaches and stiffness.

Fortunately there aren't any dinosaurs anymore, but we still end up feeling stressed. The dinosaurs have become our worries.

So what are your dinosaurs??

My Anxiety Body Signals

When you feel anxious you may notice a number of changes in your body. Circle the body signals you notice when you get anxious.

Light-headed/feel faint

Red face/Feel hot

Dry mouth

Lump in throat

Butterflies in tummy

Sweaty hands

Headache

Blurred eyesight

Shaky voice

Heart beats faster

Difficulty breathing

Jelly legs   Want to go to the toilet

Which body signals do you notice most?

Things That Make Me Feel Anxious

Draw a line between the anxious face and the things that make you feel anxious.

Going somewhere new

Spiders

Snakes

The dark

Talking with my friends

Meeting new people

Me being ill

Getting my school work right

Exams and tests

Leaving Mum/Dad

Germs or diseases

Dentists or doctors

Mum and dad being ill

Doing something in front of others

Animals

If the things you worry about aren't here, write them in the empty boxes.

My "Hot" Diary

Complete the diary when you notice strong feelings of anxiety. Write down the day and time, what was happening, how you felt and what you were thinking.

Date and time	What was happening?	How did you feel?	What were you thinking?

My Physical Activities

What physical exercise or activities do you enjoy?

| Cycling | Running | Swimming |

| Skate boarding | Roller blading | Dancing |

| Going for a walk | Taking dog out | Going to the park |

| Working out | Cleaning my room | Cleaning the car |

| Doing things in the garden | Kicking a ball | |

If the activities you enjoy aren't here then write them in the empty boxes.

Controlled Breathing Diary Sheet

Before you start, check out your feelings and use the scale below to rate how anxious you are.

Totally relaxed	Little bit anxious	Quite anxious	Very anxious
1 2	3 4 5	6 7 8	9 10

❑ Now take a deep breath

❑ Hold it, count to 5

❑ Very slowly let the breath out

❑ As you let it out, think to yourself "Relax".

Take a deep breath and do it again. Remember to let the breath out nice and slowly.

Do this again, and then one more time.

Use the scale below to rate how you are feeling now

Totally relaxed	Little bit anxious	Quite anxious	Very anxious
1 2	3 4 5	6 7 8	9 10

If there is no difference in your ratings, don't worry. Have another go and remember that the more you practise, the more you will find it helps.

My Special Relaxing Place

Think about your relaxing place and draw or describe it. This could be a real place you have been or a picture you may have created in your dreams.

- Think about the **colours and shapes** of things.
- Imagine **sounds** – seagulls calling, leaves rustling, waves crashing on the sand.
- Think about the **smell** – the smell of pine from the trees, the salty sea, cakes baked fresh from the oven.
- Imagine the sun warming your back or the moonlight shining through the trees.

This is your special relaxing place. To practise using your relaxing place:

- Choose a quiet time when you will not be disturbed.
- Shut your eyes and imagine your picture.
- Describe it to yourself in lots of detail.
- As you think of your picture, notice how calm and relaxed you become.
- Enjoy it and go there whenever you feel anxious.

Remember to practise.

The more you practise, the easier you will find it to imagine your picture and the quicker you will become calm.

My Feelings Toolbox

You will find a number of ways to control your anxious feelings which you can keep in your "toolbox". Write them down to help you remember.

❑ Physical exercises that helps me relax are:

❑ My relaxing activities are:

❑ Mind games I could use when I am anxious are:

❑ Distraction exercises I could use are:

❑ My relaxing place is:

Remember – controlled breathing can quickly help you gain
control of your feelings.

My Worrying Thoughts

Write the situation that makes you worried in the box. When you think about facing that situation, fill out the thought bubbles with some of the thoughts that race through your mind.

My scary or worrying situation is

Tumbling Thoughts

What worrying thoughts keep tumbling round and round in your head?

Materials and Worksheets from *Anxiety* by Paul Stallard published by Routledge

Thinking Traps

- **TRAP 1:** The **negative glasses** only let you see the negative things that happen.

 Negative glasses find the things that went wrong or weren't quite good enough. Finding and remembering the negative things will make you think that you always fail and will make you anxious.

- **TRAP 2:** Anything positive or good that happens is rubbished so that **positive doesn't count**.

 Rubbishing anything positive as unimportant or lucky means that you don't acknowledge your successes, never accept that you can cope or believe that success is due to what you do.

- **TRAP 3:** Negative things are **blown up** and become bigger than they really are.

 Blowing things up results in events becoming more frightening and scary.

- **TRAP 4:** Makes us **expect things** to go wrong so that we become

 "Mind readers" who think they know what everyone else is thinking or **"fortune tellers"** who think they know what is going to happen.

Expecting things to go wrong will make you feel more anxious.

- **TRAP 5: Disaster thinking** makes us think that the worst thing we could imagine will happen.

 People who have panic attacks often think like this and imagine that they will become seriously ill and die.

What thinking traps do you get caught in?

The Cool Cat

Which thought would make the cat feel most anxious?

How Would They Feel?

Mr Evans the head teacher walked into Amy and Luke's class and asked to see them before they went home at the end of the day.

GOOD, I bet he wants to ask us to do something

Oh NO. He wants to tell me off for dropping litter

Amy and Luke had very different thoughts.
How would they feel?

Worksheet: Possible Solutions?

What I want to achieve:

One way of doing this is:

❑

Or I could do:

❑

Or I could do:

❑

Or I could do:

❑

Or I could do:

❑

Which Solution Should I Choose?

Once you have a list of possible ideas the next step is to think about the negatives (−) and positives (+) of each solution. You may want to ask someone to help you do this.

When you have finished look at your list and choose the best solution for your challenge.

My challenge is:		
Possible solution	Positives (+)	Negatives (−)
1.		
2.		
3.		
4.		
5.		
6.		
7.		
My best solution is:		

My Experiment

1. What do I want to check out?

2. What experiment could I do to check this out?

3. How can I measure what happens?

4. When will I do this experiment and who will help?

5. My prediction – what do I think will happen?

6. What actually happened?

7. What have I learned from this experiment?

 Materials and Worksheets from *Anxiety* by Paul Stallard published by Routledge

My Record of Achievement

The FEARS I have faced

The WORRIES I have conquered

The CHALLENGES I have coped with

My Ladder to Success

Write the goal that you would like to achieve at the top of the ladder. Write the steps that will take you there, with the easiest at the bottom.

My goal is:

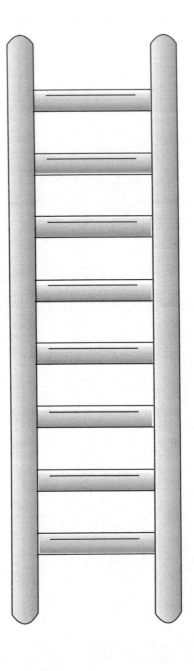

Materials and Worksheets from *Anxiety* by Paul Stallard published by Routledge

References

Albano, A.M. & Kendall, P.C. (2002). Cognitive behavour therapy for children and adolescents with anxiety disorders: Clinical research advances. *International Review of Psychiatry*, *14*, 129–134.

Alfano, C.A., Beidel, D.C. & Turner, S.M. (2002). Cognition in childhood anxiety: Conceptual, methodological, and developmental issues. *Clinical Psychology Review*, *22*, 1209–1238.

Alfano, C.A., Beidel, D.C. & Turner, S.M. (2006). Cognitive correlates of social phobia among children and adolescents. *Journal of Abnormal Child Psychology*, *34*(2), 189–201.

American Academy of Child and Adolescent Psychiatry. (2007). Practice parameter for the assessment and treatment of children and adolescents with anxiety disorders. *Journal of the American Academy of Child and Adolescent Psychiatry*, *46*(2), 267–283.

American Psychiatric Association. (1994). *Diagnostic and Statistical Manual of Mental Disorders* (4th edition). Washington, DC: APA.

American Psychiatric Association. (2000). *Diagnostic and Statistical Manual of Mental Disorders* (4th edition – Text Revision). Washington, DC: APA.

Angold, A. & Costello, E.J. (1993). Depressive comorbidity in children and adolescents: Empirical, theoretical and methodological issues. *American Journal of Psychiatry*, *150*, 1779–1791.

Baer, S. & Garland, E.J. (2005). Pilot study of community-based cognitive behavioural group therapy for adolescents with social phobia. *Journal of the American Academy of Child and Adolescent Psychiatry*, *44*(3), 258–264.

Baldwin, J.S. & Dadds, R. (2007). Reliability and validity of parent and child versions of the Multidimensional Anxiety Scale for children in community samples. *Journal of the American Academy of Child and Adolescent Psychiatry*, *46*(2), 224–232.

Barlow, D.H. (2002). *Anxiety and Its Disorders: The Nature and Treatment of Anxiety and Panic* (2nd edition). New York: Guilford Press.

Barrett, P.M. (1998). Evaluation of cognitive-behavioural group treatments for childhood anxiety disorders. *Journal of Clinical Child Psychology*, *27*(4), 459–468.

Barrett, P.M., Dadds, M.R. & Rapee, R.M. (1996a). Family treatment of childhood anxiety: A controlled trial. *Journal of Consulting and Clinical Psychology*, *64*(2), 333–342.

Barrett, P.M., Duffy, A.L., Dadds, M.R. & Rapee, R.M. (2001). Cognitive behavioural treatment of anxiety disorders in children: Long-term (6 year) follow-up. *Journal of Consulting and Clinical Psychology*, *69*(1), 135–141.

Barrett, P.M., Rapee, R.M., Dadds, M.R. & Ryan, A.M. (1996b). Family enhancement of cognitive style in anxious and aggressive children. *Journal of Abnormal Child Psychology*, *24*(2), 187–203.

Barrett, P., Webster, H. & Turner, C. (2000). *FRIENDS: Prevention of Anxiety and Depression in Children: Group Leader's Manual*. Bowen Hills, Australia: Australian Academic Press.

Beck, A.T. (1967). *Depression: Clinical, Experimental, and Theoretical Aspects*. New York: Harper & Row.

Beck, A.T. (1971). Cognition, affect, and psychopathology. *Archives of General Psychiatry*, *24*, 495–500.

Beck, A.T. (1976). *Cognitive Therapy and the Emotional Disorders*. Madison, CT: International Universities Press.

Beck, A.T., Emery, G. & Greenberg, R.L. (1985). *Anxiety Disorders and Phobias: A Cognitive Perspective*. New York: Basic Books.

Beidel, D.C. (1991). Social phobia and overanxious disorder in school-age children. *Journal of the American Academy of Child and Adolescent Psychiatry*, *30*(4), 542–552.

Beidel, D.C., Turner, S.M. & Morris, T.L. (1999). Psychopathology of childhood social phobia. *Journal of the American Academy of Child and Adolescent Psychiatry*, *38*(6), 643–650.

Bennet-Levy, J., Westbrook, D., Fennell, M., Cooper, M., Rouf, K. & Hackmann, A. (2004). Behavioural experiments and conceptual underpinnings. In J. Bennett-Levy, G. Butler, M. Fennell, A. Hackmann, M. Mueller & D. Westbrook (eds), *Oxford Guide to Behavioural Experiments in Cognitive Therapy*. Oxford: Oxford University Press.

Bernstein, G.A., Lyne, A.E., Egan, E.A. & Tennison, D.M. (2005). School-based interventions for anxious children. *Journal of the American Academy of Child and Adolescent Psychiatry*, *44*(11), 1118–1127.

Birmaher, B., Khetarpal, S., Brent, D., Cully, M., Balach, L., Kaufman, J. & Neer, S.M. (1997). The Screen for Child Anxiety Related Emotional Disorders (SCARED): Scale construction and psychometric characteristics. *Journal of the American Academy of Child and Adolescent Psychiatry*, *36*, 545–553.

Bogels, S.M. & Brechman-Toussaint, M.L. (2006). Family issues in child anxiety: Attachment, family functioning, parental rearing and beliefs. *Clinical Psychology Review*, *26*(7), 834–856.

Bogels, S.M. & Siqueland, L. (2006). Family cognitive behavioural therapy for children and adolescents with clinical anxiety disorders. *Journal of the American Academy of Child and Adolescent Psychiatry*, *45*(2), 134–141.

Bogels, S.M. & Zigterman, D. (2000). Dysfunctional cognitions in children with social phobia, separation anxiety disorder, and generalised anxiety disorder. *Journal of Abnormal Child Psychology*, *28*(2), 205–211.

Cartwright-Hatton, S., Roberts, C., Chitsabesan, P., Fothergill, C. & Harrington, R. (2004). Systematic review of the efficacy of cognitive behaviour therapies for childhood and adolescent anxiety disorders. *British Journal of Clinical Psychology*, *43*, 421–436.

Cartwright-Hatton, S., Tschernitz, N. & Gomersall, H. (2005). Social anxiety in children: Social skills deficit, or cognitive distortion. *Behaviour Research and Therapy*, *43*, 131–141.

Chambless, D. & Hollon, S. (1998). Defining empirically supported treatments. *Journal of Consulting and Clinical Psychology*, *66*, 5–17.

Cobham, V.E., Dadds, M.R. & Spence, S.H. (1998). The role of parental anxiety in the treatment of childhood anxiety. *Journal of Consulting and Clinical Psychology*, *66*(6), 893–905.

Compton, S.N., March, J.S., Brent, D., Albano, A.M., Weersing, R. & Curry, J. (2004). Cognitive-behavioural psychotherapy for anxiety and depressive disorders in children and adolescents: An evidence-based medicine review. *Journal of the American Academy of Child and Adolescent Psychiatry*, *43*(8), 930–959.

Costello, E.J. & Angold, A. (1995). A test–retest reliability study of child-reported psychiatric symptoms and diagnoses using the Child and Adolescent Psychiatric Assessment (CAPA-C). *Psychological Medicine*, *25*(4), 755–762.

Costello, E.J., Angold, A., Burns, B.J., Stangl, D.K., Tweed, D.L., Erkanli, A. & Worthman, C.M. (1996). The Great Smoky Mountains Study of Youth: Goals, design, methods, and the prevalence of DSM-III-R disorders. *Archives of General Psychiatry*, *53*, 1129–1136.

Costello, E.J., Mustillo, S., Erkanli, A., Keeler, A. & Angold, A. (2003). Prevalence and development of psychiatric disorders in childhood and adolescence. *Archives of General Psychiatry*, *60*, 837–844.

Creswell, C. & Cartwright-Hatton, S. (2007). Family treatment of child anxiety: Outcomes, limitations and future directions. *Clinical Child and Family Psychology*, *10*(3), 232–252.

Dadds, M.R., Barrett, P.M., Rapee, R.M. & Ryan, S. (1996). Family process and child anxiety and aggression: An observational analysis. *Journal of Abnormal Child Psychology*, *24*, 715–734.

Daleiden, E.L. & Vasey, M.W. (1997). An information processing perspective on childhood anxiety. *Clinical Psychology Review*, *17*, 407–429.

Dierker, L.C., Albano, A.M., Clarke, G.N., Heimberg, R.G., Kendall, P.C., Merikangas, K.R., Lewinsohn, P.M., Offord, D.R., Kessler, R. & Kupfer, D.J. (2001). Screening for anxiety and depression in early adolescence. *Journal of the American Academy of Child and Adolescent Psychiatry*, *40*, 929–936.

Drinkwater, J. (2004). Cognitive case formulation. In P. Graham (ed.), *Cognitive Behaviour Therapy for Children and Families* (2nd edition). Cambridge: Cambridge University Press.

Durlak, J.A., Fuhrman, T. & Lampman, C. (1991). Effectiveness of cognitive-behaviour therapy for maladapting children: A meta analysis. *Psychological Bulletin*, *110*, 204–214.

Eley, T.C. & Gregory, A.M. (2004). Behavioural genetics. In T.L. Morris. & J.S. March (eds), *Anxiety Disorders in Children and Adolescents* (2nd edition, pp. 71–97). New York: Guilford Press.

Epkins, C.C. (1996). Cognitive specificity and affective confounding in social anxiety and dysphoria in children. *Journal of Psychopathology and Behavioural Assessment*, *18*, 83–101.

Epkins, C.C. (2000). Cognitive specificity in internalizing and externalizing problems in community and clinic-referred children. *Journal of Clinical Child Psychology*, *29*(2), 199–208.

Essau, C.A., Conradt, J. & Petermann, F. (2000). Frequency, comorbidity, and psychosocial impairment of anxiety disorders in German adolescents. *Journal of Anxiety Disorders, 14*(3), 263–279.

Foley, D.L., Pickles, A., Maes, H.M., Silberg, J.L. & Eaves, L.J. (2004). Course and short-term outcomes of separation anxiety disorder in a community sample of twins. *Journal of the American Academy of Child and Adolescent Psychiatry, 43*(9), 1107–1114.

Francis, G., Last, C.G. & Strauss, C.C. (1987). Expression of separation anxiety disorder. The roles of age and gender. *Child Psychiatry and Human Development, 18*(2), 82–89.

Ginsburg, G.S. & Schlossberg, M.C. (2002). Family based treatment of childhood anxiety disorders. *International Review of Psychiatry, 14*, 143–154.

Ginsburg, G.S., Silverman, W.K. & Kurtines, W.K. (1995). Family involvement in treating children with phobic and anxiety disorders: A look ahead. *Clinical Psychology Review, 15*(5), 457–473.

Goodwin, R.D. & Gotlib, I.H. (2004). Panic attacks and psychopathology among youth. *Acta Psychiatrica Scandinavica, 109*, 216–221.

Graham, P. (2005). Jack Tizard Lecture: Cognitive behaviour therapies for children: Passing fashion or here to stay? *Child and Adolescent Mental Health, 10*(2), 57–62.

Greco, L.A. & Morris, T.M. (2002). Parent child-rearing style and child social anxiety: Investigation of child perceptions and actual father behaviour. *Journal of Psychopathology and Behavioural Assessment, 24*, 259–267.

Greco, L.A. & Morris, T.L. (2004). Assessment. In Morris, T.L & March, J.S. (eds), *Anxiety Disorders in Children and Adolescents* (2nd edition). New York: Guilford Press.

Hayward, C., Killen, J.D., Kraemer, H.C., Blair-Greiner, A., Strachowski, D., Cunning, D. & Taylor, C.B. (1997). Assessment and phenomenology of non-clinical panic attacks in adolescent girls. *Journal of Anxiety Disorders, 11*(1), 17–32.

Hayward, C., Varady, S., Alban, A.M., Thienemann, M., Henderson, L. & Schatzberg, A.F. (2000). Cognitive-behavioural group therapy for social phobia in female adolescents: Results of a pilot study. *Journal of the American Academy of Child and Adolescent Psychiatry, 39*, 721–726.

Henker, B., Whalen, C.K. & O'Neil, R. (1995). Worldly and workaday worries: Contemporary concerns of children and young adolescents. *Journal of Abnormal Child Psychology, 23*(6), 685–702.

Herjanic, B. & Reich, W. (1982). Development of a structured psychiatric interview for children: Agreement between child and parent on individual symptoms. *Journal of Abnormal Child Psychology, 10*, 307–324.

Heyne, D., King, N.J., Tonge, B., Rollings, S., Young, D., Pritchard, M. & Ollendick, T.H. (2002). Evaluation of child therapy and caregiver training in the treatment of school refusal. *Journal of the American Academy of Child and Adolescent Psychiatry, 41*(6), 687–695.

Hudson, J.L. & Rapee, R.M. (2001). Parent–child interaction and anxiety disorders: An observational study. *Behaviour Research and Therapy, 39*, 1411–1427.

Hudson, J.L. & Rapee, R.M. (2002). Parent–child interactions in clinically anxious children and their siblings. *Journal of Clinical Child and Adolescent Psychology, 31*, 548–555.

Hughes, A.A. & Kendall, P.C. (2007). Prediction of cognitive behaviour treatment outcome for children with anxiety disorders: Therapeutic relationship and home-work completion. *Behavioural and Cognitive Psychotherapy, 35*, 487–494.

Kaufman, J.D, Birhamer. B., Brent, D., Rao, U., Flynn, C., Moreci, P., Williamson, D., & Ryan, N. (1997). Schedule for Affective Disorders and Schizophrenia for School-Age Children – Present and Lifetime Version (K-SADS-PL): Initial reliability and validity data. *Journal of the American Academy of Child and Adolescent Psychiatry*, *36*(7), 980–988.

Kazantzis, N., Deane, F.P. & Ronan, K.R. (2000). Homework assignments in cognitive and behavioural therapy: A meta-analysis. *Clinical Psychology Science and Practice*, *7*, 189–202.

Kazdin, A.E. & Weisz, J. (1998). Identifying and developing empirically supported child and adolescent treatments. *Journal of Consulting and Clinical Psychology*, *66*, 19–36.

Kearney, C.A., Albano, A.M., Eisen, A.R., Allan, W.D. & Barlow, D.H. (1997). The phenomenology of panic disorder in youngsters: An empirical study of a clinical sample. *Journal of Anxiety Disorders*, *11*(1), 49–62.

Kendall, P.C. (1984). Behavioural assessment and methodology. In G.T. Wilson, C.M. Franks, K.D. Braswell & P.C. Kendall (eds), *Annual Review of Behaviour Therapy: Theory and Practice*. New York. Guilford Press.

Kendall, P.C. (1994). Treating anxiety disorders in children: Results of a randomized clinical trial. *Journal of Consulting and Clinical Psychology*, *62*, 100–110.

Kendall, P.C. & Chansky, T.E. (1991). Considering cognition in anxiety-disordered children. *Journal of Anxiety Disorders*, *5*, 167–185.

Kendall, P.C., Flannery-Schroeder, E., Panichelli-Mindel, S.M., Southam-Gerow, M., Henin, A. & Warman, M. (1997). Therapy for youths with anxiety disorders: A second randomized clinical trial. *Journal of Consulting and Clinical Psychology*, *65*(3), 366–380.

Kendall, P.C. & MacDonald, J.P. (1993). Cognition in the psychopathology of youth and implications for treatment. In K.S. Dobson and P.C. Kendall (eds), *Psychopathology and Cognition* (pp. 387–427). San Diego, CA: Academic Press.

Kendall, P.C. & Pimentel, S.S. (2003). On the physiological symptom constellation in youth with generalized anxiety disorder (GAD). *Journal of Anxiety Disorders*, *17*(2), 211–221.

Kendall, P.C., Safford, S., Flannery-Schroeder, E. & Webb, A. (2004). Child anxiety treatment: Outcomes in adolescence and impact on substance use and depression at 7.4 year follow-up. *Journal of Consulting and Clinical Psychology*, *72*(2), 276–287.

Kim-Cohen, J., Caspi, A., Moffit, T.E., Harrington, H., Milne, B.J. & Poulton, R. (2003). Prior juvenile diagnoses in adults with mental disorder: Developmental follow-back of a prospective-longitudinal cohort. *Archives of General Psychiatry*, *60*, 709–717.

King, N.J. & Ollendick, T.H. (1992). Test note: Reliability of the Fear Survey Schedule for Children – Revised. *The Australian Educational and Developmental Psychologist*, *9*, 55–57.

King, N.J. & Ollendick, T.H. (1997). Annotation: Treatment of childhood phobias. *Journal of Child Psychology and Psychiatry*, *38*(4), 389–400.

King, N.J., Tonge, B.J., Heyne, D., Pritchard, M., Rollings, S., Young, D., Myerson, N. & Ollendick, T.H. (1998). Cognitive behavioural treatment of school-refusing children: A controlled evaluation. *Journal of the American Academy of Child and Adolescent Psychiatry*, *37*(4), 395–403.

Kortlander, E., Kendall, P.C. & Panichelli-Mindel, S.M. (1997). Maternal expectations and attributions about coping in anxious children. *Journal of Anxiety Disorders*, *11*(3), 297–315.

Krohne, H.W. & Hock, M. (1991). Relationships between restrictive mother–child interactions and anxiety of the child. *Anxiety Research, 4*(2), 109–124.

Last, C.G., Francis, G. & Strauss, C.C. (1989). Assessing fears in anxiety disordered children with the Revised Fear Survey Schedule for Children (FSSC-R). *Journal of Clinical Child Psychology, 18*, 137–141.

Last, C.G., Hansen, C. & Franco, N. (1998). Cognitive behavioural treatment of school phobia. *Journal of the American Academy of Child and Adolescent Psychiatry, 37*, 404–411.

Last, C.G., Hersen, M., Kazdin, A., Orvaschel, H. & Perrin, S. (1991). Anxiety disorders in children and their families. *Archives of General Psychiatry, 48*, 928–945.

Last, C.G., Phillips, J.E. & Statfeld, A. (1987). Childhood anxiety disorders in mothers and their children. *Child Psychiatry and Human Development, 18*(2), 103–112.

Leitenberg, H., Yost, L. & Carroll-Wilson, M. (1986). Negative cognitive errors in children: Questionnaire development, normative data, and comparisons between children with and without symptoms of depression, low self-esteem and evaluation anxiety. *Journal of Consulting and Clinical Psychology, 54*, 528–536.

Leung, P.W.L. & Poon, M.W.L. (2001). Dysfunctional schemas and cognitive distortions in psychopathology: A test of the specificity hypothesis. *Journal of Child Psychology and Psychiatry, 42*(6), 755–765.

Lonigan, C.L., Vasey, M.W., Phillips, B.M. & Hazen, R.A. (2004). Temperament, anxiety and the processing of threat relevant stimuli. *Journal of Clinical Child and Adolescent Psychology, 33*, 8–20.

Manassis, K., Mendlowitz, S.L., Scapillato, D., Avery, D., Fiksenbaum, L., Freire, M., Monga, S. & Owens, M. (2002). Group and individual cognitive behavioural therapy for childhood anxiety disorders: A randomised trial. *Journal of the American Academy of Child and Adolescent Psychiatry, 41*, 1423–1430.

March J.S., Parker J., Sullivan K., Stallings P. & Conners, C.K. (1997). The Multi-dimensional Anxiety Scale for Children (MASC): Factor structure, reliability, and validity. *Journal of the American Academy of Child and Adolescent Psychiatry, 36*, 554–565.

Marks, I.M. (1969). *Fears and Phobias*. New York: Academic Press.

Martin, M., Horder, P. & Jones, G.V. (1992). Integral bias in naming of phobia-related words. *Cognition and Emotion, 6*, 479–486.

Masi, G., Millepiedi, S., Mucci, M., Poli, P., Bertini, N. & Milantoni, L. (2004). Generalized anxiety disorder in referred children and adolescents. *Journal of the American Academy of Child and Adolescent Psychiatry, 43*(6), 752–760.

Masi, G., Mucci, M., Favilla, L., Romano, R. & Poli, P. (1999). Symptomatology and comorbidity of generalized anxiety disorder in children and adolescents. *Comprehensive Psychiatry, 40*(3), 210–215.

Meltzer, H., Gatward, R., Goodman, R. & Ford, T. (2003). Mental health of children and adolescents in Great Britain. *International Review of Psychiatry, 15*, 185–187.

Mendlowitz, S.L., Manassis, M.D., Bradley, S., Scapillato, D., Miezitis, S. & Shaw, B.F. (1999). Cognitive behaviour group treatments in childhood anxiety disorders: The role of parental involvement. *Journal of the American Academy of Child and Adolescent Psychiatry, 38*(10), 1223–1229.

Miller, L.C., Barrett, C.L. & Hampe, E. (1974). Phobias of childhood in a pre-scientific era. In A. Davis (ed.), *Child Personality and Psychopathology: Current Topics*. New York: Wiley.

Mills, R.S.L. & Rubin, K.H. ((1990). Parental beliefs about problematic social behaviours in early childhood. *Child Development*, *61*(1), 138–151.

Mills, R.S.L. & Rubin, K.H. (1992). A longitudinal study of maternal beliefs about children's social behaviours. *Merrill Palmer Quarterly*, *38*(4), 494–512.

Mills, R.S.L. & Rubin, K.H. (1993). Socialization factors in the development of social withdrawal. In K.H. Rubin & J.B. Asendorpf (eds). *Social Withdrawal, Inhibition and Shyness in Childhood*. Hillsdale, NJ: Lawerence Erlbaum Associates.

Mills, R.S.L. & Rubin, K.H. (1998). Are behavioural and psychological control both differentially associated with childhood aggression and social withdrawal? *Canadian Journal of Behavioural Science*, *30*, 132–136.

Moore, P.S., Whaley, S.E. & Sigman, M. (2004). Interactions between mothers and children: Impacts of maternal and child anxiety. *Journal of Abnormal Psychology*, *113*, 471–476.

Muris, P., Dreessen, L., Bogels, S., Weckx, M. & van Melick, M. (2004). A questionnaire for screening a broad range of DSM-defined anxiety disorder symptoms in clinically referred children and adolescents. *Journal of Child Psychology and Psychiatry*, *45*, 813–820.

Muris, P., Kindt, M., Bogels, S., Merckelbach, H., Gadet, B. & Moularet, V. (2000a). Anxiety and threat perception abnormalities in normal children. *Journal of Psychopathology and Behavioural Assessment*, *22*(2), 183–199.

Muris, P., Meesters, C., Merckelbach, H., Sermon, A. & Zwakhalen, S. (1998). Worry in normal children. *Journal of the American Academy of Child and Adolescent Psychiatry*, 37, 7, 703–710.

Muris, P., Merckelbach, H. & Damsma, E. (2000b). Threat perception bias in non-referred, socially anxious children. *Journal of Clinical Child Psychology*, *29*, 348–359.

Muris, P., Merckelbach, H., Ollendick, T., King, N. & Bogie, N. (2002). Three traditional and three new childhood anxiety questionnaires: Their reliability and validity in a normal adolescent sample. *Behaviour Research and Therapy*, *40*, 753–772.

Muris, P., Merckelbach, H., Schmidt, H. & Mayer, B. (1999). The revised version of the Screen for Child Anxiety Related Emotional Disorders (SCARED-R): Factor structure in normal children. *Personality and Individual Differences*, *26*, 99–112.

Myers, K. & Winters, N.C. (2002). Ten-year review of rating scales. 11: Scales for internalising disorders. *Journal of the American Academy of Child and Adolescent Psychiatry*, *41*(6), 634–659.

Nauta, M.H., Scholing, A., Emmelkamp, P.M.G. & Minderaa, R.B. (2001). Cognitive behaviour therapy for anxiety disordered children in a clinical setting: Does additional cognitive parent training enhance treatment effectiveness? *Clinical Psychology and Psychotherapy*, *8*, 300–340.

Nauta, M.H., Scholing, A., Emmelkamp, P.M.G. & Minderaa, R.B. (2003). Cognitive behaviour therapy for children with anxiety disorders in a clinical setting: No additional effect of a cognitive parent training. *Journal of the American Academy of Child and Adolescent Psychiatry*, *42*(11), 1270–1278.

Newman, D.L., Moffit, T.E., Caspi, A., Magdol, L., Silva, P.A. & Stanton, W.R. (1996). Psychiatric disorder in a birth cohort of young adults: Comorbidity, clinical significance and new case incidence from ages 11–21. *Journal of Consulting and Clinical Psychology*, *64*(3), 552–562.

Ollendick, T.H. (1983). Reliability and validity of the Revised Fear Survey Schedule for Children (FSSC-R). *Behaviour Research and Therapy*, *21*, 685–692.

Ollendick, T.H., King, N. & Muris, P. (2002). Fears and phobias in children: Phenomenology, epidemiology and aetiology. *Child and Adolescent Mental Health, 7*(3), 98–106.

Padesky, C. & Greenberger, D. (1995), *Clinician's Guide to Mind over Mood*. New York: Guilford Press.

Perrin, S. & Last, C.G. (1992). Do childhood anxiety measures measure anxiety? *Journal of Abnormal Child Psychology, 20*, 567–578.

Perrin, S. & Last, C.G. (1997). Worrisome thoughts in children clinically referred for anxiety disorders. *Journal of Child Clinical Psychology, 26*, 181–189.

Pine, D.S., Cohen, P., Gurley, D., Brook, J. & Ma, Y. (1998). The risk for early-adulthood anxiety and depressive disorders in adolescents with anxiety and depressive disorders. *Archives of General Psychiatry, 55*, 56–64.

Prins, P.J.M. (1985). Self-speech and self-regulation of high and low anxious children in the dental situation: An interview study. *Behaviour Research and Therapy, 23*, 641–650.

Prins, P.J.M. & Hanewald, G.J.F.P. (1997). Self-statements of test anxious children: Thought-listing and questionnaire approaches. *Journal of Consulting and Clinical Psychology, 65*(3), 440–447.

Prins, P.J.M. & Ollendick, T.H. (2003). Cognitive change and enhanced coping: Missing mediational links in cognitive behaviour therapy with anxiety-disordered children. *Clinical Child and Family Psychology Review, 6*(2), 87–105.

Prochaska, J.O., DiClemente, C.C. & Norcross, J. (1992). In search of how people change. *American Psychologist, 47*, 1102–1114.

Puliafico, A.C. & Kendall, P.C. (2006). Threat-related attentional bias in anxious youth: A review. *Clinical Child & Family Psychology Review, 9*, 162–180.

Rapee, R.M. (1997). Potential role of childrearing practices in the development of anxiety and depression. *Clinical Psychology Review, 17*(1), 47–67.

Rapee, R.M. (2001). The development of generalised anxiety. In M.W. Vasey & M.R. Dadds (eds), *The Developmental Psychopathology of Anxiety*. New York: Oxford University Press.

Reich, W. (2000). Diagnostic Interview for Children and Adolescents (DICA). *Journal of the American Academy of Child and Adolescent Psychiatry, 39*(1), 59–66.

Reynolds, C.R. & Paget, K.D. (1981). Factor analysis of the revised children's manifest anxiety scale for blacks, males and females with national innovative sample. *Journal of Consulting and Clinical Psychology, 49*, 352–359.

Reynolds, C.R. & Richmond, B.O. (1978). What I think and feel: A revised measure of children's manifest anxiety. *Journal of Abnormal Child Psychology, 6*, 271–280.

Robins, L.W., Helzer, J.E., Ratcliff, K.S. & Seyfried, W. (1982). Validity of the Diagnostic Interview Schedule Version II: DSM-III diagnoses. *Psychological Medicine, 12*, 855–870.

Rollnick, S. & Miller, W.R. (1995). What is motivational interviewing? *Behavioural and Cognitive Psychotherapy, 23*, 325–334.

Rynn, M., Barber, J., Khalid-Khan, S., Siqueland, L., Dembiski, M., McCarthy, S. et al. (2006). The psychometric properties of the MASC in a pediatric psychiatric sample. *Journal of Anxiety Disorders, 20*, 139–157.

Schniering, A.A. & Rapee, R.M. (2002). Development and validation of a measure of children's automatic thoughts: The children's automatic thoughts scale. *Behaviour Research and Therapy, 40*, 1091–1109.

Schniering, A.A. & Rapee, R.M. (2004). The relationship between automatic thoughts and negative emotions in children and adolescents: A test of the content-specificity hypothesis. *Journal of Abnormal Child Psychology*, *113*(3), 464–470.

Schuckit, M.A. & Hesselbrock, V. (1994). Alcohol dependence and anxiety disorders: What is the relationship? *American Journal of Psychiatry*, *151*, 1723–1734.

Schwartz, R.M. & Garamoni, G.L. (1986). A structural model of positive and negative states of mind: Asymmetry in the internal dialogue. In P.C. Kendall (ed.), *Advances in Cognitive-Behavioural Research and Therapy* (Vol. 5). New York: Academic Press.

Shaffer, D., Fisher, P., Dulcan, M.K., Davies, M., Piacentini, J., Schwab-Stone, M.E. *et al.* (1996). The NIMH Diagnostic Interview Schedule for Children, Version 2.3 (DISC-2.3): Description, acceptability, prevalence rates, and performance in the MECA study. *Journal of the American Academy of Child and Adolescent Psychiatry*, *35*, 865–877.

Shaffer, D., Fisher, P., Lucas, C., Dulcan, M.K. & Schwab-Stone, M.E. (2000). NIMH Diagnostic Interview Schedule for Children version IV (NIMH DISC-IV): Description, differences from previous versions and reliability of some common diagnoses. *Journal of the American Academy of Child and Adolescent Psychiatry*, *39*(1), 28–38.

Shortt, A.L., Barrett, P.M., Dadds, M.R. & Fox, T.L. (2001). The influence of family and experimental context on cognition in anxious children. *Journal of Abnormal Child Psychology*, *29*(6), 585–596.

Silverman, W.K. & Albano, A.M. (1996). *Anxiety Disorders Interview Schedule for Children for DSM-IV (Child & Parent Versions)*. San Antonio, TX: Psychological Corporation/Graywind.

Silverman, W.K. & Dick-Niederhauser, A. (2004). Separation anxiety disorder. In T.L. Morris & J.S. March (eds), *Anxiety Disorders in Children and Adolescents*. New York: Guilford Press.

Silverman, W.K., Kurtines, W.M., Ginsburg, G.S., Weems, C.F., Lumpkin, P.W. & Carmichael, D.H. (1999a). Treating anxiety disorders in children with group cognitive behavioural therapy: A randomised clinical trial. *Journal of Consulting and Clinical Psychology*, *67*(6), 995–1003.

Silverman, W.K., Kurtines, W.M., Ginsburg, G.S., Weems, C.F., Rabian, B. & Serafini, L.T. (1999b). Contingency management, self-control and educational support in the treatment of childhood phobic disorders: A randomized clinical trial. *Journal of Consulting and Clinical Psychology*, *67*(5), 675–687.

Silverman, W.K., La Greca, A.M. & Wasserstein, S. (1995). What do children worry about? Worries and their relation to anxiety. *Child Development*, *66*(3), 671–686.

Silverman, W.K. & Ollendick, T.K. (2005). Evidence-based assessment of anxiety and its disorders in children and adolescents. *Journal of Clinical Child and Adolescent Psychology*, *34*(3), 380–411.

Silverman, W.K., Saavedra, L.M. & Pina, A.A. (2001). Test–re-test reliability of anxiety symptoms and diagnoses using the Anxiety Disorder Interview Schedule for DSM-IV: Child and Parent Versions (ADIS for DSM-IV: C/P). *Journal of the American Academy of Child and Adolescent Psychiatry*, *40*, 937–944.

Siqueland, L. & Diamond, G. (1998). Engaging parents in cognitive behavioural treatment for children with anxiety disorders. *Cognitive and Behavioural Practice*, *5*, 81–102.

Siqueland, L., Kendall, P.C. & Steinberg, L. (1996). Anxiety in children: Perceived family environments and observed family interaction. *Journal of Clinical Child Psychology*, *25*(2), 225–237.

Soler, J.A. & Weatherall, R. (2007). *Cognitive Behaviour Therapy for Anxiety Disorders in Children and Adolescents (Review)*. The Cochrane Library, Issue 3. Chichester, UK: Wiley.

Spence, S.H. (1997). Structure of anxiety symptoms among children: A confirmatory factor-analytic study. *Journal of Abnormal Child Psychology, 106,* 280–297.

Spence, S.H. (1998). A measure of anxiety symptoms among children. *Behaviour Research and Therapy 36,* 545–566.

Spence, S.H., Donovan, C. & Brechman-Toussaint, M. (1999). Social skills, social outcomes and cognitive features of childhood social phobia. *Journal of Abnormal Psychology, 108*(2), 211–221.

Spence, S.H., Donovan, C. & Brechman-Toussaint, M. (2000). The treatment of childhood social phobia: The effectiveness of a social skills training based, cognitive-behavioural intervention, with and without parental involvement. *Journal of Child Psychology and Psychiatry, 41*(6), 713–726.

Spielberger, C.D., Edwards, C.D., Montuori, J. & Lushene, R. (1973). *State–Trait Anxiety Inventory for Children.* Palo Alto, CA: Consulting Psychologists Press.

Stallard, P. (2002). *Think Good Feel Good: A Cognitive Behaviour Therapy Workbook for Children and Young People.* Chichester, UK: Wiley.

Stallard, P. (2005). *A Clinician's Guide to Think Good Feel Good: A Cognitive Behaviour Therapy Workbook for Children and Young People.* Chichester, UK: Wiley.

Stallings, P. & March, J.S. (1995). Assessment. In J.S. March (ed.), *Anxiety Disorders in Children and Adolescents* (pp. 125–147). New York: Guildford Press.

Taghavi, M.R., Dalgleish, T., Moradi, A.R., Neshat-Doost, H.T. & Yule, W. (2003). Selective processing of negative emotional information in children and adolescents with generalised anxiety disorder. *British Journal of Clinical Psychology, 42,* 221–230.

Taghavi, M.R., Neshat-Doost, H.T., Moradi, A.R., Yule, W. & Dalgleish, T. (1999). Biases in visual attention in children and adolescents with clinical anxiety and mixed anxiety–depression. *Journal of Abnormal Child Psychology, 27*(3), 215–223.

Toren, P., Wolmer, L., Rosental, B., Eldar, S., Koren, S., Lask, M. *et al.* (2000). Case series: Brief parent–child group therapy for childhood anxiety disorders using a manual based cognitive-behavioural technique. *Journal of the American Academy of Child and Adolescent Psychiatry, 39*(10), 1309–1312.

Treadwell, K.R.H. & Kendall, P.C. (1996). Self-talk in youth with anxiety disorders: State of mind, content specificity and treatment outcome. *Journal of Consulting and Clinical Psychology, 64*(5), 941–950.

Turner, S.M., Beidel, D.C. & Costello, A. (1987). Psychopathology in the offspring of anxiety disorder patients. *Journal of Consulting and Clinical Psychology, 55,* 229–235.

Vasey, M.W., Daleiden, E.L., Williams, L.L. & Brown, L. (1995). Biased attention in childhood anxiety disorders: A preliminary study. *Journal of Abnormal Child Psychology, 23,* 267–279.

Warren, S.L. & Sroufe, L.A. (2004). Developmental issues. In T.H. Ollendick & J.S. March (eds), *Phobic and Anxiety Disorders in Children and Adolescents: A Clinician's guide to effective psychosocial and pharmacological interventions* (pp. 92–115). New York: Oxford University Press.

Waters, A.M., Lipp, O.V. & Spence, S.H. (2004). Attentional bias toward fear related stimuli: An investigation with non-selected children and adults and children with anxiety disorders. *Journal of Experimental Child Psychology, 89,* 320–337.

Weems, C.F., Berman, S.L., Silverman, W.K. & Saavedra, L.M. (2001). Cognitive errors in youth with anxiety disorders: The linkages between negative cognitive errors and anxious symptoms. *Cognitive Therapy and Research, 25*(5), 559–575.

Weems, C.F., Silverman, W.K. & La Greca, A.M. (2000). What do youth referred for anxiety problems worry about? Worry and its relation to anxiety and anxiety disorders in children and adolescents. *Journal of Abnormal Child Psychology, 28*(1), 63–72.

Weems, C.F., Silverman, W.K., Rapee, R. & Pina, A.A. (2003). The role of control in anxiety disorders. *Cognitive Therapy and Research, 27*(5), 557–568.

Weems, C.F., Silverman, W.K., Saaverda, L.M., Pina, A.A. & Lumpkin, P.W. (1999). The discrimination of children's phobias using the Revised Fear Survey Schedule for Children. *Journal of Child Psychology and Psychiatry, 40*, 941–952.

Weems, C.F. & Stickle, T.R. (2005). Anxiety disorders in childhood: Casting a nomological net. *Clinical Child & Family Psychology Review, 8*(2), 107–134.

Whaley, S.E., Pinto, A. & Sigman, M. (1999). Characterizing interactions between anxious mothers and their children. *Journal of Consulting and Clinical Psychology, 67*(6), 826–836.

Wittchen, H.U., Nelson, C.B. & Lachner, G. (1998). Prevalence of mental disorders and psychosocial impairment in adolescents and young adults. *Psychological Medicine, 28*, 109–126.

Wood, J., McLeod, B.D., Sigman, M., Hwang, C., & Chu, B.C. (2003). Parenting and childhood anxiety: Theory, empirical findings and future directions. *Journal of Child Psychology and Psychiatry, 44*(1), 134–151.

Wood, J.J., Piacentini, J.C., Southam-Gerow, M., Chu, B.C. & Sigman, M. (2006). Family cognitive behavioural therapy for child anxiety disorders. *Journal of the American Academy of Child and Adolescent Psychiatry, 45*(3), 314–321.

Woodward, L.J. & Fergusson, D.M. (2001). Life course outcomes of young people with anxiety disorders in adolescence. *Journal of the American Academy of Child and Adolescent Psychiatry, 40*(9), 1086–1093.

World Health Organization. (1993). *International Classification of Mental and Behavioural Disorders, Clinical Descriptors and Diagnostic Guidelines* (10th edition). Geneva, Switzerland: World Health Organization.

Index